The Inspiring History of a Special Relationship

by Nancy Carver

Nancy Carver
c/o America's National Churchill Museum
501 Westminster Avenue
Fulton, MO 65251

Cover art by Michael Anderson, Michael Anderson Studios

Design by Stan Gellman Graphic Design

Published by Binding Solutions, St. Louis, MO

ISBN 978-0-578-76171-8

"Study history, study history.
In history lie all the secrets of statecraft."

—Winston Churchill, May 27, 1953[1]

Contents

PART TWO
Special Relationship: British History Explains British-American Ties

PART THREE
Special Relationship: Christopher Wren's Church

Foreward

In his preface to *A History of the English-Speaking Peoples*, published in 1956, Winston Churchill noted that "Every nation or group of nations has its own tale to tell." The same sentiment applies to colleges and universities, though the tales that are told are not always destined to be written into history books.

This book is an exception.

The stories in this volume reveal insights about the concept of the Anglo-American "special relationship" and its relevance and importance. It is a familiar phrase today, but remarkably few recognize or realize it was first used by Winston Churchill in his seminal "Sinews of Peace" address delivered in Westminster College's gymnasium on March 5, 1946. Provocative and powerful, the impact the 'Iron Curtain' speech (as it is commonly called) had on world affairs during the Cold War reverberated loudly throughout the second half the 20th century. Churchill's words spoken on Westminster's campus nearly 75 years ago continue to inform and influence leaders and institutions that uphold freedom, justice and democracy today.

Readers of this book will find how the history of Westminster College and Missouri's Callaway County intersects with Winston Churchill and President Harry Truman's visit to Westminster's campus in 1946. It also examines how several centuries of British historical narrative served as an extended preamble for Churchill's concept of the special relationship.

Standing in the center of the tale is Sir Christopher Wren's remarkable church of St. Mary the Virgin, Aldermanbury, a British-built monument all but destroyed in World War II and rebuilt by Westminster College in the 1960s. Its relocation from central London and reconstruction in Mid Missouri on Westminster's campus is perhaps the most remarkable symbol of the enduring bond between Britain and the United States. As Churchill wrote in a letter to the college on November 22, 1962, the church of St. Mary the Virgin, Aldermanbury continues "to symbolize in the eyes of the English-speaking peoples the ideals of Anglo-American association on which rest, now as before, so many of our hopes for peace and the future of mankind."

On behalf of the college, I wish to express gratitude to the author, Churchill Fellow of Westminster College, Nancy Carver for sharing this remarkable story anew.

Special and significant thanks go to Churchill Fellow Richard Mahoney and the estate, family, and friends of Westminster's 19th president, Dr. Robert L.D. Davidson, who established the Robert L.D.Davidson Endowment at America's National Churchill Museum at Westminster College. This generous funding support made the publication of this book possible.

In publishing this book, Westminster College is proud to perpetuate the expression of the special relationship and to share it with those who care about the college and its extraordinary role in hosting women, men and monuments that have shaped—and will continue to shape—our campus, country and world.

Donald P. Lofe, Jr.
President
Westminster College, Fulton Missouri

July, 2020

Dedication

Prior to the United States entering World War II, American citizens could not legally join the armed forces of foreign nations. The harsh penalty for doing so was the loss of citizenship. In spite of the country's position, a large number of American citizens volunteered to fly with the Royal Air Force (RAF). This book is dedicated to the three RAF Eagle Squadrons organized with American volunteers and to the entire 8th United States Army Air Force (USAAF) into which the eagle squadrons, whose official chapel is St. Mary the Virgin, Aldermanbury, were incorporated after December 1941.

The service of the 8th USAAF, as illustrated in this book's history of Britain, exemplifies the special relationship that helped win World War II. The courageous and heroic men who were stationed in England at former RAF airbases flew what many described as "suicide missions" over strategic targets in Germany. Their mission centered on "ending Germany's ability to wage war and gaining control of the air to ensure a successful Allied Forces' land invasion"[2] at some point in the war. Their bombing missions lasted from 1942-1945.[3]

Germany's pilots were among the best in the world. The 8th USAAF faced a formidable enemy and heavy casualties occurred. But the men of the Mighty Eighth were brave, determined, and relentless. On many occasions, the flak was so thick that you could almost walk on it. Still, the men kept on fighting. Their precision bombing missions continued despite the carnage that resulted. The valor of the 8th USAAF crewmembers made the Germans redeploy munitions and aircraft from other areas to defend themselves. The Mighty 8th helped win the war.

Although the following words of Churchill were said in 1940, they definitely applied to the 8th USAAF. "Never in the field of human conflict was so much owed by so many to so few."[4]

The United States Government pardoned members of the Eagle Squadron in 1944. The country owes them and all of the men of the 8th USAAF a debt of gratitude. Future generations of Britons and Americans should always remember these heroes.

Acknowledgments

Writing is not a solitary occupation. Good writing requires the assistance and input of other people. I was lucky to have two people who ensured that I profiled Churchill correctly and wrote the history of Britain as it actually happened. For their willingness to lend their expertise and help, I am very grateful.

Richard J. Mahoney served as the Churchillian expert. A fan of Churchill for many years, I imagine he has read almost every book published about Churchill and there are many. A true Renaissance man, he tapped into his reservoir of knowledge to impart wisdom, facts, and details that kept me on course. He is an excellent person to steer the ship and keep one from death by drowning in irrelevant material. In addition to all things Churchill, Richard also helped with the publication of this book, including the cover design.

When it came to British history, I turned to the best teacher I never had. Robert Blackey taught British history at my alma mater, California State University, San Bernardino (CSUSB), for fifty years. The old adage, "Ask a Teacher for Help," is definitely true. In addition to teaching, Robert had the added expertise that came from editing the teaching column in the news magazine of the American Historical Association. Luckily, he agreed to help me with the part of my book that deals with British history. Thanks also to CSUSB for hiring exceptional teachers.

I am also indebted to Cravath, Swaine & Moore LLP for its help with this book. Philip Boeckman, who is the Managing Partner of the

London office as well as the Co-Head of the Capital Markets practice for EMEA, is also the Chairman and Senior Fellow of America's National Churchill Museum Board of Governors, as well as a member of the Board of Trustees for Westminster. He provided valuable assistance and insight. He also had the advantage of having attended Westminster College.

I appreciate the help I received from other firm members. Edwin Smith, assisted by Jean Doherty, the Manager for Document Processing, did a superb job of editing and questioning various items in the book. His work allowed me to review my research and re-write as necessary. Kwasi Yeboah, another member of the firm, assisted by taking photographs of the Gardens at the previous site of St. Mary the Virgin, Aldermanbury in London.

The text of the *Sinews of Peace* speech and quotes from other speeches, works, and writings of Winston S. Churchill are reproduced with permission of Curtis Brown, London on behalf of The Estate of Winston S. Churchill.

Thanks to Baxter Watson who, as a student and member of the Skulls of Seven, escorted Winston Churchill into the college gymnasium so that he could give his famous speech. Baxter remembered much of what happened that day and had the foresight to take a photo of Churchill included in this book.

Thanks to Timothy Riley, Sandra L. and Monroe E. Trout Director and Chief Curator, Tyler Oberlag, and the staff of America's National Churchill Museum for their continued help with museum archives. Thanks also to the International Churchill Society, Hillsdale College's Churchill Project, the Harry S. Truman Museum and Library, the Margaret Thatcher Foundation, and the English Speaking Union in the United States for making much of their holdings available on their respective websites.

The staff of the Kirkwood Public Library, the St. Louis County Public Library, the St. Louis City Public Library, and the John M. Olin Library, Washington University, St. Louis, helped me locate books that I needed or helped me acquire them through inter-library loan. I appreciate their help.

Newspapers contained a wealth of information. The *St. Louis Post Dispatch* archives were particularly valuable. Due to the church's location in Missouri, the paper did many, very detailed articles about its history. I found other newspapers using the services of Genealogybank and Ancestry. I also found the Library of Congress newspapers helpful in my research.

Thanks to the late Nick T. Cave, an alumnus of Westminster, whose oft-told tales of the school made me curious about the school's history.

Thanks also to the following people who helped me in various ways: Drew Carver, John C. Carver, Suzanne Richardson, Steve Stinson, Vera Fairbanks, Esley Hamilton, Michael Evreux, Al and Kay Villagran, Don Wiegand, Samuel Rushay, the late Ed Tilles, Martha Schmidt Brown, and Paddy McNamara. A special thanks goes to Tim Corbet (class of 1970), who lent me the school newspapers and his 1969 yearbook.

Thanks to Fred Taussig, Westminster alumnus, for his creative, innovative, and skilled approach to book printing and binding and to his cadre of workers at his company, Binding Solutions.

My appreciation also goes to Teresa Thompson and to the staff of Stan Gellman Graphic Design for their excellent work on the interior design and interior cover flaps for this book.

I am indebted to Michael Anderson of Michael Anderson Studios for his artistry in design of the book cover, which beautifully illustrates Churchill's phrase "special relationship."

As always, thanks to my son, Benjamin Parke.

Any errors in this book are entirely my own. While I received a great deal of help, I am responsible for ensuring that the words are properly placed in the book and the history is properly documented. Writers are fallible and can miss suggested edits.

Introduction

On March 4, 1946, Winston Churchill boarded a Baltimore & Ohio (B&O) train in Washington, DC, with President Harry Truman and his military aide Brigadier General Harry Vaughan. They were headed to Fulton, Missouri, for a scheduled speech by Churchill on the campus of Westminster College, where Vaughan once played college football. Accompanying the men were thirty-three news writers, thirteen radiomen, ten newsreel men, four still photographers, three communications men, members of both staffs, an officer from New Scotland Yard, and Secret Service agents.[5]

The exact nature of the speech did not receive publicity and that piqued the interest of numerous reporters and members of the public who wondered what the former wartime Prime Minister planned to say. Approximately 25,000 – 30,000 people met in Fulton to hear the speech. Many farmers from surrounding areas "where fancy mules, saddle horses and purebred cattle are famous" helped pack the crowd waiting to catch a glimpse of Churchill.[6] Only 3,000 or so lucky visitors actually gained admittance to the filled-to-capacity school gymnasium to see Churchill deliver the speech.[7]

Traveling to Fulton by train took most people by surprise. The *Dallas Morning News* claimed, "Few people ever go to Fulton." Now it seemed that everyone was on the way to Fulton. Another newspaper reported that an invitation from the United States President to Churchill made the visit particularly noteworthy.[8]

Due to the speech, four words became part of the world's lexicon that year. Two were "Iron Curtain" and two were "special relationship." The topic—a warning about the coming conflict with Soviet Russia—was not well received. Many people found the latter words disturbing. War weary, they wanted no part of anything that might draw the country into further conflicts. "Uncle Joe" Stalin was a friend, they thought. Confused by Churchill's speech, they lambasted it.

Churchill first used the term "special relationship" in his speech at Westminster College, though he had used the concept of fraternal relationship previously. As Richard Langworth noted on his Hillsdale College site, Churchill used it in a 1943 speech at Harvard.[9] Probably initiated by President Roosevelt, the occasion signified the president's intent to "keep their relationship in good repair." Churchill had made an effort to help Roosevelt acquire an honorary degree from Oxford. Roosevelt, a Harvard alumnus, thought he should return the favor by helping Churchill get an honorary degree from Harvard. Due to pressing war needs, Churchill could not meet the traditional requirement for being in Cambridge during June Commencement ceremonies. Harvard made a rare exception for him to receive it in September of 1943.[10]

Those individuals who heard Churchill's speech at Harvard that fine September day commented on its excellence. Sentences such as, "The price of greatness is responsibility," still resonate today. But Churchill also remarked "victory is possible through partnership with the British Commonwealth." He explained that both the United States and Great Britain held the same values—"common conceptions of what is right and decent." He also emphasized their common notion of "fair play … impartial justice … and love of personal freedom." Later in the speech he emphasized "the rights and dignity of man," which he also knew they shared. Toward the end of the speech, he remarked, "Nothing will work soundly or for long without the united effort of the British and American peoples. If we are together, nothing is impossible."[11]

By the time Churchill came to Westminster College, the war had ended. Churchill believed that a continued strong relationship between Britain and America might prevent further conflict. While his speech may not have convinced others immediately, it does explain how a British heritage church in Fulton is now also an American heritage church. A special relationship did exist, if not for providing security as Churchill envisioned in 1946, but for circumventing seemingly impossible obstacles together.

In 1969, Westminster College dedicated the relocated Church of St. Mary the Virgin, Aldermanbury to the memory of Winston Churchill and the speech he gave at its campus in 1946. Though the church burned in the Great Fire of London in 1666, twenty-four stairs managed to survive. In 1677, Sir Christopher Wren included them in the redesigned and resuscitated church that still required a great deal of wood. A cupola was added later. As luck would have it, the church again suffered damage during World War I due to incendiary devices dropped by hostile forces. Once again, the church damage received repair only to be horribly damaged in World War II when enemy planes rained bombs on it. The walls, the interior columns, and the 12th century stairs, which constituted a majority of the church, survived.

Bravely undertaking the task of relocating one of the English war-damaged churches, Westminster College began its journey into the seemingly impossible adventure. This book tells the story of that huge endeavor as well as the special relationship with England that made the relocation possible. It entwines the history of Britain and the church with the common history that they share with the United States. It explores how the history of their shared values, developed through the centuries, affected the special relationship described in Churchill's speech at Westminster. In doing so the history and genius of Sir Christopher Wren also becomes part of that relationship. The genius of Churchill and Wren, one the great communicator and one the great architect, are entwined forever in the church that memorializes Churchill's prescient speech.

History is a subject that Churchill knew well. Beginning in 1898, he wrote forty-three history books that filled seventy-two volumes.[12] His life experiences gave him a unique perspective and he used that in his prose. A prolific and gifted communicator, he used his abilities to make history engrossing. Readers found the value in it and voraciously filled their individual appetites with his messages. Churchill understood that history books and other prose can change minds and reveal truths otherwise unknown to others. He used that to his advantage.

This history is divided into three parts. The first part tells the history of the speech that Churchill gave at Westminster College, including the critical responses to it. The second part describes the history that affected the church and the common history of Britain and the United States that Churchill believed gave the two countries a special relationship. The third part provides more information about the church and shows how the special relationship made it possible for a small college in a small Midwestern town in America to negotiate the relocation of an iconic British heritage church from the city of London to Fulton, Missouri. The subject headings in Part Two are meant to help the reader understand the significance of each period as history is retold from the beginnings of London until the end of World War II in the European theater.

The importance of the church and its relocation to Westminster College cannot be overestimated. It is a monumental memorial to Winston Churchill and his "Iron Curtain" speech. More than that, it symbolizes the ability of both people and countries to survive the most tragic circumstances in a courageous and awe-inspiring way. It is a magnificent building that symbolizes a stance against tyranny and shows that when people come together for a common purpose great things can happen. For these reasons, its continued preservation is important as both a memorial and an inspiration in the worst of times. It shines a light on man's ability to overcome incredible adversity and challenges and the ability to seize and prosper from the opportunities that may seem hidden from view.

The two life-size sculptures of Churchill, one by Don Wiegand and one by Franta Belsky, both of which stand outside the church, are also important monumental sculptures made in honor of Winston Churchill. The first depicts Churchill as he describes the "Iron Curtain" in his *Sinews of Peace* speech and the other one, according to the sculptor, depicts Churchill as he appeared in World War II, "at the turning point of the history of the Western world—standing foursquare, defiant, against a headwind."[13] They both impart the same confidence, certainty, and strength of a man who believed that as individuals we control our futures and are "captains of our fate." This Churchill saying also references an Ernest Henley poem, *Invictus*, which supposedly also inspired Nelson Mandela to persevere.[14]

Only 20 yards from the Belsky statue stand eight slabs from the Berlin Wall that separated East Germany from the rest of Germany. The graffiti faced wall depicts a man and a woman making a "breakthrough" to freedom as they move from East to West. It is an important symbol of the end of the Cold War just as the Wiegand sculpture captures the beginning of the same war.

The history of Britain is extensive, but this book will not address all of it. Only that portion that in some direct or indirect way has affected the relationship between Britain and the United States, or the history of the church, is considered important for the purposes of this book. Churchill thought that if Americans understood their common roots with Britain, they would better understand why a fraternal relationship between Britain and the United States is important. Relationships often have their ups and downs, and the relationship between these two countries is no different. As history shows, the relationship was sometimes suspicious, strained, tumultuous, cold, and violent, particularly during events leading up to and including the Revolutionary War. Due to their common culture and heritage, the two peoples have managed to forge more cooperative, interdependent, supportive, symbiotic, collaborative, and beneficial relationships post-independence. These relationships typically help each other economically and politically. While these relationships may at times be strained or weakened, the two countries often try to work out their disagreements in a way that meets the goals, or at least some of the goals, of each.

Churchill said in his book, *The History of the English-Speaking Peoples,* that due to their common heritage both the United States and Britain "have become conscious of our common duty to the human race." He used the term "English-Speaking Peoples" for want of another phrase to describe "those independent nations who derive their beginnings, their speech, and many of their institutions from England and who now preserve, nourish and develop in their own ways." This book explains the common heritage, the different paths each country took, and the evolution of shared values through the centuries that enable both nations to "become more conscious of {their} duty to the human race."[15]

All of these sinews of history, retold from the beginnings of London, are part of a fascinating story of determination, ingenuity, resilience, endurance, and survival that honors the life of Winston Churchill and his prescient speech at Westminster College in Fulton, Missouri. They form an uplifting story of the power of people to overcome the unimaginable and create the seemingly impossible.

Churchill once said, "The longer you can look back, the farther you can look forward."[16] Looking back at the history of the church and its former site, as well as the common history of the United States and Britain, the reader can understand how history affected the church, imagine its future, and realize the need to preserve it for future generations.

PART ONE

Special Relationship: Winston Churchill's Sinews of Peace (Iron Curtain) Speech

This sculpture by Don Wiegand stands outside the church and depicts the Sinews of Peace (Iron Curtain) *speech at the exact time that Churchill utters his famous, unexpected words, "iron curtain." For many, the speech marked the beginning of the Cold War. Included with permission from the sculptor Don Wiegand and Dave Ulmer, photographer.*

CHAPTER 1

The Venue: Westminster College, Fulton, Callaway County, Missouri

When word of Churchill's impending visit to the Westminster College first broke, people wondered how a small school could have secured a visit from Winston Churchill, an iconic figure, former prime minister, and war hero, when larger, well-known schools could not. One reason had to do with a very important connection to a notable alumnus close to the president. The other reason had to do with the history of the County of Callaway and the school, as well as their religious and political influence.

Before Missouri became a state, the French occupied a significant part of the Missouri territory. Well-suited for agricultural purposes, the land's attraction had to do with its ability to function as a prosperous trading post. The French believed such posts possessed the most economic value in the late eighteenth century and early nineteenth centuries.

In 1803, the United States signed an agreement with France to purchase the Louisiana Territory of which the Missouri territory was a part. Eventually, the residents wanted to become the 23rd state. Objections arose due to the issue of slavery. At the time, twenty-two states formed the United States. Eleven of them were "slave" states and the other eleven were "free" states. Agreeing to a twenty-third state would upset the perceived balance of power regardless of whether the new state was a "slave" state or a "free" state. Due to the existence of some 2,000 slaves in the area that was proposed for statehood, many fearful people earnestly believed that Missouri would become a "slave" state and increase the power of the current southern states.

Finally, Henry Clay helped broker a compromise that seemed to solve the problem. The Missouri Compromise of 1820 approved the designation of two new states. Maine would be a "free" state and Missouri would become a "slave" state and the 24th state in the Union.[17] Not everyone in the state of Missouri was happy about the new designation, since many Missourians opposed slavery. Nevertheless, Missouri became a state on August 12, 1821. Thirty years later, the Kansas-Nebraska Act of 1854 nullified the Missouri Compromise, which the Supreme Court declared unconstitutional in 1857 by stating that Congress had no right to designate a "slave" state.[18]

Despite all the political wrangling, Missouri continued to have a deeply divided population. The location of Missouri made it a border state between the North and South. The western border between Kansas and Missouri experienced constant violence ever since the Kansas-Nebraska Act of 1854. Violence broke out due to the actions of jayhawkers and bushwackers. Originally thought to be fighters for or against slavery, the guerrilla fighters had other motives. They terrorized and killed innocent civilians, primarily in the border areas of Missouri and Kansas, under the guise of political purpose to extract monetary reward. Sometimes, the thrill of killing satisfied them. On August 25, 1863, "Union General Thomas E. Ewing issued Order No. 11 to forcibly remove all residents of Jackson, Bates, Cass Counties, and that part of Vernon County in the district. Exceptions applied to inhabitants of Kansas City, Westport, and Independence, and those people who lived within a mile of those three locations, or one of the nearby military posts in Hickman's Mills (now Hickman Hills), Pleasant Hills, and Harrisonville." Those individuals allowed to remain in these locations had to prove their loyalty.[19]

During the Civil War, the Missouri governor had pro-southern leanings while many St. Louisans had more pro-northern leanings. General Nathaniel Lyon served as the Union Commander of the St. Louis Arsenal, which stored a large number of weapons. A similar arsenal stored weapons in Liberty, Missouri; however, pro-Confederate sympathizers raided it and seized most of the weapons.[20] Alerted to the possibility that the Missouri State Guard located near the St. Louis Arsenal might try a similar approach to seize weapons from the St. Louis Arsenal, Lyon initiated a surprise attack to capture the Guard at Camp Jackson. Parading and humiliating the captured men through the streets of St. Louis led to a riot and what became known as the "Camp Jackson Affair." Twenty people died and tension heightened between people on each side of the political spectrum.[21]

Unable to seize the weapons, Claiborne Fox Jackson, the Governor of Missouri, realized the enormity of the Union threat and eventually fled the state. He set up an alternative government with a provisional capital in Neosho, Missouri, before moving to Arkansas.[22] The Missouri Constitutional Convention of 1861 officially declared Missouri a Union State; however, a star symbolizing Missouri became part of the Confederate flag after the departing Governor Jackson's alternative government joined the Confederacy on November 28, 1861.[23]

Only 25 miles from the center of Missouri's government in Jefferson City, the County of Callaway largely remained pro-Confederate. Established in 1820 and laid out in 1825, Callaway had a population that largely came from the upper southern states of Virginia and Kentucky and many residents had a Scotch-Irish ancestry. Their business transactions prior to the war depended heavily on the South. The county, along with six other neighboring counties, became known as "Little Dixie" due to their southern leanings, agricultural economy, culture, and politics. People immigrated to the area due to the fertile nature of the land. They believed the climate was similar in many respects to the states from which they left, though the winters could be harsher.[24] Examples of this immigration are the related Thurmond and Rothwell families whose families originally lived in Albemarle, Virginia. The lure of good tobacco land and land for other familiar crops in Callaway County and nearby Pike County inspired such pioneering spirits to move to less populous locations in Missouri, often near the western border of the country.

The early settlers planted cotton and tobacco but both proved labor-intensive and Callaway County never gained a huge share of either market. They found hemp, which was used to bind cotton bales, more profitable and it became a leading crop in the 1860s.[25] Aside from hemp, the agricultural land found its best use for grain and stock farming. The mule industry also proved profitable. Mules, hardworking and courageous animals, became a major business. They could be used for a variety of work and would prove invaluable in the Mexican, Civil, and First World Wars. They could also do a great deal of work on the farm, reducing the need for mechanized tools and laborers.[26]

Laborers sometimes meant slaves. The slave population in the seven counties of "Little Dixie" was the highest in the state. In 1860, the slave population in the state represented 10% of the total population, and in "Little Dixie" it represented almost 30% of the state's slave population. Lafayette County and Saline County had the largest number of slaves. Slaves were found more often near the Missouri River due to the "rich agricultural land and the industry that it attracted." Both required more workers.[27] Despite the overall concentration of so many Missouri slaves in Little Dixie, no large plantations existed. Only 4% of the slaveholders owned 20 or more slaves and 500 acres of land.[28]

Corte Sans Dessein, the first and now-defunct settlement in Callaway County, almost became the site of the state capital, which by law had to be centrally located and within 40 miles of the Osage River. Too many problems related to validating ownership of the land defeated that goal.[29] The southern side of the river ended up being the chosen location. Named after Thomas Jefferson, Jefferson City was laid out by Daniel Morgan Boone, Daniel Boone's son. Similarly, Callaway County took its name from Boone's grandson, Captain James Callaway, who lived in St. Charles, Missouri. Serving noteworthy terms as a deputy sheriff in St. Charles and as a leader of companies of rangers, Callaway never lived in Callaway County.[30] The use of his name reflected the enormous state pride in the presence of the Boone family in Missouri.

During the Civil War, a home guard force of Callaway residents attempted to defend their homes from invading Union forces, and the legend of Kingdom City, Callaway County was born. Legend has it that one Jefferson Jones, the leader of the militia, signed a treaty with the Union to prohibit any further military action in the city. According to the same legend, Callaway thus became the Kingdom of Callaway, which seceded from the Union. Largely fabricated, the story depicts a treaty that never happened and a county that did not secede from the Union. It is possible that an agreement did exist to protect Callaway, though Union forces later occupied Fulton for most of the war. Jones did come up with the title "kingdom" and it stuck, providing years of great celebration for the bygone era of rugged, independent, and strong individuals and the creation of a great story.[31]

The City of Fulton resembled Callaway in its pro-Confederate leanings. A small city with numerous churches and people with deeply held religious convictions, its powers in charge balked at a proposal to use the name of the French Count Volney, a philosopher whose real name was Constantine Francois de Chasseboeuf. Sometimes referred to as an atheist, a freethinker, a spy, and an infidel, Volney did not seem an appropriate name for a Christian community. His friendship with Thomas Jefferson did little to persuade people otherwise.[32] Members of the County Court immediately decided to pursue a more conservative approach. They named the city Fulton, after Robert Fulton, who invented the steamboat. Fulton's father, a church deacon, helped build a Presbyterian church in Pennsylvania.[33]

In the early 1850s, the local Presbyterians began planning for a Presbyterian college in Fulton. The *St. Louis Republican,* formerly the *Missouri Gazette,* announced the establishment of a new school in Fulton by the Old School Presbyterians in 1852. According to the paper, Fulton is "an old well-settled, populous, and wealthy."[34] In 1837, a schism occurred in the Presbyterian Church. The Old School Presbyterians favored Calvinist orthodoxy, conservative views, adherence to the Westminster Confession of Faith.[35] They also had a strong belief in the word of God contained in the bible. The views of the church meshed with those views of the Presbyterian populous in Fulton.

The local Presbyterian Church chartered Fulton College in 1851 as an independent college. Neither the presbytery nor the synod owned it.[36] When the Synod of Missouri decided to establish a Synodical College, it decided on Fulton due to its location near the center of influence of the Presbyterian Church in Missouri. The new school held a ceremony to dedicate its new cornerstone. During the 1853 ceremony, officials placed a bible and a copy of the Westminster Confession of Faith document in the cornerstone.[37] The new school name, Westminster College, referenced the Westminster Confession of Faith to which it adhered.

Both subsequent schisms within the Presbyterian Church and the Civil War impacted the school. Despite its southern leanings, Westminster did not close its doors during the war years. It became the only outstate (i.e., outside the metropolitan areas of St. Louis and Kansas City) Missouri post-secondary school to remain open. Of course, many professions during this time period, even physician and attorney positions, relied more on apprenticeships than college degrees. Still, possession of a degree reflected some degree of status.

Enrollment at the college did not decline during these years. Perhaps some students did not relish fighting other people in their community, including friends and family members. Both possibilities were more likely to occur for men who came from states that bordered the north and south.

To guard against problems at school, officials instituted rules that prohibited certain actions, such as duels and political discussions that might otherwise occur in a potentially volatile environment.[38] At school commencements, politically charged words were avoided, though seemingly innocuous words could cause potential problems for the speaker. At the conclusion of their studies, many dutiful students patriotically left for war and the confederacy took its fair share of new soldiers.

Meanwhile, the Presbyterian Church experienced division during the Civil War. The Old School made a decision to stay neutral on the subject of slavery, believing at the time that it was not a religious issue. Some southern church members formed a new Presbyterian Church of the Confederate States; however, it did not include the church in Missouri.[39]

Westminster is no longer under the auspices of the Presbyterian Church. While the early religious belief of the church meshed with the southern and pioneer history of Fulton and the college, today's environment is more expansive and inclusive. The Church of St. Mary the Virgin, Aldermanbury is nondenominational and open to people of all faiths. The City of Fulton is moderately conservative and Christian; however, many different faiths are reflected in its demographics. Students are taught that all people are children of God and deserve to be free. The residents have long moved on from issues related to the Civil War. They now view themselves as Midwesterners. Very patriotic, the city honors residents who fought in various wars. By 1946, almost 2,000 students served in the Civil War and foreign wars. Fifty-four of them were killed in action.[40]

Having Harry Truman, a Democrat, native Missourian and President of the United States visit the city was nothing short of exhilarating for Westminster students and residents alike. Fultonians believed that Harry was one of them. He had a similar background, including Scotch-Irish ancestors who once lived in Virginia and Kentucky. Like many of them, he came from a family of farmers with pro-southern leanings during the Civil War. Truman's grandparents, Solomon and Harriet Young, felt the brutality of harassment when Union soldiers came to their farm. The soldiers almost hanged Harry's uncle trying to locate the father who was away on business. When they finally left, they carried large amounts of stock, food, and valuables with them. The Young's situation didn't improve. After Ewing signed Order Number 11, the family had to forcibly evacuate their home. Soldiers destroyed all their grain and hay. Both of these events occurred despite Solomon's signing a required oath pledging loyalty to the Union.[41]

Fultonians in 1946 also knew that Presbyterians held a special place in Truman's heart due to his wife. He spoke about them in his remarks in Alexandria, Virginia, where he participated in the laying of the cornerstone for the Westminster Presbyterian Church. He said, "Every denomination has made its particular contribution to our Nation, and certainly the Presbyterians have done their share … Indeed, the democratic nature of our Government owes much to the democratic experience of the Presbyterian Church. I can brag a lot on the Presbyterians because I started {attending} a Sunday school in the Presbyterian Church when I was 6 years old, and that is where I met Mrs. Truman."[42] He may not have planned the trip for that reason but it probably didn't hurt.

Without a doubt, the people of Fulton loved Harry. Now they learned that Harry planned to bring Winston Churchill to their city. They couldn't believe it, but they knew that only Harry could manage to do something so thrilling. Harry loved Missouri and his actions showed that Harry loved Fulton. They couldn't wait to start the parade and celebrate.

CHAPTER 2

Ideas Begin at the Old Fishing Hole

Some of the most fascinating stories begin with unlikely events and this one is no different. It begins with a fishing trip taken by Franc L. McCluer, president of Westminster College in Fulton, Missouri in 1945.

McCluer took Westminster College to new heights in some difficult situations. During his tenure, which lasted from 1933 to 1947, he faced numerous challenges caused by the effects of the Great Depression and the conscription of men into military service during World War II.[43] Only thirty-seven years old when he took over as president, McCluer dealt with numerous financial adversities that required a gifted leader to overcome. Indefatigable, he faced and overcame all of the challenges with ingenuity and resolve. Enrollment did drop below the 200 mark at one point during his tenure, but the college continued due to his ability to change programs to encourage increased demand.

In 1946, enrollment in the college stood at just 225 students.[44] During the 1940s, only a small percentage of students actually graduated high school, and an average of just 6% of the adult population actually graduated from college. War and its impact on finances hurt the college. Congress provided some relief. Passed into law on June 22, 1944, the GI Bill or The Servicemen's Readjustment Act of 1944, its official name, helped many veterans of World War II obtain educational opportunities otherwise denied them. By 1947, the number of college graduates almost doubled.[45] Though Westminster was a small school, it benefited from the GI Bill.

McCluer, who graduated from high school in Fulton and Westminster College, held a strong belief in the necessity of education. He once gave a commencement address in which he said, "The founders of the American experiment in constitutional liberty realized that only an educated citizenry can be a free citizenry" but also emphasized that "one is not free if his neighbor is enslaved." His strong religious faith compelled him to try to educate others to understand that "the right to be free is inalienable in a person because he is a creature of God." He also further told an audience in Richmond that, "the training of youth in the mastery of ideas provides the understanding and the appreciation of values vital to our democratic way of life. People, not dictators, must make the decisions of the future."[46] He spoke to Washington University graduates in St. Louis about the "rights of man" and he cautioned high school graduates about "shallow thinking that leads people to accept the opinions of others rather than their own ideas through critical thought."[47] His humanitarianism and strong faith made him a popular figure at Westminster. Many parents sent their sons to the school based on the strong faith of its leader and the culture of the school.

McCluer's faith also provided him with a belief that determination could help him accomplish the goals he set for both the public good and the good of Westminster. Born Francis Lewis McCluer, he later became known as "Bullet" due to his rapid-fire oratory skills in college debates,[48] McCluer was no slouch. Hard work came naturally to him. He expected others to follow the work ethic model that he set. His leadership ability also transferred to the public sphere where he worked feverishly and successfully as a major player in helping design and promote the adoption of a revised state constitution for Missouri.[49] That constitution, approved by Missouri voters, remains in place today. Due to his leadership in that effort, McCluer attracted many calls to take public office, but his devotion to Westminster kept him at the college.

That devotion made him constantly on the lookout for new ideas to build on the reputation and stature of the college. One exciting idea came during one of his vacations. A fishing enthusiast, McCluer found great relaxation in the sport. He found it a good opportunity to think about the future. On the day in question, he thought about the best person to give the annual John Findley Green Foundation lecture.

Endowed by Mrs. John Findley Green, the lectures honored her late husband, a former attorney with the firm of Judson, Green, and Hardy in St. Louis and a distinguished alumnus. Mrs. Green intended that the lectures promote a better understanding of political, economic, or social problems of international significance. Previous speakers spoke about international and foreign affairs during an approximate one-hour lecture on a particular topic. The college administration temporarily canceled the lectures for the duration of the war, but Westminster had decided to resume the lectures in 1946 to seek a better understanding of how to achieve long-lasting peace and prosperity.

Hoping to find a celebrated speaker, the college began a search for an international figure. They wanted someone who could command a stage, receive international attention, and speak on world affairs and policy with conviction and great foresight.

While trying to hook his own fish, an idea suddenly came to McCluer. Why not lure the biggest catch of all—Winston Churchill?

Franc Lewis McCluer, B.A., M.A., Ph.D. Eleventh president of Westminster College. Photo courtesy of Westminster College.

CHAPTER 3

The Idea Germinates

Having an idea is one thing. Making it grow and develop is another thing. For that to happen on a college campus requires the input of a number of people. Bullet McCluer thought he had a great idea but he first needed to run it by his most trusted advisor, Ida Belle, his wife, who heartily agreed with him. Now he needed to broach the idea with the college trustees.

Returning to the campus, he brought several of the trustees together in a room. Among them was John Raeburn Green of St. Louis. Since Green was the son of the man for whom the Green Lecture had been named, his input was critical. After the trustees agreed with McCluer, he next talked to Thomas H. Van Sant who worked at the Callaway Bank in Fulton. Both men had been former classmates at Westminster and Van Sant had established a great friendship with President Truman over the years. Since he knew the president personally, he probably knew best how he might react to such a request. Van Sant thought the idea was terrific. Whether it panned out or not, the idea should be tested. For help with that, Van Sant suggested Major General Harry H. Vaughan, another former classmate and current military aide to President Truman.

If you want someone to carry the ball and make a touchdown, a former football player with a strong allegiance to Westminster would be the right person to handle the task. But Harry Hawkins Vaughan was more than that. Born in Glasgow, Missouri, he possessed no real background for his ultimate career but he was a decorated veteran and Truman admired veterans.[50] A quiet man at home, he was sometimes described as a "bull in a china shop" away from home. One newspaper called him a "Sunday School Teacher with a Mule Skinner's Vocabulary." He may have had his faults but Vaughan was Truman's friend and Truman believed in loyalty.[51]

They first met in 1917 at Camp Doniphan, Fort Sill, Oklahoma. When Vaughan first saw him, Truman stood on the receiving end of a severe tongue lashing by a military general. Vaughan made a noisy entrance to distract the general's attention. He played the right move. The general switched his attention to Vaughan and forgot about his first "whipping boy." Truman and Vaughan gave each other a smile when the general wasn't looking. Years later, Truman designed a special medal for his friend. The inscription read, to "the best whipping boy."[52] It was not the first medal that Vaughan received. Both he and Truman fought in the horrible trench warfare of the Argonne Offensive and other World War I battles. Vaughan received his first medal, the Silver Star, for his heroic efforts in the world war.

The two men stayed in touch. Eventually, Vaughan became secretary to Truman during Truman's first term as a US Senator from Missouri. After Truman became vice president, he created a new military aide position that he filled with his good friend. Vaughan became a major general while serving in that position.[53]

Although he was a war hero, Vaughan did not always exercise good sense. Several years after Churchill's visit to Fulton, a newspaper reported that he told an audience in Alexandria, Virginia, that Churchill was "a garrulous old gentleman who uses 20 words where 10 would do." Churchill supposedly forgave him and even sent him an autographed portrait to show that there were no hard feelings.[54] That misstep was just Harry, an affable man with excessive gestures (or "hoof and mouth disease" as one newspaper stated)[55] but a loyal confidant and good friend. His affability probably sprang from his ability as "a gifted story-teller (sic) and after-dinner speaker."[56]

Vaughan believed in loyalty to his school as well as to his friends. A fierce advocate of the education provided by Westminster College, he did what he could to support its efforts. When his friend, Bullet McCluer, the "short, stout and peppery mainspring of the college," paid him a visit in Washington, DC, he eagerly greeted his 1916 classmate.[57] Bullet appeared in his usual energetic way and wasted no time in stating the purpose of his visit. "Mr. Churchill is going to be in the United States in the spring. It sure would be great if we could get him to come out to the college and talk." Vaughan suggested that a letter be written. McCluer was one step ahead of him. He handed the letter to Vaughan. "Let's go and see what the Boss thinks about that," replied Vaughan. He then quickly called Matt Connelly, Truman's Appointments Secretary, to find out if they could meet with the President. Fortunately, the President had a few minutes at that very moment. The two men rushed to his office. Vaughan "stuck his head in and said, 'Boss, I've found you've got five minutes free and I've got a guy here from Missouri who wants to see you—Bullet.'"[58]

Graciously, Truman said, "Well, come in, Bullet. How are you?" After a brief conversation, Vaughan interjected. "He's got a letter he wants you to look at." After taking the letter and reading it, Truman said, "I think that's a good letter. That might work. Wait a minute." With that, he took his pen and wrote at the bottom of the letter, "This is a wonderful school in my home state. Hope you can do it. I'll introduce you. Best regards, Harry Truman."[59] He looked back at the visitors and told them, "Now you send him that."[60]

According to Vaughan, Bullet brimmed with excitement. A few weeks later, he called Vaughan, though Vaughan said if "he'd had the window and his head out the window, he wouldn't have needed the phone." Breathlessly, Bullet said, "Mr. Churchill said that he will come and make this talk and that it will be the only public appearance that he will make during his trip to the United States."[61]

Success. All that was left to do was make preparations for the visit. They had no idea what was about to happen.

CHAPTER 4

Westminster and Fulton Prepare

Stepping out at the Ritz is quite different than a community gathering in a small city of fewer than 10,000 people. The latter event brings together the strength and bonds of people who have forged relationships over the years. The local food is typically simple but delicious. The volunteer cooks are the men and women who prepare everyday meals for their families and know the way to their stomachs. The event is usually filled with laughter and plain talk. Everyone has a good time, and their hearts are filled with good cheer and the memory of another day together. Fultonians wanted Churchill to understand what the heart of America loved. They were sure he would love it too.

Obviously, a fabulous parade had to be arranged. Every special event required one and this one would be exceptional. The parade route would display British and American flags as well as photos of their British guest. Bunting in red, white, and blue would adorn the streets. Cameras would be at the ready. Excitement would fill the air.

The city did not immediately know how many visitors might arrive but they soon found that over 15,000 people had requested admission for the Gymnasium where Churchill would speak. To make sure that everyone could hear, exterior sound systems were utilized. Technicians installed additional loudspeakers at different locations, including the neighboring women's college, William Woods College. Arrangements were made with other local communities for visitor housing but local residents, already set to house their friends and relatives, agreed to throw open their doors for visitors wanting to stay the night. Such is life in a small, friendly city.

The University of Missouri in Columbia also agreed to help by providing additional seats for the gymnasium, which normally could seat fewer than 3,000 people. College buildings, scrubbed and polished, awaited the distinguished visitors.[62] Residents pitched in by agreeing to make sandwiches for the crowd. Clarence Littrell ordered thousands of hot dogs.[63] Local eateries would never be able manage the anticipated crowd. The school found cooks to prepare the ham for lunch and the roast beef for dinner. Everyone agreed they would be the best he had ever eaten. The Midwest group of citizens was set to display its culinary skills.

Residents understood that travel might be difficult. The train didn't stop in Fulton but accessing it by car was not difficult. Parking might be a problem but the residents came up with solutions to every known problem to make the visit stress-free. A community of neighbors, they knew how to work together to solve problems. They would be ready.

CHAPTER 5

Winston Churchill Arrives and Heads for the Beach

When Churchill landed in New York at the beginning of his visit to America, a crowd of reporters begged for information. The scene took place on the dock of Pier 90. The *Queen Elizabeth* had slid into the dock" only minutes previously. Aside from Churchill and his wife, there were 12,000 Canadian troops onboard and supposedly 1500 cases of Scotch whiskey, a possible beverage exaggeration.[64]

Before disembarking, Churchill did make a speech to the Canadian soldiers on the trip. Generally upbeat, it ended with a description of a ship at sea. According to Churchill, the waves that beat against the ship have no purpose. They "bump around, tireless and ineffective." By contrast, the ship withstood the waves since it had a purpose. Purpose is what kept Churchill going after his defeat in the previous British election. He had a purpose and he came to America to fulfill the purpose of helping Britain and the United States make the world a safer place.[65]

Understandably fatigued after a grueling war and term as prime minister, Winston let Americans know that his doctor required that he rest for a month before taking on additional work. He chose a destination not unfamiliar to New Yorkers. After a couple of days in

Washington DC, he headed for the warmer clime in Florida. As the *Augusta Chronicle* reported,

> He has lived through a strenuous decade, which has sapped much of his physical strength and vigor, and the beloved old warrior is entitled to enjoy the refreshing tonic afforded by the beauty of the landscape and the warmth of the Florida sunshine.[66]

While certainly entitled to rest, Churchill found that the press still tracked his every move. Hunted by reporters and photographers, he did not escape visibility at his temporary residence at the home of Col. Frank Clarke in Miami Beach. Clarke knew a great deal about the perils of war. He owned ships that the Allies used in World War II. More importantly, his eldest son, captured by the Japanese, spent four years as a prisoner of war. In appreciation of Churchill's war efforts and his friendship, Clarke paid for most of Churchill's travel expenses, though Churchill did give him a check that he never cashed.[67]

Thanks to the media, most people now knew Churchill had the use of a large, six-foot-wide bed, a bed size that was unusual for the time.[68] They also knew about his getaway to Cuba, his visit to the racetrack, his swims in the ocean, and his paint sketches of the islands and beaches of greater Miami. Nothing, it seems, escaped the press.

Even Van Johnson, the actor, almost moved into the fray. After spotting Churchill in a swimming pool, he supposedly said to his press agent, who was with him, "Wouldn't it be wonderful if Churchill started to drown and we saved him. Boy what a story."[69] They both thought better of trying to do a shameless stunt. In fact, the entire story may have been a shameless pitch for press coverage.

At the beginning of his sojourn, Churchill did sit down for a brief interview. In response to his statement that he only came to Florida for relaxation, a reporter asked him to say just ten words about his experience. He said, "I've been asked to say just ten words—or thereabouts ten—which come very readily to my mind, and that is the great pleasure I have in feeling the genial sunshine of Miami Beach." He paused and then said, "One too many. One too many." He had counted the words. There were actually more than one too many, but he did say "thereabouts."[70]

During his stay in Miami Beach, Churchill wrote to Prime Minister Clement Atlee and explained that he intended to reference fraternal association in his speech at Westminster, just as he previously had done at Harvard. He informed Atlee that both Truman and Secretary of State James F. Byrnes seemed to like that approach "very well," which is one indication that both parties had some awareness of the speech.[71]

According to reports, Truman planned to meet with Churchill in Florida at an unannounced location, presumably the presidential yacht. Their meeting supposedly would include a discussion about the upcoming speech in Fulton, though the exact nature of the discussion remained secret.[72] Due to a national crisis related to striking workers, Truman's plans unraveled and he was unable to meet with Churchill. According to C-SPAN, "almost five thousand strikes affecting 4.6 million people occurred in 1946. The need for higher wages due to increased costs of living motivated workers to strike."[73] Not concentrated in particular sectors, strikes were widespread and created a difficult and contentious time for the workers and government alike.

But Churchill did meet with Secretary of State James F. Byrnes and Churchill's longtime friend, Bernard Baruch, to discuss the loan that Britain hoped to get from America. New Yorker Baruch, the son of a Confederate field surgeon, Jewish financier, and former economic and political advisor to Woodrow Wilson and Franklin Roosevelt, served on a number of governmental committees under a number of presidents. Among other things, he consulted on dealing with the Depression and preparing the country economically for war.[74] In 1947, he coined the term "cold war" to describe relations with the Soviet Union, though others credit George Orwell.[75] At the end of his career in public service, he developed the "Baruch Plan," which he thought would protect American atomic bomb secrets and control their manufacture. His plan involved using an international agency to monitor and protect the weapons from being made by countries that might use them for nefarious reasons. Soviet Russia rejected the plan.[76]

Truman did not like Baruch but Baruch was well respected by Congress and very influential in matters dealing with the government.[77] Anti-Semitic remarks by Henry Ford were an affront to Baruch who followed tzedakah, the religious obligation to do what is just and right.[78] This form of religious social justice is particularly good, according to Maimonides' eight levels of charity when the donor helps Jews with loans or partnerships so that the recipient can eventually become independent.[79]

The war had taken a huge financial toll on the British economy. People were struggling just to find enough food to eat. Churchill believed that as a private citizen he could influence the outcome of the congressional vote, perhaps by speaking to Congress. The latter event did not happen; however, Byrnes and Baruch could definitely help the outcome. Very careful not to affect the planned speech in Fulton, Churchill made sure that his discussion on this matter remained secret unless specifically asked to comment on the possibility of a loan.

Reply is what he did when the *Miami Daily News* posed the question.

> We suffered far more than any country during the war. Some other countries were overrun, but they were not fighting. We were fighting and using up our credit. We borrowed all we could and now we must use all we can get.[80]

He explained the same problem to both Byrnes and Baruch. After a long conversation, Churchill believed that Baruch, who previously opposed using American money for socialism and nationalization, would not oppose the idea any more. Baruch had previously said, "It was an American interest to see that Britain did not collapse, but not an American interest to have her pay her debts to those we have defended." Nevertheless, after much discussion, Churchill said that Baruch left the meeting "most anxious not to be unfriendly to our country, for which he has expressed the most ardent admiration." For that reason, Churchill did not believe he would oppose the loan.[81] Undoubtedly, Churchill included an appeal to social justice in his discussion with Baruch. (Note: Truman signed the British Loan Bill for $3,750,000,000 on July 15, 1946, "terming it a major step to carry out a program for reviving and expanding international trade.")[82]

While Churchill did meet with some success while "relaxing" in Miami, his trip to America was laced with some sadness. The death of Harry Hopkins, Franklin Roosevelt's closest advisor on foreign policy, was the saddest event. Military personnel often complained that Hopkins and Churchill discussed and agreed on military decisions that they could not override.[83] Churchill clearly admired Hopkins.

> He was a true leader of men and alike in ardor and wisdom. In times of crisis he has rarely been excelled. His love for the causes of the weak and poor was matched by his passion against tyranny, especially when tyranny was for the time triumphant. To dynamic, compulsive, and persuasive force he added humor and charm in an exceptional degree. We do well to salute his memory. We shall not see his like again.[84]

Despite the initial sadness upon hearing of Hopkins' death, Churchill very much enjoyed his stay in Miami Beach. Before his vacation ended, Churchill received an honorary degree from the University of Miami.[85] It was one of several honorary degrees that he received during his American trip. One could not say that the American trip was not educational.

CHAPTER 6

On Board the Train to Fulton

Filled with politicians, public servants, reporters, and photographers, the train to Fulton had a mix of personnel guaranteed to entertain Churchill. One person often omitted is Inspector Williams of New Scotland Yard. Security may have prevented his first name from being used; however, his appellation proved intriguing. For a nation enamored of Sherlock Holmes mysteries, the inclusion of someone from the Yard seemed very exciting. *The Milwaukee Journal,* on top of such detail, opined, "At long last there will be an opportunity to observe a genuine Scotland Yard man in the flesh and not through the eyes of A. Conan Doyle." Still covering all the details, the newspaper predicted audible gasps when Americans heard a certain song scheduled to be sung during the visit. "God Save the King," seemed a friendly, but perhaps shocking, choice of music for descendants of American patriots who sang "My Country 'Tis of Thee," to the same tune rather than a song praising a king.[86] (Note: When Queen Elizabeth II took the throne, "Queen" replaced "King.")

A former St. Louisan also appeared on the roster of train goers. Captain Clark M. Clifford, who grew up in St. Louis, served as special counsel to President Truman.[87] An accomplished individual, Clifford successfully ran Truman's campaign for the presidency in 1948. An undergraduate and graduate of law school at Washington University in

St. Louis, Clifford probably relished the idea of returning to Missouri as much as he enjoyed the prospect of spending more time with Winston Churchill.

Matthew J. Connelly, the president's appointment secretary and gatekeeper, joined the group. Press secretary Charles G. Ross, a high school friend of Truman's, also came. He would die in 1950 while holding a press conference. He "died at his post," said Truman, who was very upset at the death of his long-time and trusted friend.[88] Interestingly, Ross stated in 1931, when he worked for the *St. Louis Post Dispatch,* that a president should never pick a newspaperman to fill the press secretary's position. He believed that the reporters would treat the person on their own terms. If the press secretary reacted differently, he thought the press would be resentful.[89]

Another passenger, Ted Marks, who hailed from Kansas City, was born in England. He served in Battery B of the Missouri National Guard and fought in World War I. He met Truman while still in service. Fond of veterans, particularly ones from Missouri, Truman became good friends with Marks, who was a member of Truman's wedding party. A tailor by trade, he made many of Truman's suits for many years. He served as a Veterans Placement Officer in the Federal Government, a job he owed to Truman.[90] Westminster College trustee, John R. Green, the son of the man for whom the Green Lectures at Westminster College was named, rounded off the party of close friends and political advisors with Truman.

The inclusion of so many people associated with Missouri did not surprise those who knew Truman well. Proud of Missouri, he promoted both the state and its people. When it came to trusting people, he trusted Missourians.

Churchill brought others to the group. Among them were Frank Clarke, his host in Miami Beach, and Charles Campbell, British embassy information officer. Campbell attended the Bretton Woods Conference in New Hampshire, a conference that worked on issues dealing with the establishment of an international monetary system.[91] The one woman in the entire group, who rarely received recognition, was Edith Nina "Jo" Sturdee, later Lady Onslow. Jo Sturdee commented about the kindness of Dorothy, the Countess of Halifax, while in America. Interestingly, she later married the countess's nephew. Jo Sturdee typed the *Sinews of Peace* speech.[92]

A number of reasons popped up in the media to explain why the group traveled by train. The most logical one is that Churchill and Truman both wanted more time to get to know each other. They had met only briefly in Potsdam before Churchill had to return to England in time for the election results.

It seems clear that the men did discuss the speech again at some point during the trip, though Truman vigorously denied any knowledge of the speech. According to Churchill, he did show a copy of his speech to Truman while on the train, several hours before he took to the stage. In a telegram to Ernest Bevin sent a couple of days after the speech, Churchill mentioned that Truman "thought it admirable and would do nothing but good."[93] Clifford also mentioned the fact that Truman read a copy of the speech on the train. Truman previously avoided reading it so that he could claim ignorance of its content. When given a copy on the train, he did read it, according to Clifford.[94]

One other matter also proved important as the train motored to Missouri. Truman told Churchill that he planned to send the body of the Turkish Ambassador to the United States back to Turkey on board the *U.S.S. Missouri*, "one of the most powerful battleships in the world." His purpose in doing so was to send a message to Russia that Americans held both Turkey and Greece in high regard and that no untoward aggressive actions by the Russians would be tolerated.[95] Though he did not discuss the Long Telegram (An eight thousand word telegram from Foreign Service Officer, George Kennan, chargé d'affaires, who wrote his views on Soviet aggression and American policy.) with Churchill, the contents had been shared with others. Churchill may have received some information about it before the train ride.[96] According to Clifford, Truman was growing distrustful of Stalin but did not want to appear as though he was endorsing Churchill's speech. As the President of the United States, rather than an ordinary citizen, he had the obligation to try to "try to keep the channels of communication open with Russia." Truman also seemed to need time before making a decision on any aggressive action against Russia.[97]

The entire trip did not involve just serious matters. As the train passed Harper's Ferry, Churchill reminisced about General George McClellan at Harpers Ferry. He then captivated everyone who heard him, when he recited John Greenleaf Whittier's poem about Barbara Frietchie.[98] If they ever doubted his knowledge of history and poetry, the fellow passengers quickly changed their minds.

Clifford Clark, remembering the trip, enjoyed staying up late and talking with Churchill and Charlie Ross. He realized that Churchill was not a big drinker. According to Clark, Churchill liked to nurse his drinks for an hour and a half. His best memory was when Churchill remarked, "If I were to be born again, I would wish to be born in the United States. At one time, it was said that the sun never sets on the British Empire. Those days are gone … The United States is the hope of the future."[99]

Churchill knew something about how to make his hosts relax. He challenged them to poker. He seemed to know that Truman loved poker. Truman's mild-mannered looks may have belied the fact that Truman was a very competitive individual and card games to him were not just games. They were tests of skill. Churchill had learned to play the game during the Boer War and supposedly loved the game. When Churchill was out of hearing range, Truman urged everyone to play his best but to make it professional. At least one objection came from one of the men, who thought Churchill made the perfect pigeon. As the game wore on, Truman started to worry. When Churchill left for a few moments, he urged his fellow players to let Winston start winning. Truman didn't want to fleece his guest. They grudgingly agreed and Churchill's losses were much more palatable to both sides.[100] The Americans had avoided any international repercussions.

After a brief stop in St. Louis, the train made its way to Jefferson City where a parade welcomed Churchill to Missouri. In perfect form, Churchill gave his obligatory V for Victory sign and displayed his cigar. Soon, he was rushed to Fulton for arguably the most important speech of his career outside of public service.

Churchill Onstage at Westminster, March 5, 1946. Photo courtesy of America's National Churchill Museum.

CHAPTER 7

Fulton Welcomes Churchill

Ten thousand people gathered on the county fairgrounds for a chance to glimpse one of their wartime heroes. Many of them were veterans of the war. Among them stood or sat men disabled by war. They chose to wait and possibly meet the man who led men in battle. Women with children came to support their husbands or memorialize the men they lost during the recent war. They couldn't wait to hear the scheduled speech.[101] The speaker was not Churchill.

The year was 1875, almost 75 years prior to Churchill's speech in Fulton. Many people in Fulton had supported the Confederate cause and donned the Confederate soldiers' uniform after they left the city to join the Confederate Army. They viewed themselves as southerners and they would die southerners.

Jefferson Davis, imprisoned after the war, received invitations from a variety of organizations and locations to speak in 1875. Agriculture provided the theme of his speeches. Davis believed the topic held no political tinge and could possibly do much to restore his legacy damaged by defeat in the war. He chose Callaway due to the legend he had heard about its stance against the Union army. No longer wanting to deal with intense controversy, he hoped to speak before sympathetic crowds. So soon after the Civil War, times were different.[102]

As the years passed, other generations of Fultonians filled the city. Their view of the world became more expansive and democratic. School leadership helped make a difference. Patriotism became associated with their state and country. Fultonians now considered themselves Midwesterners and Missourians. The pride of Missouri would soon bring a British hero to their city. He abhorred tyranny just as they did. What a great day it would be.

With streets decorated, people started to line them well before Churchill's arrival. Some ambitious students chose the roofs of fraternity houses to wait for their visitors. Others brought folding chairs and packed lunches from home. All Westminster students received tickets to the gymnasium, which would be packed with people anxious to hear a speech by Churchill. Rumors spread that some had found ways to reuse the tickets by passing them to people outside the gymnasium.

Not in short supply, food awaited the thousands expected to come to Fulton that day. Columbia, Missouri, brought eight truckloads of buns and bread for the 8,000 frankfurters and 3,000 pounds of hamburgers previously furnished. St. Louis vendors set up shop to supply additional fare.[103] Predictions ranged from 20,000 to 30,000 expected visitors. Local organizations set up their own lunch stands. Without the more sophisticated tracking tools in use today, the actual number became hard to estimate. With a holiday declared, locals arrived to view the once-in-a-lifetime event.

Before arriving in Fulton, Truman and Churchill made a quick pass through the streets of Jefferson City and then began their 25-mile journey to Fulton. Liquor did not appear as a line item on any Fulton menu, but his aides found ways to smuggle some for his use. When he received the first drink, Churchill commented that he was beginning to think he arrived in Fulton, Sahara instead of Fulton, Missouri.

The news media began filling the gymnasium. A number of microphones filled the lectern. Today, they are portrayed in the 2010 Wiegand sculpture that stands before the door of the museum. Bob Paquette, who founded the Microphone Museum in Milwaukee, the world's only microphone museum, generously lent the same type of microphones to Wiegand so that their portrayal in the sculpture could be true to what actually existed in Fulton. Paquette served in the Army Air Corps from 1946-1948.[104] A film of the actual 1946 speech, featuring newsreel footage captured by news media organizations present at the speech, can also be viewed at the museum.

St. Louis radio stations KMOX, KSD, KWK, and KXOK all prepared to transmit the speech, as did KRFU in Columbia, Missouri.[105] The basement of the gymnasium held desks and typewriters for about 400 members of the press. Television, still in its infancy, did not play a part since Churchill preferred radio coverage only.[106] It didn't seem to matter. Communication of the speech was not in danger.

Before long, the presidential motorcade arrived. The crowd roared and the parade began. People held up their flags and pennants and waved them at the two men. Both men waved back to the crowd. Churchill doffed his hat, made the victory sign, and held his cigar for all to see. The Kemper Military Academy band played "The Missouri Waltz." Flashbulbs from cameras illuminated the path of the automobiles. Finally the entourage reached the college president's house, where lunch was served. Churchill loved the ham featured at the luncheon and made a very Churchillian remark, "The pig, here, has reached the highest point of evolution." He would miss the roast beef supper so that he could meet and shake hands with the mothers of 57 graduates who had been killed in the war. However, he did have time to take a quick nap before the group headed for the gymnasium for his speech.[107]

Churchill had changed to the more formal attire appropriate for the ceremony. Music began to play. As predicted, the lyrics for "God Save the King" did not become a crowd favorite once people realized the English lyrics did not match the ones sung by Americans. In keeping with the solemnity of the occasion, no audible gasps were heard.[108] God Save the King!

CHAPTER 8

The Sinews of Peace Speech[109]

Curiously, some people believe that Churchill argues for war in his speech. For some unknown reason, the title escapes them. The word "sinews", meaning tendon and signifying the source of strength, is used to form part of the overriding theme. "Peace" forms the other part. Churchill is speaking about ways in which the bonds of peace can be strengthened. He is not making a call to war. Rather, he is urging everyone to find ways in which peace can be maintained.

At the very beginning of his speech, Churchill tries to form a connection that he will highlight throughout the speech. He informs his audience that he received his education at another Westminster, a bit of history that makes the two places "kindred establishments." He also establishes that he is speaking as a private citizen, rather than a representative of the British government. This fact gives him more independence in what he is about to say. Again, he references the "kindred nation" of the United States to whom he is providing "faithful counsel."

He goes on to explain that although the two nations achieved "absolute victory" in World War II, victory came at a cost of "sacrifice and suffering." Again, he is establishing a connection by acknowledging the common sacrifice and suffering that befell people of each country. He tries to put the sacrifice in perspective by saying that it was done "for the future glory and safety of mankind," an important statement since he will touch on the need to safeguard the world later in the speech.

He gives credit to the United States for being "at the pinnacle of world power." Churchill readily admits that the war has increased the standing and power of the United States, while privately he understands it has had the opposite effect on Britain. The word "duty" is used as a reminder of his long-standing belief in duty to one's country and the world. He states that people might feel "anxious" that they might lose standing but reminds them that the present-day provides "opportunities … for both … countries," opportunities that should not be squandered.

Although the war resulted in peace, Churchill states that there is a "severe requirement" to continue on the path of "consistency of mind {and} persistency of purpose." The rationale for this path is discussed in his speech.

Finally, he reveals the "strategic concept" that is foremost on his mind. "It is nothing less than the safety and welfare, the freedom and progress, of all the homes and families of all the men and women in all the lands."

Churchill understands that presidents are constrained by popular opinion. He directs his speech to the people in hopes of increasing their knowledge of current events. He is fighting against attitudes that foster a belief in appeasement, a belief that slowed the involvement of the United States in past world wars. He references "homes" and then the "cottage or apartment homes," trying to persuade people why involvement is necessary. The use of the latter two words probably fell on deaf ears, since "cottage" in American vernacular generally refers to a summer home. Apartment homes, while numerous in heavily populated cities such as New York and Washington DC, did not have the same connection to the rest of the country. His reference to the "wage-earners {who strive} to guard … wife and children from privation and bring the family up in the fear of the Lord" is more powerful.

As he continues, he states the need to provide "security" to the homes and to shield them "from the two giant marauders, war and tyranny." Churchill understands that the citizens of the United States abhor war and tyranny, a belief shared by the citizens of Britain. He brings religion into the discussion since he understands the potency of religion on ethics, attitudes, and belief systems. He references the ruin of Europe and "large parts of Asia" to remind people of the horrors inflicted by the recent war on people worldwide. He wants people to understand that "duty" applies to people beyond their own country, for everyone suffered an unimaginable loss. It is important that he tries to suppress feelings of xenophobia, or fear of foreign strangers, so that people have a broader perspective of their duty towards their fellow man.

He then refers to the actions of "wicked men" and the "aggressive urge of mighty States" that "dissolve over large areas the frame of civilized society." By referring to the people impacted as "humble folk," he is trying to get people in the United States to realize that what is happening elsewhere in the world is relatable to them. People in the United States and people in other countries are both impacted by aggressors and wicked men. The victims in other countries are "humble folk." He tells his audience that these people cannot cope with the problems that are happening. He is hoping to elicit sympathy for their plight.

He continues and massages his words. He "shudders to visualize what is actually happening to millions {of people.}" He emphasizes their pain and says that it is "our supreme task and duty … to guard the homes of the common people from the horrors and miseries of another war." Rather than ask if they agree, he makes a definitive statement: "We are all agreed on that."

At this point in the speech, he discusses the role of the newly formed United Nations, "the successor to the League of Nations," … which is "a world organization … for the prime purpose of preventing war." He inserts the organization into the speech as one way that the world can try to assure peace. However, Churchill is secretly wary of the fledgling organization. Problems with Russia over the selection of members had become contentious. Still suffering from growing pains, the United Nations seemed incapable of immediately and successfully dealing with the magnitude of problems it faced. Further, problems related to the safeguarding of information already occurred.[110]

Four countries, the United Kingdom, Russia, the United States, and China, participated at the Dumbarton Oaks Conferences (Washington Conversations on International Peace and Security Organization) in 1944 and 1945. The purpose of the conference was to shape an organization (The United Nations Organization) to succeed the League of Nations and successfully maintain international peace and security. Approximately 50 countries had to ratify it its establishment. Roosevelt told reporters that the new organization's purpose was to deal with "some aggressor that started to run amok and seek to grab territory or invade its neighbors." Churchill, on the other hand, was more concerned about seeking a "balance of power" so that the Soviet Union did not dominate affairs in Europe. Stalin wanted to protect itself from further German or other European expansionism that might jeopardize Russia. It also had expansion plans.[111]

The actual charter prohibited force or the threat of force in international relations and required that all members "settle their disputes by peaceful means in such a manner that international peace and security are not endangered."[112]

Churchill, of course, had more imminent problems on his mind in the days before the end of the war. He also had to contend with those Americans who were more concerned about breaking up the British Empire. Problems in negotiations within the United Nations began almost immediately when Russia refused to meet directly with China. The course of the new organization did not run smoothly.[113]

Problems in safeguarding information further jeopardized the new organization. An enterprising reporter named James Reston (*The New York Times)* convinced a young Chinese delegate to provide copies of all the position papers of each of the four major players. The *Times,* in competition with its rival newspaper, *The New York Herald-Tribune,* published the papers over the course of a few days and continued to do so after representatives of the conference warned of the impact on the sustainability of the conference. Reston won the Pulitzer Prize for reporting in 1945.[114] Specifically, he received the award for articles he wrote on the Dumbarton Security Conference. Understandably, Churchill maintained concerns over security measures and more so after the atomic bomb blast in Japan. Reston, lauded as a man of integrity and an excellent journalist, died in 1995. His treatment of the position papers is more likely an expression of accepted practices of the time.[115]

Problems with the United Nations undoubtedly shaped Churchill's view of the organization in its fledgling state. It is probably why he said, "we must be certain that our temple is built, not upon shifting sands or quagmires, but upon the rock." Once again he references the Christian bible to solidify his view.[116]

For some time, Churchill had wanted to include a united air power to the United Nations and he included that in his speech. As he said, "I wished to see this done after the first world war and I devoutly trust it may be done forthwith."

He then launched into the issue of the atomic bomb, something that caused him great anxiety. Ambassador W. Averell Harriman noted that the "Russians had found in Berlin laboratories {that} Germans were working on the breaking of the atom but … did not find that they had come to any results." He also indicated that the Soviets had been working on it without a result.[117] His later interview with George Andreychin, a Bulgarian-American revolutionary, had found that the

American bomb shocked the Russians, "who thought it exposed their weakness."[118] This information, if he had it, would surely have made Churchill blanch. He did not want the Russians to have access to the atomic bomb secrets.

On the other hand, Churchill did want the United States to share information with the United Kingdom. Frustrated at the end of similar sharing of secrets during the war, he thought that a better relationship on the matter would succeed in providing more, not less, security. Also concerned about further unilateral use of the bomb from the American base in East Anglia without the knowledge or agreement of Britain, Churchill later received written agreement from Truman that it would not take such a similar unilateral action. Fear of reprisal worried Churchill and others in Britain.[119]

Speaking before the US Congress in 1952, Churchill had uttered a warning.

> If I may say this, members of Congress, be careful above all things, therefore, not to let go of the atomic weapon until you are sure, and more than sure, that other means of preserving peace are in your hands. It is my belief that by accumulating deterrents of all kinds against aggression we shall, in fact, ward off the fearful catastrophe, the fears of which darken the life and mar the progress of all the peoples of the globe.

Thus, Churchill had conflicting emotions. Both centered on the prevention of war. The first emotion involved holding tight to the weapon that might deter war and the second involved keeping the secret of it away from anyone or any country that might use it to wreak havoc in the world. The second emotion is the one he expressed in his speech at Westminster College.

Returning to Churchill's *Sinews of Peace* speech, Churchill tried to put people at ease after his mention of the atomic bomb. He added references to God and a biblical quotation. "We have at least a breathing space to put our house in order." The "brotherhood of man", with the appropriate "safeguards," can put together safeguards in a world organization. He is expressing his hope in the future of the United Nations.

Next, he deals with the issue of tyranny, something that is carefully studied in the histories of both Britain and the United States in Part II. Democratic societies detest tyranny; however, Churchill acknowledges that not all countries are democratic. Nor do they enjoy the same liberties. "Control is enforced upon the common people." He tries to assure people that it is not the duty of either country to "forcibly ensure" democracy or liberties in countries that "we have not conquered." But, he insists that both countries "must never cease to proclaim in fearless tones the great principles of freedom and the rights of man."

His paragraph is to the point, articulate, and historically accurate. The audience in front of him probably understood the meaning of the Bill of Rights and Declaration of Independence, though they may not all have understood fully the history of the Magna Carta, Habeas Corpus, and English common law. That is not to say that people were probably ignorant of such subjects. They may not have been fully educated on their history and the connection that they have to the Declaration of Independence and the Bill of Rights. Churchill may have not been a great student while attending school but his education broadened once he left it. Further, he had such a deep interest in the history of both countries that he drank in as much information as he could about that history. Not all Americans had the same thirst.

Next, he launches into the right to vote, something that both countries struggled to achieve for all people. Churchill is thoroughly convinced that free elections and the power to "choose or change the character or form of government under which they dwell" are essential. When he

Courtesy of Baxter Watson, Photographer.

sees that right being taken away from people, he becomes very upset. It is at the heart of democracy. Further, he explains that "freedom of speech" and "justice" are the "title deeds of freedom." Many Americans are familiar with the manner in which Norman Rockwell characterized Franklin Roosevelt's words on the Four Freedoms in his paintings, so there is undoubtedly an understanding among Americans of the necessity for freedom in many areas of life. Churchill believes his words will resonate with people.

Then he asks all Americans to "practice what we preach," a familiar phrase and another biblical reference. If people can successfully deal with the two "great dangers" of "war and tyranny," the existing problems related to food shortages could be addressed, and addressed quickly, so that there is no danger of denying "to all nations the inauguration and enjoyment of an age of plenty" or freedom from want, as Rockwell depicted in his paintings. Again, rather than wait for their approval, he states, "we are in full agreement."

Finally, he comes to one of the most important parts of the speech, the issue of "fraternal association" or "special relationship," an idea he has tried to convey for some time. It is also an idea he tries to convey in his "History of the English-Speaking Peoples" and at a speech that he made at Harvard University. He is not speaking about an alliance, though many people will assume that he is. He explains that he is talking about the need for the two countries, two "kindred systems of society" to grow in "friendship" and "mutual understanding." He thinks that the commonalities in their background make friendship and mutual understanding easy to achieve. He says that he is certain that an "intimate relationship and interchange between our military advisors will provide mutual security and joint use of weaponry." Using British military bases would double the power of American defense, expand British defense, and save money. Without mentioning alliances, he adds that there are already islands that both countries use together. This particular paragraph in his speech stirs the most emotion as it is misconstrued by newspapers and then by citizens who do not want to do anything that might precipitate another war. They are done with wars.

But Churchill goes on to say that the United States already has an agreement with Canada, which is part of the British Commonwealth, and it is a better arrangement than any type of alliance. He wants the same agreement to be extended to the entire British Commonwealth "with full reciprocity." He envisions that someday the United States and the British Commonwealth can have "common citizenship." Interestingly, John F. Kennedy and US Congress gave honorary citizenship to Churchill during Kennedy's presidential term.

For those who might be uncertain about forming a special relationship that rules out other countries, Churchill explains that the same type of relationship can exist with other countries that "have no aggressive point against any other countries." Again, he appeals to the religious by reminding them, "in my father's house are many mansions." Churchill pins his hopes on the United Nations, another indication that he is hopeful for its future.

To appeal to Americans in another way, he describes the special relationship as something akin to workmen working together with their "families intermingled" and their "faith in each other's purpose." If they don't "share their tools … the temple may not be built." The words "faith, hope, charity, and temple" once again are meant to relate to the religious citizenry. He references the "Temple of Peace" to highlight peace; however, the actual temple in Rome contained treasures captured in Jerusalem, something he did not mean to reference.

While considering the analogy of workmen working together, he reminds his audience that "time may be short" for action. "Allowing events to drift along until it is too late" is not an option. Peace requires "strength and security." Prevention (immediate action) is much preferable to war (the cure.) He is hoping to convince people to take peaceful actions to prevent war in the future.

His next statement, "a shadow has fallen upon the scenes so lately lighted by the Allied victory" is an introduction to the reference he will soon make to the "iron curtain." Originally, the iron curtain was used in theatrical productions to safeguard the audience in case of fire. Now Churchill is referring to what is happening in Europe as "scene so lately lighted" just as scenes are on stage. The use of both the darkness of shadow and the glow of light are meant to show the competing forces of good and evil found on the world stage. His use of words is brilliant.

Though he references the opposing forces, he wants to ensure that people don't mistake his talk as a bashing of Russia. He takes pains to express his "admiration for the Russian people and for … Stalin." He says there is "goodwill in Britain for Russia" and a "need to establish long-lasting friendships" with her. He even states that he understands the need for Russia to be "secure on her western borders and remove any trace of possible German aggression." He "welcomes Russia to her rightful place among the leading nations of the world." But, and this is a big but, he believes he must inform the world of certain "facts about the present position in Europe."

Churchill is careful to take this approach since most people think of Stalin as "Uncle Joe" who helped other countries during World War II. At this point in time, Stalin is not viewed as a villain or an aggressor. He is a friend. What Churchill is gearing up to say is that even friends may have ulterior motives.

Amazingly, at this most important point in the speech, the speaker system went out. Thanks to an intrepid worker who held two wires together for the rest of the talk, Churchill's words did not get lost.[120]

When he introduces the concept of an "iron curtain," Churchill specifically names "all the ancient capitals that lay behind it." Not all of the capitals actually fell behind the iron curtain, so why did he use them? This part of the speech is the most important part of Churchill's composition. The beat and sound had to work perfectly. The presence of so many "t," "b," and "p" sounds created the importance and emphasis he needed. The words startled any person whose mind might have drifted to another thought. People may not have known exactly where the capitals were located but they understood that they played a part in an important event that required their attention. A more descriptive analysis of these capitals is found in the next chapter. For purposes of this chapter, they form an important part of Churchill's speech. Aside from their political importance, they give movement and rhythm to the speech and energize it.

Churchill did not coin the words "iron curtain." Part of his genius was his ability to store data in the filing cabinets of his mind for later use. According to Martin Gilbert, he used the words previously in letters to Truman. He referenced a curtain in his book about World War I. Several other people used the same phrase. Researchers have noted its use by H.G. Wells, Ethel Snowden, and Vasily Vasilievich Rozanov. Joseph Goebbels used it in a similar manner to Churchill. Still other uses may be found in the future.

When considering the importance of Churchill's words as opposed to the same words used in other instances or by others, an analysis of their full meaning, relevance, and impact is important. While Churchill did not coin the phrase, it only became common parlance after he used it in his speech at Westminster College. He used the words to provide imagery in direct opposition to its normal usage, which references a theatrical curtain. He is not telling his audience that the curtain safeguards them, which is what the theatrical curtain does. He is telling them that the curtain eliminates transparency and hides what is happening with Soviet aggression. He paints a much sharper, darker, and dire picture of current world events. He is explaining that these events affect everyone, not just the countries behind the Iron Curtain. He is portraying a situation in need of immediate attention to prevent the possibility of war in the future. To emphasize his point, he uses bold words and phrases such as "a shadow has fallen," "enormous," "wrongful," "mass expulsions," "grievous," "undreamed of," "totalitarian," "profoundly alarmed," and "disturbed" to represent bold strokes on the canvas he paints of Europe and Soviet aggression. He wants his audience to visualize the problem more vividly.

He explains the situation in Berlin, a city partitioned into zones, to show that the Americans and British armies gave Russia the ability to occupy a zone that western democracies had conquered. The "build-up of a pro-Communist Germany" in that area now gives "the Germans the power of putting themselves up to auction between the Soviets and the western democracies." He adds, with emphasis, "This is not the Liberated Europe we fought to build-up. Nor is it one that contains the essentials of permanent peace."

Why is this message important? He is warning people that the safety of the world requires unity of action. He reminds people of the two world wars that thrust the United States into horrible wars, causing it to send "several millions of its young men across the Atlantic." He knows that Americans have a tendency to isolate themselves from problems that occur in nations far from their own borders. He is telling them that geographic distance does not and will not matter for "war can find any nation." He paints American soldiers as "young" in an effort to highlight the danger and make it more understandable. If Americans want to avoid the loss of young lives in the future, Churchill argues that Britain and the United States should "work with conscious purpose" for peace just as they state they want to do in the newly formed United Nations. Churchill is walking a thin line. He wants to educate people and make them understand the need for action. He does not want to immobilize them with fear.

Churchill's push for action is undoubtedly partly based on his understanding of the military imbalance in the making. Both the United States and Britain are under pressure to demobilize as quickly as possible so that loved ones can return to their families who want to put the war behind them. Meanwhile, the Soviet Union is trying to beef up its military to prepare for the possibility of future aggression. One possible alternative is to have the United Nations provide a united military force to maintain peace.

Communism, he continues, is an enormous threat to freedom and democracy. It is creating an anxious situation in Italy. He fears for France since he believes a strong France is necessary for a strong Europe. As Anne Applebaum states in her book, *Iron Curtain: The Crushing of Eastern Europe, 1944-1956,* the "French communist party won the largest number of votes in the parliamentary election of 1945."[121] To emphasize his point, he explains that communism "constitutes a growing challenge and a peril to Christian civilization." The repetitive use of religion is for a purpose. He wants people to clearly understand that their religious freedom is at stake. Even though communism isn't currently a threat within the borders of the British Commonwealth and the United States, he lets people know that it is still a threat, since it is only "in its infancy" in those two countries. His statement is a clear warning of the threat to everyday life, as the audience currently knows it.

Next, he turns to the Far East where the "outlook is anxious." He believes Americans are well informed. He reminisces about the Versailles Treaty, parts of which he strongly opposed. Yet, he says he does not have the same feeling of hope that he did after the First World War and the formation of the League of Nations, which was the precursor to the United Nations.

Nevertheless, he assures his audience that he does not want another war and he does not think one is imminent. This statement is one that is often overlooked by people who thought of him as a warmonger. Also, he denies emphatically that Soviet Russia desires war. He is "speaking out since it is his duty to do so." He reiterates that he wants to "prevent war." He speaks against appeasement by saying that people cannot "close their eyes to what is happening. There needs to be a settlement without delay to avoid the danger that he believes lies ahead."

On the plus side, he believes that "the Soviets respond to strength and despise weakness, especially military weakness." He is trying to assure people that action will not cause a negative reaction leading to war. The balance of power that Britain has tried to achieve throughout history can occur, he believes, if western democracies are united. In making that statement, he is again trying to highlight the relationship of democracy that the two countries have as well as his belief that "united we stand," a familiar American phrase. To avoid saying those exact words he injects the word "divided" and places it near the word "catastrophe" for effect.

He reminds people that the last time he saw a major problem brewing, people disregarded his warning and a world war erupted. "Germany might have been saved from the awful fate that has overtaken her." Timeliness of action, he stresses, is important so that everyone is not "sucked into the awful whirlpool." He pleads for people not to "let that happen again." The solution for peace is provided in his speech, aptly named the *Sinews of Peace.* He wants everyone to know the simplicity of such a solution and the complexity of inaction.

"Let no man underrate the power of the British Empire and Commonwealth" are the beginning words of the end of his speech. Despite their many hardships, which he describes, "they have come through the glorious year of agony." By uniting their remarkable force and energy with that of the United States, he says, "there will be no quivering, precarious balance of power to offer its temptation to ambition or adventure." With emphasis, he states that uniting the two powers will bring the "assurance of security" by nations who do not wish to "seek or lay … arbitrary control upon the thoughts of men." Fraternal association, which he finds analogous to a special relationship, is the answer that he believes will secure the "high roads of the future for all mankind."

CHAPTER 9

From Stettin in the Baltic

While working on his book, *The World Crisis,* a historical work about World War I, Churchill sent a message to his devoted wife, Clementine. Anxious to tell her about the book's progress, he said writing it gave him "a great chance to put my whole case in agreeable form to an attentive audience."[122] Similarly, Churchill's speech at Westminster is written in a clear, understandable, and "agreeable form" given its subject matter. Churchill judiciously used words in hopes that his audience could make no mistake about what he said, although many ignored his words and interpreted the speech differently. Churchill wanted to reach Americans directly and not through their politicians or the press. In that way, he believed, they would be able to make their own informed decisions about current events.

The section of the speech that may cause some difficulty for the average audience is the section on the "capitals of the ancient states." The text states the following.

> From Stettin in the Baltic to Trieste in the Adriatic, an iron curtain has descended across the Continent. Behind that line lie all the capitals of the ancient states of Central and Eastern Europe. Warsaw, Berlin, Prague, Vienna, Budapest, Belgrade, Bucharest and

> Sofia, all these famous cities and the populations around them lie in what I must call the Soviet sphere, and all are subject in one form or another, not only to Soviet influence but to a very high and, in many cases, increasing measure of control from Moscow.

To clarify what Churchill meant, while not every city was truly behind the curtain, the cities he mentioned are described as follows to indicate their history, Russian influence, and locale relative to the iron curtain pictured by Churchill.[123]

Stettin—Germany: (behind the Iron Curtain)

In 1945, the city of Stettin, which lay near the mouth of the Oder River, served as the Baltic port of Germany. During World War II, a number of bombings had reduced most of the city to ruin. In 1945, the Russian Army invaded it. Some Germans fled the city and moved further west to Germany before that happened. Many Germans still occupied the city though living conditions had been severely hampered by the effects of continuous bombings. Food shortages created other problems. Contentious discussions took place among Russia, Britain, and the United States over the question of post-war borders. Russia wanted a large part of what was then eastern Poland. In return, it suggested that a portion of eastern Germany be given to Poland. That part included Stettin. The resolution of the conflict was not easy. Both the United States and Britain wanted Stettin to remain a part of Germany. Russia said that it would turn over the area to the Polish government if border changes were approved. They did not mention that they intended communism to prevail. In the end, Stettin, which was actually divided into two parts by the Oder River, became part of Poland. The Poles changed its name to Szczecin. Communist Russia controlled much of it, including elections, until they turned it over to Poland. Nevertheless, communism, established by the Soviets, continued to have a grip on the country. As Churchill said at Westminster College, "the … Communist fifth columns … work in complete unity and absolute obedience to the directions they receive from the Communist center." Mass expulsion of Germans began when Polish residents of eastern Poland, taken over by Russia, were repatriated to the city. Churchill described these expulsions in his "Iron Curtain" speech. He said, "The Russian-dominated Polish Government has been encouraged to make enormous and wrongful inroads upon Germany, and mass expulsions of millions of Germans on a scale grievous and undreamed-of are now taking place." German street names and culture were systematically removed from Stettin. Violence became commonplace and included the "deliberate burning of buildings, rapes, arrests, and deportations."[124] Such actions did not constitute the "fruits of war." They were scurrilous, repugnant, and repulsive actions.[125]

Trieste—Now part of Italy (questionable if behind the Iron Curtain then)

The Trieste question, after World War II, centered on which country would control the city. At the time of Churchill's speech, the answer was not clear. Churchill may have included the city to gain support for keeping it out of Communist Russia's hands. He knew that the British government wanted more control over the city to protect the Mediterranean, which was vital to them. American Slovenes who lived in Ohio, primarily in the Cleveland area, paid particular attention to the mention of Trieste in Churchill's speech. Many, but not all, of them had been political refugees who left Trieste and the areas surrounding it after constant bombings destroyed their homes and occupying forces tortured and killed members of their community. Ohio offered the chance for them to maintain their culture, find employment and housing, and live without fear of political oppression in a Slovene community, which at one time had the third-largest number of Slovenes in the world. Situated on the Gulf of Trieste, a shallow bay of the Adriatic Sea, Trieste served as a seaport. At the time of the speech, Slovenes, Croatians, and small Montenegrin and Serb minorities occupied the hinterland. The entire region, disputed by Italy and the People's Federal Republic of Yugoslavia, was sometimes referred to as the Julian March (Venezia Giulia) region. After World War I, Italy annexed the region, which included Trieste. The Nazi Germans occupied Trieste during World War II. Neither of these occupations made for peaceful times. The Slovenes did not like the Nazis or the Italians. Atrocities committed by both countries instilled a deep hatred in the Slovenes for both of them. Thousands of people ended up persecuted or killed in both occupations. A German concentration camp with a crematorium in Trieste functioned as a detention and death camp for political prisoners and a detention center for Jews, who were bound for Auschwitz. Intent on punishing partisan insurgents, the Nazis sometimes burned entire villages. Both Russia and the Slovenes pushed for Trieste to become part of Yugoslavia. In 1947, Trieste became part of Italy. Slovenes felt betrayed. They did not think that the United States, in particular, understood the ethnicity of the area or its history. A British-American force administered Trieste for several months before withdrawing. Had Trieste come under Yugoslav rule, it would have been behind the Iron Curtain. Some changes did occur after 1946 and those changes affected the borders.[126]

Warsaw—Poland (behind the Iron Curtain)

The Russian Army invaded Poland, pushing out the German occupying force. The Nazis had destroyed much of the city during the years of their occupation. Russia took control to ensure its placement behind the Iron Curtain. The Crimea (Yalta) agreement reached by the three parties, Britain, Russia, and the United States, called for a more broadly based form of government in Warsaw and free elections in the future. Agreements made at Yalta did not always come to fruition in reality.[127]

Berlin—Germany (west of the Iron Curtain)

In 1946, Berlin was far west of the Iron Curtain; however, Churchill wanted to make several comments about it. "An attempt is being made by the Russians in Berlin to build up a quasi-Communist party in their zone of Occupied Germany by showing special favors to groups of left-wing German leaders. At the end of the fighting last June, the American and British Armies withdrew westwards, in accordance with an earlier agreement, to a depth at some points of 150 miles upon a front of nearly four hundred miles, in order to allow our Russian allies to occupy this vast expanse of territory, which the Western Democracies had conquered. If now the Soviet Government tries, by separate action, to build up a pro-communist Germany in their areas, this will cause new serious difficulties in the British and American zones, and will give the defeated Germans the power of putting themselves up to auction between the Soviets and the Western Democracies." Churchill then emphatically stated, "This is certainly not the Liberated Europe we fought to build up." Had Churchill not included Berlin as a capital behind the Iron Curtain, he would not have had the same leeway to make these comments, which he so desperately wanted to convey.[128]

Prague—Czechoslovakia (behind the Iron Curtain)

Germans occupied the city during World War II; however, the Czech resistance joined with citizens toward the end of the war to defeat them. A few days later, the Russian Army liberated the city. Other German troops had tried to stop the resistance but the Czechs had slowed their arrival by placing obstacles in their path. The Czech people disliked the Nazis, who killed many residents of their community; they greeted the Russians with warmth. The Germans had treated the citizens better than the people in most of the areas that they occupied because they believed many of them were Aryan. Still, the Czech people hated the German occupiers. Both Churchill and General Patton had wanted to help liberate the city, but Eisenhower stopped any action on the

Edwina Sandys, Churchill's granddaughter, designed this Breakthrough *sculpture from a portion of the Berlin Wall and negotiated its relocation to Westminster. Photo courtesy of America's National Churchill Museum.*

part of the Americans and British Armies. He had conferred with Stalin on the matter and did not want to incur any more losses or antagonize the Russians any further since they had been very helpful during the war. Churchill thought that if the western allies tried to liberate the city, their help might stop the progression of communism in Czechoslovakia and surrounding areas. The lack of support from Britain and America helped turn Czechs against them and made them more inclined to favor communism. The Czechs approved of left-leaning policies of "nationalization of industries, social experiments, and expulsion of Germans and Hungarians." Atrocities continued after the liberation. As in other countries, citizens often want payback for the horrible treatment they received during an occupation. The democratic government of Czechoslovakia was toppled by a communist coup d'état. The democratic Czechoslovakia that Churchill mentioned in his speech ended.[129]

Vienna—Austria (west of the Iron Curtain)

The Allies partitioned both Austria and Vienna after World War II. Portions of the city received heavy damage during the war, but not as much as in other cities occupied by the Germans. Issues did arise with Russia, which had entered a space other than its own and, according to the Americans, had no real "interest in the restoration of Austria as a democracy." The Russians also "seized property and deported individuals without the approval of the Allied Council." Americans believed that the Russians wanted to destroy the existing government and take whatever they could. Churchill probably considered these issues as a threat to democracy and thus included Vienna as a capital behind the Iron Curtain.[130]

Budapest—Hungary (behind the Iron Curtain)

By the end of January 1945, three-fourths of Budapest had fallen to the Russians. The 2nd Ukrainian Front captured the railroad station in Buda and the Russians soon captured the rest, including Pest on the other side of the Danube.[131] The Nazis left the country devastated and lost 625 tanks and more than 14,700 men while trying to maintain their hold on it. In October of the previous year, the Germans, with the help of Premier Ferenc Szalasi, the Fascist leader of Hungary, carried out a horrific pogrom to exterminate thousands of Jews living in the country. Though many had obtained the necessary paperwork required to leave the country, their oppressors destroyed the passes and beat their holders. A forced march of 120 kilometers to the Hungarian border took place for those who survived. At least one-fourth of the 100,000 Jewish people on the march died before reaching the border. Their suffering was only part of the total suffering experienced by Jews during the German occupation. By the time Budapest was rescued by the Russians, it was, as one newspaper described, "a forlorn heap of wreckage."[132]

Belgrade—Yugoslavia (behind the Iron Curtain)

When President Josip Broz Tito died on May 4, 1980, he had served as president of the Socialist Republic of Yugoslavia for almost thirty years. The country included six socialist republics: Bosnia and Herzegovina, Croatia, Macedonia, Montenegro, Serbia, and Slovenia. Belgrade served as its capital. Tito had previously led the Yugoslavian guerilla movement and his people considered him their great liberator. After the agreement to transfer Trieste to Italy, Yugoslavia became a country. First controlled by the Soviet Union, Yugoslavia formed its own brand of communism under Tito. The break with Russia occurred in 1948. Yugoslavia no longer remained in the Soviet Bloc. A much-loved figure, Tito was viewed as a person who always tried to the best for his country, even if it meant breaking ties with the Soviet Union. He was ready to fight Stalin to prove it. In response, Stalin sent assassins to kill Tito on 22 separate occasions. One biographer suggests that Stalin died of poisoning rather than a stroke. He claims that Tito had Stalin murdered, though that accusation was never proven. In 1995, Khrushchev apologized for Stalin's assassination attempts.[133]

Bucharest—Romania (behind the Iron Curtain)

In an effort to save his country, the King of Romania agreed to cooperate with Germany by becoming part of the Axis. He could not save the thousands of Jews brutally murdered during Nazi control of the country. When Russia "liberated" the country, they forced non-communists out of power by accusing them of failing to remove the fascists. This communist action took place not long after the agreement at Yalta in Crimea, which was meant to stop "political interference in the integrity of liberated and ex-satellite countries." As Lord Dunglass, the British Conservative politician said at the Crimean Conference on February 27, 1945,

> Therefore, a Europe of small, free, independent States is a fundamental British interest, and we interpret this Clause as covering the right of Poland and other sovereign States to real independence. We could never be a party to a process under which a whole range of the smaller countries of Europe was drawn, by a mixture of military pressure from without and political disruption from within, into the orbit of another and a greater Power. The communists took control of the country.

Interestingly, Dunglass also questioned whether Russia's "actions would correspond to her pledged word," noting that Russia is "very good at keeping things under her hat."[134]

Sofia—Bulgaria (behind the Iron Curtain)

In 1941, Bulgaria united with Germany and became an Axis satellite state. In so doing, it declared war on both Britain and the United States. Its declaration did not include Russia, which invaded the country in 1944 without resistance. Four days later, an armistice was signed. Although no Allied ground fighting occurred in the country, the United States did provide air power. A number of its aviation crewmembers ended up being captured and imprisoned in Bulgaria. While that is a fact, it is also a fact that Russia actually invaded Bulgaria and took control of the country. That is the point at which the three Great Powers started to diverge on their special interest in Bulgaria. Russia did share a background with Bulgaria that included commonality in race, language and religion. However, they had not engaged in any fighting there prior to their takeover of the country near the end of the war. Before World War II, the British government had helped Bulgaria achieve independence from Turkey. They grew concerned about it falling into the hands of communism after the war ended, something that they strenuously opposed. The United States wanted to help the country move in a more democratic direction. Despite the opposition of Britain and the United States, Russia quickly gained control of the country and its army. They quickly eliminated people with opposing views from any other discussion. Despite the initial efforts at improving the independence of Bulgaria and other countries, the attempt to initiate a democratic shift in Sofia failed. The western Allies became concerned about elections and the freedoms accorded its citizens. The freedom of speech, the press, religion, choice of politics, and the freedom to peacefully assemble were some of the freedoms specifically addressed. The actions that Russia took to suppress these freedoms did not meet the conditions laid out by the Crimean agreement. Both Britain and the US protested.[135]

CHAPTER 10

Reviews

In the theater, the reviews are all-important. They can make or break a show. Watch an old movie about a show on Broadway and one scene will include the theater cast waiting to read the reviews in the wee hours of the morning. If the critic says the show is a bomb, that usually means it's lights out for the show. If the critic says the show is wonderful, the cast can relax, for a short time at least. Most shows do not fall into either category. Most shows get mixed reviews. Surely Churchill knew that. If so, the reviews did not disappoint.

Quotes from a wide range of newspapers are found in clippings on Churchill during 1946. Some people hated the speech. Some people loved it. Some responses gave mixed reviews. Some people inserted their own political ideology. Some people spiced their language with ad hominem remarks. Everyone, it seems, had an opinion.

Communication requires a good speaker and a good listener. As James C. Humes pointed out in his book, *The Sir Winston Method,* "The Ear is one-tenth the organ of the eye." Elaborating, he explained, "There is no tube that carries all your words to the listener's ears."[136] Based on the criticism appearing in the news media, not everyone heard every word. Some may not have listened at all. Some may have waited to read what someone else wrote. Some may have just wanted to express their frustrations about something unrelated to the speech. Some newspapers relied on Associated Press articles. It is interesting today to read what was said almost 75 years ago. Some people misunderstood the meaning of the words "alliance," "fraternal associations," and "special relationships." Some people thought that dual citizenship and shared military bases meant military involvement. Some people thought it posed a threat for the United Nations. Some people had no sympathy for the British. Some people believed in isolationism. Weary of war, many people thought Churchill promoted yet another one in his speech. Those people who correctly understood Churchill's words had polar opposite opinions.

Nevertheless, the Fulton speech shocked the world, which wasn't ready to hear about Soviet misdeeds. Churchill had tried to highlight the need to protect democracy by quickly dealing with situations that could impact freedoms and lead to war and tyranny. He believed the common ideals of Britain and the United States would make them want to work together for better worldwide security. His audience, for the most part, needed time to digest the impact of Soviet expansion. They needed time to remember the close relationship that Britain and the United States shared for many years and what Soviet expansion meant to the basic freedoms they enjoyed.

Included in this section are quotes from 1946 as well as quotes almost 75 years later. Comparing the two periods reveals striking differences.

1946 Comments (March 6-8, 1946)

Advocate (Baton Rouge, LA):

"Churchill's suggestion of an alliance between Great Britain and the United States may not sit well with Anglophobes in this country. His indictment of Russian foreign policy may not sit well with communists … but he voiced the fears and hopes of millions of plain people who hope that the recent war was the last but who fear that the seeds of another war are being sown."

Atlanta Constitution (Atlanta, GA):
"Mr. Churchill in one breath declares he does not believe Russia wants war, but in another he would set up a military alliance against her. In another he expresses high admiration and regard for Marshal Stalin but follows with a denunciation of Stalin policies. It was not a sound speech."[137]

Beaumont Journal (Beaumont, TX) by Marquis Childs:
"Churchill's speech, it seems to me, overlooks a vital truth. That is that you cannot fight the Communist menace by armed alliances."

Boston Traveler (Boston, MA):
"A beautiful plea for the continuance of British imperialism"—Harold J. Laski, British Labor Party Chairman

"It will be time enough for Churchill to criticize Russian expansionist policy when he and the Labor government have liquidated the British Empire."—Fenner Brockway, Independent Labor Party secretary

Chicago Daily News (Chicago, IL) by William H. Stoneman:
"Nothing would be more dangerous or more calculated to put American friendship in jeopardy than an attempt to frame British foreign policy on a presumption of assured American backing."

Daily Nonpareil (Council Bluffs, IA):
"One (school of thought) hold(s) that it would bring hidden distrust out into the open and force a showdown; the other that it would bolster belief that security must entail spheres of influence."

Chicago Daily Times (Chicago, IL):
{Why mutual citizenship?} "Because as a realist in world affairs, Mr. Churchill knows that the one hope of preserving the peace lies in binding together closer and closer the ties between nations whose aspirations and ideals for justice and freedom are similar."

Chicago Daily Times by Carleton Kent:
"The big ovation was for the fat pink-faced type with the determined dewlaps who wore the scarlet gown and black shovel hat and the set expression of contempt for Communists and left-wingers."

Chicago Daily Times by Irving Pflaum:
"He spoke of the iron curtain that has descended across Europe, from Stettin to Trieste—but he said nothing of India, Indo-China or Indonesia, or of the tyranny in Spain."

Chicago Sun (Chicago, IL):
"Winston Churchill was fighting for his world. It is a world which no longer exists in reality. To follow the standard raised by this great but blinded aristocrat would be to march to the world's most ghastly war. Let Mr. Truman's rejection of the poisonous doctrines declared by Mr. Churchill be prompt and emphatic."

Dallas Morning News (Dallas, TX):
{Reuters, London} "But, whether applauding or condemning, political observers here recognized that Churchill's speech was inspired by an urgent desire to prevent the disaster of a fresh war by giving warning of a danger which he genuinely believes to be very real."

Dayton Beach Morning Journal (Daytona, FL):
"Churchill expressed admiration for the Russian people and Marshal Stalin. He repudiated the idea that 'a new war is inevitable' still more 'that it is imminent.'"

Detroit Free Press (Detroit, MI):
"Anglo-American cooperation is one thing and re-entry into the British Empire is another."

Las Vegas Review-Journal by Alex H. Singleton (Las Vegas, NV):
"Churchill spoke at Fulton, Missouri, yesterday as a private citizen.

But the fact that he was introduced by President Truman lent perhaps even more importance to his words than if they had been voiced on the floor of the commons in Churchill's role of leader of His Majesty's Government."

Evansville Press (Evansville, IN):
"Happily, we have a moral alliance with England. In Churchill's noble words: 'The great principles of freedom and the rights of man, which are the joint inheritance of the English-speaking world and which, through Magna Carta, the Bill of Rights, the Habeas Corpus, trial by jury and the English Common Law, find their most famous expression in the Declaration of Independence."

Evening Star (Washington, DC):
{Associated Press} "Parliamentary circles predicted today that Winston Churchill's speech in Fulton, Missouri, might have repercussions in the House of Commons …"

Milwaukee Sentinel (Milwaukee, WI):
"He has made a great speech, and he has lifted the whole problem of British and American relations with Russia to an honest and realistic level."

Newark Star-Ledger (Newark, NJ):
{Editor's Opinion} "Nothing since Britain's ordeals in the war has served to bring the American people as close to the British in sentiment as this forthright, timely and inspired message from the leader whom the British people will not follow in the details of domestic policy, but whom they fervently follow in the great march of history toward the safeguarding of our civilization."

New York Times (New York, NY):
"He came with a message of such interest and importance to our country, to his, and to the world at large, that he converted his presence at Fulton into a historic event."

Omaha World-Herald (Omaha, NE):

"The master political physician diagnosed the world's ills rather accurately only to come up with the wrong prescription. For the forging of a British-American military alliance at this time would be a disruptive rather than a unifying force in world affairs."

Philadelphia Record (Philadelphia, PA):

"In the event that Britain and Russia went to war, is there any doubt as to what America would do—sooner or later? We were almost too late last time. If we are too late next time there will never be another chance."[138]

Repository (Canton, OH):

{Associated Press} "A disturbing new element beset suspicion-riddled Big Three relations today—Winston Churchill's plea for quick creation of an Anglo-American alliance."

Richmond Times Dispatch (Richmond, VA):

{Associated Press} "The President, however, made no reference to the suggested Anglo-American alliance and strictly refrained from any criticism of Russia."

St. Louis Post-Dispatch by Dorothy Thompson (St. Louis, MO):

"… there has been a disposition to play down the seriousness of the situation, and to hope that a conciliatory attitude would be more fruitful than a firm stand. But the fact is that nearly every agreement made by the Soviet Government in Teheran and Yalta, all of which contained extraordinary concessions to the Soviets, has been cynically violated."

San Antonio Light (San Antonio, TX):

"It is to be hoped that the significance of the dramatic sponsorship of his great speech by the president of the United States is that we have come at last to the end of our humiliating road of appeasement of Russia …"

San Francisco Chronicle (San Francisco, CA):
"Simultaneously, the 70,000,000 here and their British brothers ought to climb out of the quandary and take a stand for the application of reason to this world situation—that is, they ought to, seeing their whole futures depend on it."

Times Picayune (New Orleans, LA):
{Associated Press} "The former prime minister's call for sharing of bases and military preparations found some support, but most senators said they want no formal alliance because it might arouse suspicion on the part of Russia and because it would link the United States too closely to British foreign policies."

The Springfield (MA) Republican:
"Churchill's opinions could be read or heard in nearly a score of countries where the English language is either the mother tongue or the second language of somewhere between 300 and 600 million people."

"If worse comes to worst—which the Republican does not anticipate—the English-speaking democracies will hang together, as they have hitherto since the 20th century opened, against any totalitarian or antidemocratic conquest of the spirit of mankind."

Congressional Responses (1946)

Senator Johnson (Democrat) Colorado:
"There already is an unwritten alliance for mutual protection. I'm very sure we are not ready now to have a military alliance that would impose on us the duty of enforcing Britain's foreign policy."

Senator Brewster (Republican) Wyoming:
"Until such time as Russia rolls up the iron curtain, close co-operation between the United States, Britain and other members of the United Nations is essential."

Senator Pepper (Democrat) Florida:

{Churchill has spoken} "in his best Marlborough manner for glorious imperialism—but it is always British imperialism."

Senator Maybank (Democrat) North Carolina:

He agreed with Churchill on most of what he said; however, he "doubted that a military alliance with Britain would curb the tendency of Russia for indefinite expansion."

Senator Connally (Democrat) Texas and Senator George (Democrat) Georgia:

Both men agreed "the United States, Great Britain and Canada should retain the secret of the atomic bomb until test United Nation controls are set up."

Senator Wheeler (Democrat) Montana:

"... found Churchill's address confirmation of fears he said he had expressed before this country became involved in war."

Senator Aiken (Republican) Vermont:

"I'm not ready to enter a military alliance with anyone. Britain, the United States and Russia should pull together to make the United Nations work."

Senator Tydings (Democrat) Maryland:

"I wish we might have what I thought we had—a five power alliance to enforce the peace."[139]

Representative Colmer (Democrat) Mississippi:

"A great speech by a great man—a realistic speech by a realistic man."

Representative Smith (Republican) Ohio:

"A military alliance between the United States and Great Britain would mean a third World War, with the United States carrying the burden as it did in the last war."

Representative May (Democrat) Kentucky:
"The United States should take no position on any military alliances until Russia has been given a chance to state her aims through the United Nations."

Representative McCormick (Democrat) Massachusetts:
Russia "has been unwilling to date to co-operate for world peace."

Representative Savage (Democrat) Washington:
"Churchill proposes a return to power politics."

Representative Ellis (Republican) West Virginia:
"A build-up for the British loan."[140]

British Press Responses (1946)

The Times:
"Anglo-American friendship is an essential element in British policy, but it can never be its sole and all-sufficient foundation or an excuse for failing to pursue independent action along lines which British interests and prosperity require."

The Daily Mail:
"Russia's disastrous course can and must be arrested. Who can doubt that the way to do it is the one proposed by Mr. Churchill."

The Yorkshire Post:
"Mr. Churchill's proposals are 'the one remedy that can rid the freedom-loving powers of their present grievous anxieties.'"

The News Chronicle:
"Churchill is not trying "to foist Anglo-American military domination on the world. He is proposing to join the two countries to enable them

to 'be strong enough and united enough to give effective leadership to an all-embracing society of nations.'"[141]

Other Notable Responses:

Robert F. Patterson, Secretary of War Response:
"I know of no problem as important to the Nation as that of its defense in the times ahead."[142]

Trygve Lie, UNO Secretary General Response:
"If we look out at the world, we must acknowledge that it is no bed of roses."[143]

W. Averell Harriman, former Ambassador to Russia Response:
"The future course of events between the United States and Russia depends principally on us."[144]

James Roosevelt (son of Franklin D Roosevelt) Response:
Churchill's words are "harmful to world peace."[145]

Eleanor Roosevelt Response:
"Instead of running an armament race against each other and building up trade cartels and political alliances, the nations of the world should join together, each contributing a certain amount of military strength to be used only against an aggressor. I do not wonder that the elder statesmen think this a revolutionary move in the international situation. There are two possibilities here—the old way and the new way. We have seen that the results of the old way were war and destruction, and we may still see starvation and pestilence stalk the earth as a result of the old way. May it not be wise to try the new way?"[146]

Randolph Churchill (son of Winston Churchill) Response:
"The fact is that Churchill in his speech nowhere called for an alliance.

What he did call for was the continuation of the intimate military arrangements which did so much to assure our recent victory. This would be something infinitely more far-reaching and effective than any alliance … {the speech's} purpose was to outline a plan, not for making war but for preserving peace."

Clark Clifford, (Oral Interview with Jerry N. Hess, Truman Library, April 13, 1971):
When asked to comment on Churchill's vision for a British-American alliance, Clark, who came to Fulton with Churchill in 1946, said he didn't think that the idea was "appealing" to Truman. As some suspected, he opined that Britain wasn't in a good bargaining position after the war. They had had "economic, political, and military" problems.[147]

Responses 50 Plus Years Later:

St. Louis Public Radio: (2017):
"Following World War II, British Prime Minister Winston Churchill, in 1946, delivered one of the most famous speeches of the 20th century. Known officially as the 'Sinews of Peace,' Churchill's speech came to be known as the "Iron Curtain" speech, and it foreshadowed the Cold War."

Washington Times: (2019):
"It was here in Fulton that Churchill, who had just been turned out of office, delivered his "Iron Curtain" speech, describing the advent of the divided world that would characterize much of the latter half of the 20th century."

Business Insider (2017):
"This speech, titled "The Sinews of Peace," ended up sounding the alarm on the fracturing relationship between the post-war superpowers."

Wall Street Journal by Sarah Backer writing for Westminster College (2018):
"This week, The Wall Street Journal named the National Churchill Museum on the Westminster College campus as one of the top 10 places worldwide to visit in 2019. In the article published Oct. 23, Missouri is listed as the sixth most-intriguing destination in the world, with the National Churchill Museum in Fulton, MO, specifically singled out for its historic tie to Sir Winston Churchill's "Iron Curtain Speech," and its convenient location between the urban centers of Kansas City and St. Louis."

Fox News (2018):
"Known colloquially as "the Iron Curtain Speech," this event had an important impact on framing the primordial threat to world peace in the post-World War II period—the Cold War—and to focusing attention on the leading global alliance motivated to protect world peace, the Anglo-American Special Relationship."

BBC by Sean Coughlan (2005):
"Unlike the nugget-sized phrases of modern political speeches, this speech by Churchill is a piece of classical oratory, heavy with literary language and imagery. It is not so much a sound-bite as a sound three course meal."

The Hill by Tobias T. Gibson (2016):
"Though not well-received initially, in many ways this speech laid the foundations for the West's anti-communism policies. In addition, arguably the foundations of US national security policies and institutions, as well as diplomatic norms, were based on this speech."

Radio Free Europe, Radio Liberty by Sonia Winter (1996):
"But Churchill's 1946 speech is generally regarded as his most significant and far-reaching, not counting his wartime oratory. Its

major tenets ring as sound and true today, with as much relevance as they did half a century ago."

Council on Foreign Affairs, The Water's Edge by James M. Lindsay (2014):
"Despite the public disavowals, Churchill's speech influenced the Truman administration's emerging thinking on how to deal with Moscow."

The Deseret News (Salt Lake City, UT, 2014):
"Churchill proved correct in his characterization of the Soviets' desire to expand and conquer. The Soviet Union did indeed project its power over Europe in as brutal a fashion as Churchill feared. Soviet forces violently put down challenges to their power in East Germany in 1953, in Hungary in 1956 and in Prague in 1968."

"Local Communist parties, beholden to their masters in Moscow, introduced police states in every one of the Soviet satellite nations. East German's secret police force, the Stasi, dwarfed its fascist predecessor the Gestapo. Additionally, communist agents attempt to foment revolution and destabilize governments around the world."

Dave Stinson, Westminster Vice President, standing on sandstone base that formerly held a church column in London. Photo courtesy of Steve Stinson.

CHAPTER 11

Alliances versus Special Relationships

President George Washington's 1796 Farewell Address warned of permanent military alliances and advised the nation to "steer clear of permanent alliances with any portion of the foreign world." His concern centered on the possibility that the country could be drawn into foreign wars that did not affect the national interest. He did not want to "interweave our destiny with that of any part of Europe, entangle our peace and prosperity in the toils of European ambition, rivalship, interest, humor or caprice."[148] Similarly, President Thomas Jefferson, in his inaugural address, called for "honest friendship with all nations, entangling alliances with none."[149]

When people heard Churchill's speech, they latched onto the word, "alliance," which is normally attached to permanent military agreements. Words are important. When improperly launched, they can create unintended explosions. An avid historian, Churchill explained that the common ideals and common thirst for basic rights made both countries averse to war and tyranny. Their quest for equal justice, legal rights, and free speech joined them in a special relationship. He further explained that the common background of both countries formed a special relationship forged by the common desire to seek freedom for all people, eliminate tyranny, and prevent war. He repeatedly said that his speech was not a call to war but a call to strengthen the bonds of peace. By peace, he explained he meant worldwide peace.

The following imagined dialogue captures the sentiments expressed in critiques of the speech. It includes a response to each concern. The response information is contained in Churchill's *Sinews of Peace/Iron Curtain* speech.

Why should our two countries have a special relationship? It sounds like it may not be in our best interest.

> … the principles of freedom and the rights of man … are the joint inheritance of the English-speaking world and which through the Magna Carta, the Bill of Rights, the Habeas Corpus, trial by jury, and the English common law {which all began in Britain} find their most famous expression in the American Declaration of Independence.

We fought with you to gain our independence. You are the "redcoats." When the "redcoats are coming," watch out! What benefit do we derive from a special relationship?

> Neither the sure prevention of war, nor the continuous rise of world organization will be gained without what I have called the fraternal association of the English-speaking peoples. This means a special relationship between the British Commonwealth and Empire and the United States.

When you speak of "shared military bases, shared study of potential dangers, similarity of weapons and manual instructions, and interchange of officers and cadets at technical college," we think you mean we should gear up for war.

… I repulse the idea that a new war is inevitable, still more that it is imminent. It is because I am sure that our fortunes are still in our own hands that we hold the power to save the future.

We sympathize with the Russian people and their trials and tribulations during the war. Uncle Joe is a friendly guy. He would never harm us. We haven't heard of all the problems that you are describing.

I have a strong admiration and regard for the valiant Russian people and for my wartime comrade, Marshal Stalin. There is deep sympathy and goodwill in Britain—and I doubt not here also—towards the peoples of all the Russias and a resolve to persevere through many differences and rebuffs in establishing lasting friendships. We understand the Russian need to be secure on her western frontiers by the removal of all possibility of German aggression. We welcome Russia to her rightful place among the leading nations of the world. We welcome her flag upon the seas. Above all, we welcome constant, frequent and growing contacts between the Russian people and our own people on both sides of the Atlantic. It is my duty however, for I am sure you would wish me to state the facts as I see them to you, to place before you certain facts about the present position in Europe.

These countries are so far away from where we live. I am concerned about my family and my country. I don't want to hear about other people's problems. We have sunk into our cushion of isolation and don't want to get up from the couch. Wake us if they threaten the United States.

If now the Soviet Government tries, by separate action, to build up a pro-Communist Germany in their areas, this will cause new serious difficulties in the British and American zones, and will give the defeated Germans the power of putting themselves up to auction between the Soviets and the Western Democracies.

I still don't see why I should care about these small countries that are far away from me.

Our difficulties and dangers will not be removed by closing our eyes to them. They will not be removed by mere waiting to see what happens; nor will they be removed by a policy of appeasement. What is needed is a settlement, and the longer that it is delayed, the more difficult it will be and the greater our dangers will become.

We are just getting settled after a long and horrible war. We don't want more war. We are tired of war.

If (our two countries) become divided or falter in their duty and if these all-important years are allowed to slip away then indeed catastrophe may overwhelm us all.

Duty? My duty is to my family and my country. I don't want my country to be dragged into another war.

The United States stands at this time at the pinnacle of world power. It is a solemn moment for the American Democracy. For with primacy in power is also joined an awe-inspiring accountability to the future. Opportunity is here now, clear and shining for both our countries. To reject it or ignore it or fritter it away will bring upon us all the long reproaches of the after-time.

The United Nations will safeguard our freedom. Let's allow it to do its job.

> Would a special relationship between the United States and the British Commonwealth be inconsistent with our over-riding loyalties to the World Organization? I reply that, on the contrary, it is probably the only means by which that organization will achieve its full stature and strength.

Churchill's lengthy experience in combat gave him a first hand understanding of the horrors of war. He knew that the destructive forces that last long after victory is declared could forever change a nation. Though he didn't object to economic alliances or friendly alliances that help spread the democratic ideals he sought, he saw the danger in alliances that dragged a country into a war not in its best interest.

Churchill also long lamented the fact that the United States chose not to participate in the League of Nations, an organization promoted by President Wilson. But he also understood the political differences that made it impossible for many legislators to support Wilson's stance. Churchill had high hopes for the United Nations but he realistically knew it had growing pains to overcome before it reached the level of maturity needed to deal with a world crisis.

For that reason, and his abiding faith in the power of the United States, Churchill pinned his hopes on a fraternal or special relationship with the United States. He knew that the United States had met numerous challenges, including war with Britain, to achieve a democratic state where freedom, liberty, and rights of all men were valued and respected. He understood British history and well knew the obstacles and challenges that it met to achieve the same democratic ideals. Working together in a special relationship, the two countries, Churchill believed, could help oppressed countries deal with tyrannical governments by using the peaceful tools of communication and negotiation.

This sculpture stands outside the Church of St. Mary. Douglas Fairbanks, the Hollywood Legend, was instrumental in obtaining the services of Belsky. Photo courtesy of Westminster College.

Repeatedly, Churchill emphasized, "The price of greatness is responsibility."[150] Duty to one's fellow man is the by-product of great achievement. Freedom has its responsibilities.

> "For with great power is also joined an awe-inspiring accountability to the future. If you look around you, you must feel not only the sense of duty done but also you must feel anxiety lest you fall below the level of achievement.[151]

In other speeches, he explained the need to perform one's duty in the following way.

> … victory or defeat are things which happen, but duty is a thing which is compulsory and has to go on irrespective, and carries with it its own rewards whatever the upshot of the struggle may be.[152]

The question remains whether Presidents Washington and Jefferson would oppose a relationship to improve safety and security, thus avoiding future war. The answer is no. Both men issued warnings but did not campaign against any alliances. The United States did not abandon alliances when they clearly benefited the country. Normally, economic growth benefits the country. Washington wanted people to be careful lest alliances be formed out of bias as opposed to real needs of the country. For example, Jefferson favored the French after the execution of Louis XVI during the French Revolution while others could not comprehend the level of violence that resulted in the execution of the French king. Washington warned that people consider the overall proposal for an alliance. Simply put, it is hard to make general pronouncements. The essence of Washington's speech is that every situation is different but emotion should not cloud judgment or a decision about whether an action is in the best interest of the country.

Both Washington and Jefferson spoke in an age when the country was in its formative years. Still fragile, the United States needed to concern itself with issues that dealt with its continued growth and prosperity. Problems in other countries seemed outside its self-interest. They could not possibly imagine the country's position at the end of World War II when, as Churchill noted in his speech, it stood at the "pinnacle" of strength. It had great power capable of dealing with situations that affected "equal and exact justice to all men."[153] These goals were in the best interest of both nations and related to the principles that "formed the constellation"[154] under which both countries lived. They could "safely trust temporary alliances for extraordinary measures,"[155] i.e., the safety and security of all nations. They could take a road that "leads to peace, liberty, and safety."[156] A road that does not require military or permanent union but a temporary united effort, a special relationship, that leads to a better world.

Margaret Thatcher spoke before the General Assembly of the Commonwealth of Virginia in 1995 and said the following words about Churchill's speech and the special relationship that existed since the speech.

> The Iron Curtain of which Churchill spoke did indeed descend, and barely a chink of light showed through it. Then one day it was torn down, and scrapped, due in great measure to the 'union of hearts based upon conviction and common ideals' between your country and mine. Over the last fifty years, the United States and Great Britain have stood together, stalwart defenders of liberty against every form of tyranny.

When Margaret Thatcher spoke before the English-Speaking Union in New York on December 7, 1999, she stated, "Churchill displayed what President Ronald Reagan would later describe as 'that special attribute of great statesmen—the gift of vision, the willingness to see the future based on the experience of the past.'" She went on to explain the same rationale that Churchill used for special relationships to defend freedom, liberty and the rights of man. Then she added the following words:

> As Churchill urged us, 'We must never cease to proclaim in fearless tones the great principles of freedom and the rights of Man which are the joint inheritance of the English-speaking world.'[157]

Helping to spread freedom, liberty and the rights of Man through communication and negotiation is, as Churchill stated, the best approach to achieving peace and collective security. Churchill's concept of a special relationship is tied to the idea of first rallying countries that share democratic ideals, regardless of what path they travel and what form of democracy they choose, to start the process of maintaining worldwide peace. He looked to a mature United Nations to continue that process.

Truman shovels first dirt for rebuilding the Church of St. Mary the Virgin. Photo courtesy of America's National Churchill Museum.

CHAPTER 12

Truman Acts

In September of 1946, Clark Clifford presented his report on Soviet activity to President Truman, who had requested it. Although it contained more details than Churchill's speech, the basic message remained the same. The Soviets had committed a number of acts that ran counter to agreements made at Potsdam and Yalta and to agreements made in the development of the United Nations Charter. The text of these findings is among the holdings of the Truman Presidential Library and Museum, Ideological Foundations of the Cold War.

Churchill's speech had a disquieting effect on Stalin as evidenced by his telegram to Truman and his subsequent interview by *Pravda*. His "secret" response, issued in the form of a telegram, arrived at the White House just one day after Churchill's Speech. Attached to it was a "top secret" telegram from a General Smith who interviewed him the night of the speech. Both messages have been declassified and they reflect Stalin's concern about the possibility of aggressive actions on the part of the United States. He specifically states that in the past Churchill tried to instigate war against Russia and he now believes the US and Britain have formed an alliance General Smith assures him that there was no alliance and that the primary interest of the US had to do with world justice and security and that "this responsibility extended to small nations as well as large." He also makes it clear that the United States is interested in "arriving at a basis of understanding with Russia to benefit the future of the world."[158]

Stalin states that he considers Churchill's *Sinews of Peace* speech an "unfriendly act" and an "unwarranted act." It clearly threatens Stalin, who begins discussing the need to "reduce armaments." More discussion ensues during which Stalin seems to gain clarity and calm. He declines President Truman's invitation to the White House, stating that his doctor would not allow such a visit.[159]

In his *Pravda* interview, published in many newspapers, Stalin takes a more belligerent approach. He refers to Churchill as a "warmonger" who visits the United States to take up his cause. He refers to the speech as "a dangerous act, calculated to sow the seeds of discord among allied states and to cause difficulty in their collaboration."[160]

Stalin's interview contains three key elements. First, he claims that Churchill uses the same racial strategy that Germany employed by seeming to imply that only English-speaking nations are "full fledged nations" that can "dominate other nations." Stalin's response implies that if the Soviet Union refuses to accept that assumption, war is inevitable. He adds that Churchill failed to understand that the rest of the world would not accept a new slavery and domination, by a nation of English-speaking people or not, after their experience in the war with Germany.[161]

Secondly, Stalin rails about the five long years of fighting on the part of Russia against the Germans. He states that those years made Russia unwilling to undergo another threat to its independence. The notion of having to concede anything to Churchill angers Stalin. He considers Churchill's description of the Iron Curtain "slander." His evidence is that the agreement at Potsdam gave all four states authority to made decisions related to Vienna and Berlin. He does not admit to any plans for expansion but avers that the growth of communism is a natural phenomenon in reaction to the previous fascist rule of Europe. According to Stalin, other people view communists as "trustworthy, brave, self-sacrificing fighters against the fascist regime and that they view them as a party that does what it can for the freedom of the people."[162]

Lastly, Stalin repudiates Churchill's claims of totalitarianism in the countries of Poland, Romania, Yugoslavia, and Bulgaria. He asserts that these countries have several forms of government whereas England is only ruled by one, "the Laborites," whom he says deprives others of their right of input. He strongly believes that Churchill's idea of democracy is to let "fascist hide-outs" take control of the four countries.[163]

Reverting to his stance that Russia experienced great loss in World War II, Stalin highlights the great toll that the Soviet Union experienced fighting with the Germans. Seven million Soviets died and those captured often ended up in German forced labor camps. He interprets Soviet expansion as the result of people wanting to align themselves with governments that are peaceful and loyal. Although he doesn't believe that the United States or Britain appreciates the Soviet contribution in World War II, he states that other nations "gratefully appreciate their contributions."[164]

With Stalin's help, *Pravda* puts a different spin on the European situation. Although pravda actually means "truth," the veracity of the speech seems lost on the recipients.

According to a Chicago newspaper article written on March 11, 1946, American troops in Wuerzburg, Germany, were warned by their commanding officer, Lt. Col. Frank Ebey, not to criticize Russia. The officer had heard that some people in the United States agreed with Churchill's speech, including members of the military. He told his men that the Soviets were friends of the United States and since they were representatives of the United States, he would not "tolerate disparaging remarks against {Russia}." He went on to say, "… millions of Russian soldiers and civilians died to save our skins" and that "propaganda should not cause them to hate the Russians." Churchill's speech had not convinced him to change his opinion.[165]

Truman gave Clark Clifford the task of assessing the relationship of the United States and Russia in September of 1946. Clifford's subsequent report was long, detailed, and thorough. After reading it, Truman asked for all copies of it. He said, "If this got out, it would blow the roof off of the White House, it would blows the roof off the Kremlin. We'd have the most serious situation on our hands that has yet occurred in my administration." Approximately 20 years later, Clifford gave the memo to Arthur Krock, who published it in his book. A copy of the report can be found on the Harry S. Truman Library and Museum website.[166]

The Truman Doctrine issued on March 12, 1947, a year and one week after the *Sinews of Peace* speech, is an effort to contain Soviet expansion and support free people who "resist attempted subjugation by armed minorities or by outside pressures" during the Cold War. Churchill's speech paved the way for its acceptance by the American people.

PART TWO

Special Relationship: British History Explains British-American Ties

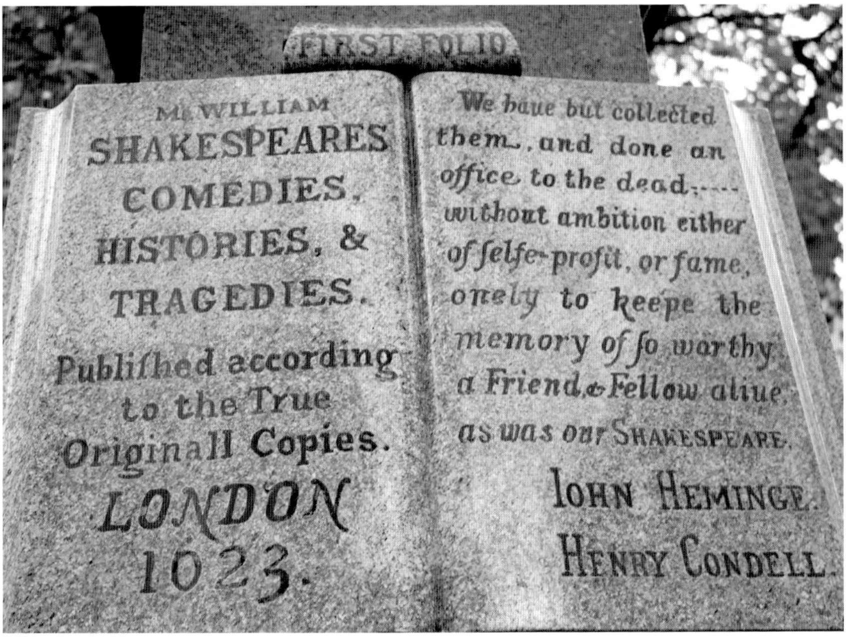

This sculpture is found in the gardens at the former site of the church of St. Mary the Virgin, Aldermanbury in London, England. Photo courtesy of Kwasi Yeboah.

CHAPTER 13

Why History?

It may seem a bit far afield to include a history of Britain in a book about the meaning of the term "special relationship"; however, British history explains the ties that have bound the United States and Britain for centuries. Some people claim that the two countries only began to share a relationship in the nineteenth or twentieth century. Churchill did not agree. He wrote his *History of the English-Speaking Peoples* to educate people, particularly Americans, on the common ties that existed since the founding of London. This history, centuries long, is included here to refresh our collective memories about our common ties, including our struggles for freedom and democracy.

A de facto relationship is how Churchill would describe the relationship between the United States and Britain. In his opinion, their common heritage gave them a "distinctive position and character." While he knew that their "beginnings" were the same, he understood that they "preserved, nourished, and developed their speech and many of their institutions in their own ways." He had no problem with that, since he never viewed the special relationship as a "lockstep" relationship. Churchill emphasized their common language, law, and literature to illustrate their relationship. He also gave detailed descriptions of the paths they took to gain their various freedoms, e.g., speech, assembly, voting, and religion. They each came to the realization that monarchies do not represent the law of the land. Britain declared them answerable to the law. The United States placed its emphasis on the people rather than the king or queen.[167]

One of the most important aspects of the quest for freedom dealt with religion. Today, both countries have many diverse religions. Their history is littered with severe discriminatory practices related to religion. The majority that ruled in the land or in particular areas, left others to either hide their religious preference or fight back against religious intolerance. Eventually, discrimination gave way to more tolerant attitudes and freedom of religious choice but the way was not smooth. They each experienced bumpy rides. Even today, forms of discrimination do exist in some ways though both countries have tried to work toward a separation of church and state. Britain still allows some bishops to hold seats in Parliament. Old ways are hard to change. The United States, which mandates freedom of religion, has its own problems. It has not been an easy path to walk for either country.

This book also describes basic legal rights for which both countries fought. It shows how the British attainment of these rights affected the United States' creation of its Constitution, Declaration of Independence, and judicial system. It shows how these entities sprang from events that occurred in British history. It also shows how language evolved in both countries and how literature in Britain affected literature in America. Further, it shows how each country changed in its attitudes toward the freedom to vote and freedom of speech and how the attainment of these freedoms led to their establishment of democratic forms of government.

Treaties and alliances are discussed to show how they influenced economic expansion, which led each country to progress and attain more influence in the world.

The history of the Church of St. Mary the Virgin, Aldermanbury is discussed to show how the history of Britain affected its own history.

Finally, this book shows why each country abhors tyranny and why they believe they have a duty to the human race as a whole. Although the words *special relationship* gained immediate negative publicity after Churchill's speech, they remain important words for both countries. The two countries' kinship, shared ties, and successful forms of government owe much to the long-enduring special relationship that represents a deep concern for the welfare of all people and the shared love for the freedoms that democracy imparts to all people under its rule.

Churchill repeatedly tried to impress the need for his country to always maintain a friendship with America. He believed that such an arrangement benefited Britain's safety and place in the world, which is why he often said, "Never be separated from the Americans."

He made a more detailed pronouncement of the need for a special relationship in 1918.

> Deep in the hearts of the people of these islands … lay the desire to be truly reconciled before all men and all history with their kindred across the Atlantic Ocean, to blot out the reproaches and redeem the blunders of a bygone age, to dwell once more in spirit with them, to stand once more in battle at their side, to create once more a union of hearts, to write once more a history in common.[168]

Bust of Shakespeare at former London site of St. Mary the Virgin. Photo courtesy of Kwasi Yeboah.

CHAPTER 14

The Gardens of St. Mary the Virgin, Aldermanbury

Today

Public gardens can be relaxing places to visit. Just like parks, they give the visitor a chance to unwind and enjoy the abundant beauty of nature. They are places to meditate and opportunities to block out stress and inhale the freshness of life. The garden on the footings of St. Mary the Virgin, Aldermanbury near the old Roman wall in London, England, provides a respite for people wishing to escape the chaos of city life. As Max Ehrmann said in his prose poem, *Desiderata,* they can "go placidly amid the noise and the haste and remember what peace there may be in silence."[169] The garden of St. Mary the Virgin, Aldermanbury also represents a story that fires the imagination and lifts the spirit.

Built in 1966, the garden's primary purpose is to erase the wounds of any scar left by the removal and transplant of the church that once stood on its grounds. In actuality, the garden does much more than that. It is a monument to the history of both the site and the church.

Interspersed among the natural elements of the garden are monuments to John Heminges, Henry Condell, and William Shakespeare. The poet/playwright was a dear friend and "fellow" of both Heminges and Condell to whom he left six shillings and eight pence each in his will to buy "mourning rings," a finger ring that is worn by someone in memory of a deceased friend or loved one. The act showed Shakespeare's great affection for both men.[170]

Shakespeare supposedly attended the Church of St. Mary, though definitive evidence is lacking. He did live less than a ten-minute walk from the church when he lodged with a family named Mountjoy on Silver Street in 1604 and perhaps longer, so it is certainly possible that he attended the church. By contrast, both Heminges and Condell, who collected and published Shakespeare's work at their own expense, are listed in parish records as members. Both actors served as church wardens and were buried at St. Mary's.[171]

Heminges and Condell, of course, are extremely important in our understanding of William Shakespeare, arguably the most famous poet/playwright in literary history. Without them, at least 18 of his plays would never have been published. Heminges and Condell also categorized the plays by listing them as histories, comedies, and tragedies. Both men were shareholders in the Globe Theater, a leading London theater that showcased Shakespeare's plays and a theater of which Heminges was a founding member. At one time, the two men owned half of the theater. Both of them performed with Shakespeare and made appearances before Elizabeth I, James I and Charles I.[172]

In 1896, the parish of St. Mary the Virgin, Aldermanbury decided the time had come to honor both of these men and their accomplishments. Charles Clement Walker, of Lilleshall Old Hall, County Sallop, donated a monument for a memorial. Walker and his brother made their fortunes by constructing some of the largest structures in Britain and abroad for purifying and storing gas.[173] On July 15, 1896, Rt. Hon. The Lord Mayor of London, Sir G. F. Faudel Phillips, Bart., unveiled it in the churchyard, where it still stands. Henry Irving and other well-known actors of the day attended the ceremony. Charles Walker also wrote a book about the two men. At the end of it, he wrote that since their were no likenesses of the two men available to sculpt a bust similar to the one that they had for Shakespeare a decision was made to sculpt a “model of the First Folio.”[174]

Another celebration took place on April 21, 1923, at the church. Its timing coincided with the Tercentenary of the First Folio. The Lord Archbishop of Canterbury, Lord Davidson of Lambeth, gave an address in memory of Heminges and Condell. He hailed their work in saving the work of Shakespeare. For that reason, he concluded, “… we are their debtors beyond all reckoning …”[175]

These literary connections between Shakespeare and the church are important symbols of the term “special relationship” as described by Winston Churchill who emphasized the relationships formed in literature when he spoke at Harvard in 1943. There can be no greater literary connection than with the famous playwright.

The types of words and the use of language in Shakespeare’s play are also good examples of what Churchill meant by the special relationship of language, a reference that he used in his speech at Harvard. Supposedly, Shakespeare coined at least 1700 new words, depending on who does the crediting. Whether these words existed prior to his use is subject to debate. A dictionary did not exist at the time he wrote his plays, so Shakespeare may have been the first to write down the words he heard from a multitude of sources. It is true that Shakespeare had a facile use of the English language, which evolved greatly during the period in which he wrote his plays and which became closer to contemporary English. If the words Shakespeare used already existed, he definitely had a good understanding of the existing culture and the formation of new words, although that understanding did not come to him through formal education. Shakespeare’s treatment of words is powerful even today. He enriched a language that needed enriching despite its inclusion of words from other languages. He treated words in a different way than most writers of his day, e.g., by using nouns as adjectives or creating compound words with two different words.

Whether he created the words or not, his playful and creative use of words still excites those who read the plays or use the words without realizing where they originated in written form.[176]

Americans and Britons have tremendous love for the works of Shakespeare as evidenced by the number of books sold and plays and festivals held in their countries. His themes and subject matter continue to attract millions of followers but his words and use of language leave his audience spellbound.

In addition to the monuments of Shakespeare and his folio publishers, visitors are treated with views of other parts of the landscape. When the Corporation of London acquired the land after the church removal, it combined it with residual land from the Wood Street Police Station and laid it out as a garden. While not exceptional, the garden provides a visual of the entire expanse of the church that once stood on its grounds. The footings of the church are clearly visible. The mind is left to imagine the former structure and its impact on the area prior to the Blitz of London.

Like many of the places in this book, the gardens are a fascinating place to visit and the first stop for a tour that takes the visitor on a journey described in this book. At this initial stop, the tourist views the former London site of the church and envisions its existence in London's youth, before it had even acquired the name "London". Understanding the history helps the visitor learn that the past is prologue, as the figures in front of the National Archives in Washington, DC proclaim.

CHAPTER 15

British History and Ties with the United States

Roman London

Circa 50 CE – 410 CE[177]

The founding of London, Churchill's view of Romans, Boudicca's revolt, Walls and security, Roman administrative genius, Justice and order in Londinium, Type and impact of early construction, Beginning of religion and the English language

Most Americans remember the year 1492, when Christopher Columbus accidentally discovered lands unknown to Europeans. After all, most teachers drilled that occasion, along with the names of the ships, the Nina, Pinta, and Santa Maria, into the heads of their students at a very early age. Thanks to President Benjamin Harrison's designation, Columbus Day became a national holiday. Americans are reminded of the event each October.[178] Unhappily, the truth is not always as depicted by explorers or some historians. Hoping to find a new route to India, our national "Wrong Way Corrigan," named the first Americans "Indians." Since they already had tribal names and didn't ask for a new name, the various tribes remained unimpressed by the appellation. As for the "discoverer," some people believe Columbus may not have been the first to discover the New World. Others argue whether Columbus Day should exist when the man it honors does not seem worthy of such a celebration in light of today's revelations about his conduct.

London's founding is not attributed to one individual's exploration nor is the exact date of the Roman invasion known, let alone the names of their ships. Christopher Wren discovered evidence of Roman occupation when he began excavating sites after the Great Fire of London in 1666. According to authors Christian E. Hauer and William A. Young, that occupation occurred sometime between 43 and 50 and brought us the geographic area with its name—Londinium.[179]

Excavations found no evidence of a pre-Roman city. Earlier people did not form a town but roamed the land as hunters and gatherers.[180] The Romans thought Londonium could be used as a port location due to its existence on the River Thames. While Londinium did not reach the size of modern day London, its importance lay in its use by the Romans as a port for trade and commerce. The Roman wall served as the perimeter of the old City of London.[181] Also of importance, the infrastructure and construction material used by the Romans offered powerful resistance to the elements.

Although Londinium did not have strategic importance to the Romans, Emperor Claudius believed conquering such areas proved the power of the Romans while also adding to its revenue stream by taxation and money derived from the trade of food, minerals, and other commodities and materials.[182]

Churchill admired the Romans. According to Henry Steele Commager, who wrote the introduction to Churchill's history, *Marlborough: His Life and Times*, Churchill "admired Roman accomplishments in law, government, empire so he rejoiced in Roman virtues of order, justice, fortitude, resoluteness magnanimity." In fact, Commager said that Churchill believed that the British possessed similar virtues, which formed the basis for their actions. As Commager said, his belief in such virtues was straightforward. "A people who flout these virtues is doomed to decay, and … a people who respect them will prosper and survive."[183]

The sense of order and strength that Churchill admired indicated the strength and practicality of a people who had the foresight to build a fortified garrison; however, Boudicca, a British Celtic Queen with a name that had many spellings, led an uprising against the Roman occupying forces sometime around 60. Unhappy about being beaten, having to witness the sexual assault of her daughters, and losing her inheritance after the Roman occupation, this fierce woman showed considerable military and leadership skills by mustering an army against the Roman invaders and in the process setting Londinium ablaze and supposedly killing around 70,000 people.[184] The uprising forced the abandonment of the razed settlement. Boudicca's luck ran out when the Romans defeated her and recovered the land. According to legend, she poisoned herself and her two daughters rather than live under Roman occupation. Boudicca has not been forgotten. An impressive group sculpture of Boudicca and her daughters now stands close to the Houses of Parliament.

In ensuing years, the Romans made a concerted effort to form a better relationship with the existing population to avoid future problems. The constant attacks and threats from outside Britain made peace and harmony difficult, if not impossible. After they retook control from Boudicca, the Romans rebuilt the area as a planned Roman town that quickly became a large provincial capital. The fire started by Boudicca actually made it easier for the Romans to build Londinium in a way that matched their objectives.[185] Archeologists believe it became the seat of the provincial governor, thus providing the order, justice, and provincial administration so admired by Churchill. By the end of the first century, the population had grown to the tens of thousands.[186]

The founding of the Roman city included the Roman societal structure with centralized authority. Roman engineering produced a network of roads and a bridge over the River Thames that allowed commerce to flourish with other areas. Construction spurred the growth of the city.[187]

To guard against further rebellions, the Romans constructed a new and more solidly constructed fort, eventually named Cripplegate. Descriptions of Londinium sites sometimes refer to whether they are within or outside of the walls of the fort in much the same way that locations are described as inside or outside the beltway in Washington DC. Professor W. F. Grimes discovered the exact location of the fort during post-World War II excavations. Constructed in the twelfth century, the Church of St. Mary the Virgin, Aldermanbury lay within the fort, just south of the eastern gate.

Although villas normally appeared in Roman locations, no evidence is found for their existence in London. That could mean military or imperial ownership of much of the land. The Romans built most of the residences using wood, a material easily consumed by fire, which destroyed part of Londinium again sometime in the second century. These residences normally stood outside the fort. The prolonged use of wood for building purposes would result in a major disaster during the seventeenth century.

Stone buildings did appear in Londinium, as did public buildings, bathhouses, a temple, water pipes and drainage systems. Built on a grid system, streets sprang up. Evidence of a governor's palace, a forum and an amphitheater also existed. Whether the amphitheater served as a place for the military to drill and exercise or a venue for gladiator combat, sports, and entertainment is debated.[188]

Today's Leadenhall Market sits in the middle of Roman Londinium. Formerly the site of the Roman forum, it housed a Basilica, the largest Roman building north of the Alps. It also served as the home for "city administrators, law courts, an assembly hall, the treasury and shrines." The Basilica's open-air forum became a public meeting place. Ruins of the Basilica can be viewed in the basement of the hairdresser shop at 90 Churchstreet, though access is restricted. It is all that remains of a structure destroyed in retaliation for Londinium's political misstep of supporting the larcenous military commander, Carausius.[189]

Bloomberg's London Mithraeum, also known as the Temple of Mithras, Walbrook, is a museum featuring items from Londinium as well as the Temple of Mithras that archeologists found during excavation of a site prior to the construction of a new building. Representatives of Bloomberg worked closely with the Museum of London Archeology to reconstruct the temple at the site of its new Mithraeum building so that it could be located as close as possible to the one at the original site, which archeologists discovered in 1954.

In addition to advancing construction, the Romans influenced the use of food in Londinium by introducing new ways of eating and including food in their trade.[190] New foods included sauces, walnuts, onions, cabbages and olive oil, items still popular in Britain and America. Unfortunately, only the very rich could enjoy the food. Stew and porridge remained the staple for most households.[191]

The introduction of new construction and culinary methods can be attributed to the diverse background of the Romans who came to Londinium. Many men in the Roman military came from parts of the world other than Rome, which had a sizable empire. The military typically came from the countries they occupied. Despite the diversity of the military, they served the Empire and followed its lead. [192]

That lead also included some form of Christianity, though it did not reach the breadth of its existence in later periods, since the Romans practiced polytheism. Language also lacked the breadth of sophistication that it did in later eras.[193]

The English language evolved over many years, including the years of occupation by people of different backgrounds. The introduction of Latin occurred primarily in the medieval period; however, some words originated with the Romans. For example, derivatives of the word salt came from the Roman occupation when salt served a vital role in the economy due to its preservative qualities. Since it was in short supply, it became a valuable means of payment in the Roman economy. For this reason, some members of the Roman army received a portion of their salaries (a word derived from salt or "sal") in the form of salt.[194]

Despite its initial revitalization of the area, the economic status of Londinium declined over the years, probably due to repeated attacks from outside forces and the decline of the Roman Empire. As the economy declined, so did housing. The population of Londinium ebbed and flowed but is thought to range between 40,000 – 60,000 people at its height. The Romans left the area in the early fifth century when the Roman Empire began to crumble and the recall of troops became necessary for defense purposes. Without strategic importance, the need to stay in Londinium dwindled quickly and the Romans abandoned it. No evidence exists for its use during the next two centuries, though discoveries may be made in the future.[195]

Anglo-Saxon London

7th century – 1066

Identity of early occupiers, Old English as the foundation of ties between Britain and America, Influence of Anglo-Saxon law in Britain and America, Beginning of Democracy, Possible derivation of Aldermanbury name, Importance of religion, Possible construction of St. Mary

The approximate three hundred year period immediately following the Roman occupation of Londinium is commonly known as the dark ages. By all accounts, Londinium remained abandoned and the lack of written history for the dark ages makes it difficult to know exactly what transpired. That changed with the Anglo-Saxon occupation.

The Northumbrian monk, Bede, who perhaps gave a somewhat biased account of English history, described the Anglo-Saxons as "very powerful Germanic peoples." They came from parts of Germany and what we now know as Scandinavia.[196] Many of them served as mercenaries during the Roman period, though a full-blown occupation did not occur until larger groups came. Since they arrived over time, their larger presence is not considered an invasion.

Sometimes classified as tribes, though some say incorrectly, the fierce group of Anglo-Saxon warriors made many lasting contributions locally and on a much wider scale. Many scholars count language as one of their most lasting gifts. All of the different groups spoke a different dialect of the Germanic language. These different dialects eventually merged into Old English, which ultimately evolved into modern day English and provided the country with its name that is now spelled and pronounced "England."[197]

Thomas Jefferson advocated for the study of Old English. He found its Germanic roots important in education, while he viewed Latin and Greek as more "engraftments on its idiomatic stem." His facility in all of these languages played a key role in his education; however, he firmly believed that the study of Old English contributed to his lengthy involvement in the formation of the United States. From his perspective, Old English gave everyone a better understanding of a wide breadth of subjects, which is why he thought that Old English should be included in college curricula. Jefferson had also had an appreciation for Shakespeare and Milton, both of whom were associated with the Church of St. Mary the Virgin, and he thought Old English gave one a better understanding of their works. He also thought that Old English played an important role in understanding the origins of democracy, which he and some others of his time, attributed to the Anglo-Saxons.[198]

Jefferson's vast library, which ultimately became part of the now magnificent Library of Congress, contained volumes on Old English. The subject fascinated him. His advocacy of the subject ultimately led the University of Virginia to teach the first course in America on the language. While he understood that Old English evolved over time with the introduction of other languages, Jefferson believed the "basic idiom, structure and syntax, remained intact and formed the basis for the language used in America."[199]

Churchill's reference to the "English speaking people" in his "Iron Curtain" speech in Fulton referenced this same commonality that interested Jefferson. His words highlight the connection between the countries of Britain and the United States. He used the terminology to emphasize that a special relationship already existed due in part to their common language that evolved from the Old English of the Anglo-Saxons. Judging by how people seemed to respond to the term used in his speech, they were more inclined to believe George Bernard Shaw who said, "England and America are two countries separated by a common language."[200]

The early English settlers in America probably did descend from the English people, and probably the Anglo-Saxons. Three distinct groups of Germanic people—the Angles, the Saxons, and the Jutes—formed the group known as Anglo-Saxons. The term is a more modern one and not one used at the time. Apparently, the exclusion of Jutes resulted from the much larger size of the other two groups and the much larger area they occupied in Britain.

As Anglo-Saxons settled in Britain during the seventh century, many of the Saxons ended up in the kingdoms ending in "–ssex", i.e., Essex, Sussex and Wessex. The Angles settled in East Anglia, Middle Anglia,

Mercia, and Northumbria, while the Jutes primarily settled in Kent and to a lesser extent on the Isle of Wight and Hampshire. Though the groups and their dialects differed, they evolved in unison into Old English.[201]

Language was not the only contribution the Anglo-Saxons made. In Londinium, which became known by different names after the accession of Alfred the Great who ruled from 886-889, the economy improved and once more the area became an important center for trade. Londinium served primarily as a port for trade. Although that trade included exports, there is no evidence of supply warehouses for exports. The existence of the Roman Wall and Cripplegate may have hampered their erection.[202]

Anglo-Saxon law heavily influenced the way of life in what is now London and ultimately affected law in the United States. Throughout most of the Anglo-Saxon period, law was local, presumably due to the different locations occupied by members of the different tribes or Germanic groups occupying Britain. That law had its origins in Germanic law not Roman law.

History reveals that the three parts of Anglo-Saxon law dealt with the laws imposed by the king, private compilations of laws and rules, and customary law. Considered common law, the commonality applied to the location not to Britain as a whole, since no centralized government existed until King Alfred started trying to consolidate the power of the various locations into a more centralized organization.[203]

Most of the law concentrated on criminal law though reference to some private law existed. The Anglo-Saxons respected property and individual rights did exist, including the rights to juries and public hearings, something found in American law today.

The importance of the Anglo-Saxons in history captivated Thomas Jefferson, who submitted a design to the Second Continental Congress for a proposed United States Seal. Jefferson, part of a committee that included John Adams and Benjamin Franklin, thought it important to memorialize the Anglo-Saxons in some way. The contributions of the Anglo-Saxons so impressed Jefferson that he included the figures of two Anglo-Saxon warriors, Hengist and Horsa. Although he attempted to draw upon common history, others did not possess the same sentiment and his design was not approved.[204]

Nevertheless, Jefferson believed that the legal liberties enjoyed by the Anglo-Saxons, limited though they were, formed the beginning of democracy that he promoted as a founding father.[205]

Many but not all Anglo-Saxons were literate. This accounts for the scarcity of legal history, though King Alfred the Great made significant changes to codify it. Alfred preferred the use of Old English to Latin but histories typically included both languages. The *Anglo-Saxon Chronicle* narratives, first assembled by King Alfred, organized seven manuscripts that survived the period. The yearly account in the *Anglo-Saxon Chronicle* documents battles and changes in the royalty that existed prior to the Battle of Hastings.[206]

The Chronicle is not complete for all portions of the period but it is for the reigns of AEthelred, the Unready (978-1013), and Edward the Confessor (1042-1066). Unfortunately, neither of these kings possessed exceptional qualities as AEthelred's name implies; however, Edward's piety became influential after his designation as a saint. As Churchill remarked in his history, the "vigor of Alfred's posterity was exhausted and the monarchy was in a state of decline" at the end of Edward's reign.[207]

In areas they occupied, the Anglo-Saxons also brought expertise in organization and governance. Their culture included some excellence in the arts, including the wonderful poem, *Beowulf.* They gave us the first gospels written in English. Present-day shires, towns, and villages owe their existence to the local government set up by the Anglo-Saxons.

The Anglo-Saxons also gave London a royal palace that most historians believe stood in Aldermanbury—probably close to and just north of the Church of St. Mary.[208]

Despite all their contributions, the Anglo-Saxons continued their involvement in power struggles with forces within and outside of Britain, and Londinium involuntarily became part of them. These struggles had the advantage of ensuring the refurbishment and maintenance of the old Roman walls and surrounding ditch that shielded the royalty and, later in time, the Church of St. Mary the Virgin.

Though the Anglo-Saxons did much to secure the city, Viking raids occurred frequently from 830 until the end of the Anglo-Saxon occupation. Londinium burned to the ground in 842, and by 871 the Vikings took temporary control of the city. Alfred the Great led West Saxon forces in 878 when they defeated the Vikings once more.[209]

Before he died, King Alfred appointed his son-in-law, Earl AEthelred of Mercia to the position of Governor of what is now known as London, after which the city became more unique in its government. Importantly, laws started being issued from councils in the city.

AEthelred may have had a great deal to do with the name of Aldermanbury. He served as a royal alderman but his power exceeded the role of later aldermen and he enjoyed a fortified residence in Londinium for protection.

Religion became more important under Anglo-Saxon rule. Pagans when they arrived, the Anglo-Saxons began converting to Christianity beginning in the late sixth century. Monasteries began appearing throughout Britain and became important centers of learning. Churches also sprung up in most localities. To support them, ecclesiastics collected tithes of ten percent. Clashes occurred when the Vikings once again sought control over Britain. The newly Christian English nation abhorred the Danish practice of human sacrifice and clashes continued until the Viking King Cnut and his sons ruled England from 1016-1042.[210]

Whether the Church of St. Mary the Virgin can trace its origins to this period is debatable. It had two foundations that existed prior to 1437.[211] Christopher Wren used one of them when he rebuilt the church after the Great Fire of London, though no evidence for it being built prior to the Norman Conquest in 1066 currently exists. A small church was built on the current site of St. Paul's Cathedral during this period but its history is unknown. What is known is that religion continued to grow in influence, as the history of Britain illustrates. The changes in religion had a significant impact on the Church of St. Mary.

Norman and Angevin Rule
1066-1216

Rise of William the Conqueror, Expansion of Normans in key positions, Beginning of feudalism, Compilation of the Domesday Book, Changes in warfare, Construction of cathedrals, Impact of the French language on English, Influence of Common law on the American legal system, Importance of the Magna Carta in relation to the US Constitution

The son of an unmarried woman and Robert, Duke of Normandy, seemed an unlikely person to aspire to succeed Edward the Confessor as King of Britain. William the Conqueror not only aspired to the role, he exhibited great confidence that he would succeed. Confidence and strength of character are only two reasons why William has been so admired by many people.

In reality, William's claim to the throne had some substance. His father, also known as Robert the Devil, had married a sister of the late King Cnut and he had a close relationship with AEthelred's sons, Alfred and Edward. The latter son ascended to the throne after the death of King Cnut's sons, while William succeeded Robert as the Duke of Normandy.

Unfortunately, Harold, the son of the Anglo-Danish Godwin, had similar aspirations, although William insisted that both Edward and Harold had promised William that the throne would be his. Harold quickly changed his mind about deferring his aspirations after Edward the Confessor personally and inexplicably named him as his successor before he died. Conflicts in monarchical interest rarely ended peacefully. As most English schoolchildren learn, William took the Crown from Harold by defeating him at the Battle of Hastings in 1066. Sadly, Harold lost the battle and his life after a combatant arrow struck him in the eye. William moved quickly to establish his power.[212] {The battle, as well as the arrow in Harold's eye, can be seen in the Bayeux tapestry in Normandy.}

Most kings and heads of state understand, sometimes too late, control generally means eliminating people whose loyalties are with the former occupants of their position. William quickly grasped the need to weed. He replaced potentially disloyal Anglo-Saxon people with Normans loyal to him. The need to weed did not end with the elite landowners. William used the same process to replace Anglo-Saxon sheriffs and bishops with Norman ones.

His strategy worked. He soon gained control over land ownership and tax revenue, which is not to say that everyone agreed with his strategy. The English people soon learned that William had great power, which in combination with his ruthless behavior made him a force to be reckoned with. As he continued to push his agenda, the number of people in the upper echelons who possessed great wealth dwindled. William's actions not only assured that the king could control the most wealth but that more power rested with the king. The centralization of government that King Alfred attempted to start intensified with William.

William's system of government is known today as feudalism. {The name was not used in feudal times.} Historians argue whether he introduced the practice or expanded what occurred during Anglo-Saxon times. What is known is that land ownership did not apply to the serfs, who remained bound to their owners. Knights, who were above the serfs in the social hierarchy, became essential to barons for use in military service, which resulted in a more developed, organized, and warring force in support of the king. Knights received land in return for the promise of loyalty and service.[213]

Regardless of who instituted the system, feudalism definitely helped to strengthen the power of the king, which would lead to other problems in Britain and in America in later times.

To further increase his power, William had the ability to tax and derive revenue. To help him determine the inventory of land and wealth, he began the laborious process of compiling the Domesday Book, an important list of land ownership and value in Britain. Compiled county-by-county, it seems the precursor to the census used many years later in America. For the time period, the extraordinary compilation represented an unprecedented methodology. Today, it is viewed as a remarkable display of administrative genius.[214]

Interest in the administration of justice led William to improve trials and institute trials by juries. Whether or not they existed prior to his reign, trials became more widely used. He also separated ecclesiastic courts from local courts, thus helping to launch the idea of separation of church and state.[215]

In addition to wealth and power, William I focused on construction for security. Architecturally, William's construction of motte and bailey castles (i.e., castles on some form of raised earth surrounded by a ditch and a type of protective fence) helped change the conduct of war, since open field battles no longer became as important. A pious man, William also focused on the construction of many cathedrals and churches, including St. Paul's, one of four with that name that stood on the site. A later St. Paul's Church became one of Christopher Wren's most important designs. Although the exact date is not known, the construction of St. Mary probably took place when one of the Angevin kings ruled. Understanding its architectural style when initially constructed could better pinpoint the approximate date of construction.[216]

The Normans, under William I, introduced the French language and continental culture. Britain increased its connections to the rest of the world and became more cosmopolitan in attitude. French permanently changed words used in conversation and literature though French may have proved a barrier to many in the beginning. The French influence would also affect English as spoken in America.

Culturally and linguistically, the Normans ensured that the histories of both England and France became intertwined, though their eventual rivalry is evident in the history of America.[217]

After William the Conqueror died, his kingdom passed first to his son, William II (Rufus), and then to Henry I, Stephen, and briefly to Matilda, Henry I's daughter. Rufus and Henry I possessed the same ruthless behavior but Stephen was much more lax and as a result the period of his reign, the last of the Norman rule, is often identified with anarchy.

Henry II, the grandson of Henry I, became the first of the Angevin kings in 1154. He presided during the period now known as the High Middle Ages (1000-1300). His reign is most noted for the beginning of a great legal system and the establishment of common law in England, although some of his changes may have been rooted in the earlier law. He is credited with making judicial precedents more important than the previous customary law that could vary from place to place. The change had the effect of bringing one set of common law for all of England and for setting the foundation for common law trials in

England and later the United States.[218] His "Assize of Clarendon," meant to initiate judicial reform by checking the role of local judges, made use of what is now known as the grand jury.[219]

Thanks to Hollywood, Americans know about Henry II due to the movie, *The Lion in Winter*, that focused on Henry and his wife. Peter O'Toole and Katherine Hepburn play Henry II and Eleanor of Aquitaine as they plot to determine which of their children would succeed him. In reality, both Eleanor and his sons betrayed him. Henry knew he had to forgive his sons to secure succession but he never forgave his wife. A woman betraying a man proved too much for him.

The reigns of Henry II's sons, Richard I and his brother John, are best known to Americans, primarily due to the stories of Robin Hood and the Crusades, where Richard spent most of his time. The two were not loving brothers. Like many medieval royal figures, they often clashed with one another over their individual ambitions.

Legally, the reign of John had the greatest impact on Britain and America since his grandfather's reign. The growing ruthlessness with which the Normans used their power upset the barons, who found an opportunity to rebel after John's problems with the church hierarchy led to his excommunication and deposition by the Pope against him. The Pope's action gave King Philip Augustus, the French king, authority to invade England. John, who had confiscated church property after his excommunication to increase his wealth and engage in warfare, quickly saw the error of his ways and decided to make peace with the Pope by agreeing to his demands.

Unfortunately, John's struggle with the French resulted in his permanent loss of Anjou and the end of the Angevin dynasty. The loss elevated the position of France in the world hierarchy and created a rivalry that has never quite ended.

Despite his problems, John's reign resulted in the creation of the Magna Carta, which wasn't his idea. In fact, he tried to change his responsibility to abide by it. As Marc Morris indicates in his book, *King John,* the king's personality and tyranny did him in. Most people described him as cruel, routinely harsh with taxes and other burdens, and disrespectful in his behavior. He appeared to be a predator who preyed on the wives and daughters of barons and other high-ranking people. Unlike Richard, his actions in defense of the country did not possess a "boldness" of quality but rather a tepidness of action if victory could not be assured. He lacked the characteristics of a good leader. Further, he could not make genuine peace with the papacy. His downfall led to a marked change in the role of English kings.[220]

While the popular belief has been that the Magna Carta gave liberty to all, it primarily favored the barons who had wearied of heavy taxation and the prescribed military service required by John. Its language included "to all freemen of the realm and their heirs forever" is viewed as the beginning of English liberties and the foundation of many documents prepared by the American colonists after the American Revolution, including the Constitution and Bill of Rights.[221]

The Magna Carta prohibited the king from operating as a despot and limited his authority to act, particularly in an abusive way. Though the charter guaranteed other rights and liberties, the primary importance of the document is the idea that even the king answered to the law. It also provided principles of justice, including the right to a trial with judgment by one's peers. These changes in the law and the principles of justice are the reasons the document is often viewed as establishing the roots of democracy in Britain and in the United States.[222]

Despite his involvement in many military campaigns, a hero's end eluded King John. He died of dysentery.

The Plantagenet Dynasty
(1216-1485)

Loss of Anjou, Influence of the dynasty on Shakespearean plays, Losses sustained as a result of famine, Plague and war, Rise of the merchant class, Weakening of the church, Construction of St. Paul's Cathedral, Rise of universities

John's death did not mean an end of succession for his family. His son did succeed him, though the name of his dynasty, Plantagenet, is considered a subset of the Angevin Dynasty.[223] Some historians combine both dynasties and refer to the combined dynasty as Plantagenet. England lost possession of Anjou, so it could no longer claim a dynasty named for that location.

Plantagenet took its name from the father of Henry II who was nicknamed Plantagenet. The origin of his name seems to come from his surprising habit of sporting sprigs of broom (planta genista) in his helmet.[224] Why that action deserved a nickname or the name of a dynasty remains a mystery.

Despite its rather inauspicious beginnings, the Plantagenets did not die out with the end of their dynasty. William Shakespeare, whose plays were preserved by two members and church wardens of the Church of St. Mary, kept them alive by naming some of his history plays after Plantagenet kings, though such plays cannot be taken at full face value. Political expedience resulted in some tweaking of the actual history.

Receiving increasing literary attention many years after it occurred, the War of the Roses became the subject of movies and other media in the United States. The war involved the Lancasters and the Yorks, two rival branches of the dynasty, and ended when Henry VII, who had Lancastrian blood, married Elizabeth of York, after he became king.

The Hundred Years War, which actually lasted for 116 years, started when Edward III occupied the throne. Rather than one long war, the Hundred Years War actually consisted of a series of conflicts with the French over succession to the French throne. It began when Edward III pressed a claim for the throne after Philip VI of France took the duchy of Aquitaine away from England. Many years of battles with different conclusions finally resulted in England losing its land in France, which then became a major power. Aside from the staggering loss of human life and the destruction of towns and villages, the war marked a change in military weaponry with gunpowder becoming the primary choice for military strategists.[225]

In addition to losses sustained by war, there were other losses due to problems that resulted from climate change, a subject that is met with acute interest today in the United States. Cooler winters and wetter summers led to a famine that swept European nations and left millions dead. The effect of famine on human life probably contributed to another major loss of life when rats carried the Black Death (probably the Bubonic Plague) from the ports of England to the interior of the country. Unsanitary conditions in the cities contributed to the spread of the disease. At least one-third of the British population perished.[226]

The loss of life that occurred due to war, famine, and the plague contributed to the end to feudalism, which could no longer be supported by the same number of serfs.[227] Rent income fell precipitously and those lower income people who survived initially had their wages capped despite a shortage of laborers. Changes in conditions led many to give up agriculture in favor of raising sheep for the sale of its wool. Though the American South used slaves, who also lacked any rights, the South's refusal to change the driving force of the economy (agriculture), which used slave labor, eventually led to the American Civil War.

As the years progressed, the merchant class gained strength due to increased trade with areas outside of Britain. Meanwhile, the church's struggle with the king led to some weakening of its power, though it still retained control and great wealth. The cathedrals of Britain, built during this period, became symbols of that power and wealth. In 1087, work began on St. Paul's Cathedral, which was finally completed in 1310. Unfortunately, many of the churches built during this era were damaged or destroyed by the Great Fire of London, which also destroyed most of the Church of St. Mary, the Virgin and St. Paul's Cathedral.

Nationalism increased as the Middle Ages progressed even when the behavior of kings did not favorably improve. Education improved and great universities began during this period. The more sophisticated legal system of this period led to the beginnings of Parliament.[228] English became the language most used in the legal system, resulting in its eventual colloquial and literary usage.

The Battle of Bosworth Field in 1485 marked the end of the dynasty and the death of Richard III, its last ruler. Some people interpret Shakespeare's words, "My kingdom for a horse," to mean that Richard offered his kingdom for a horse. In reality, he lost his horse in the battle. Without a horse, Richard knew he would lose the battle and his kingdom. At any rate, the quote is probably a fine example of what we now call "literary license."

Tudor Rule
(1485-1603)

Henry and Elizabeth, Church of England, Reformation, The Book of Common Prayer, Renaissance, Expansion in Ireland and America, Sir Walter Raleigh, St. Mary the Virgin, Aldermanbury

For many Americans, the Tudor Dynasty remains the most fascinating and compelling. Five kings and queens comprised the dynasty but two of them captured the most attention after their reigns. Henry VIII and Elizabeth I enlivened the landscape filled with intrigue, cruelty, tyranny, excitement, religious upheaval, and significant change. With an abundance of intelligence, charm, bravado, temper, political wrangling, and decisiveness, both rulers seemed to overwhelm their roles. Countless books, movies, and television shows still manage to mesmerize audiences with tales of their rule. Although their years of governance proved much shorter than the years of the Plantagenets, the Tudors made more history or at least they made history more energetic and dynamic, if not always pleasant.

Most especially, the Tudors had a major impact on religion. To be sure, British people questioned some of the practices of the papacy and the Catholic Church and Martin Luther had posted his Theses on a church door in Wittenberg in 1517, but no open rebellion against the church in England existed at the time Henry VIII decided to divorce (technically: annulment) his first wife, Catherine of Aragon. {Note: There is some dispute about whether Luther actually posted the Theses on the door or sent them to Archbishop Maisz, while others used the printing press to communicate them more broadly.}[229] The 95 Theses seemed to give many people permission to voice their own concerns with the church and made it possible for Protestantism and the Reformation to grow in importance. While Henry did not favor Protestantism, his actions allowed the Reformation to become a greater part of English life. Somewhat fearful that the Pope might send Catholic countries to invade Britain, Henry tried not to antagonize the Pope by appearing to support Protestantism.

Nevertheless, bitter over the Pope's opposition to his request for an annulment, Henry set about separating the English Church from the control of the papacy. By the end of his reign, Henry VIII was known as the Supreme Head of the English Church by an act of Parliament. He began, under Cromwell's guidance, the dissolution of England's monasteries, both selling and giving away lands to England's wealthy landowners. After paying the monasteries debts, he pocketed the rest.[230]

The religious change did not develop easily after Henry's death, but a Reformation happened nonetheless. Each successive Tudor ruler imposed an interpretation of Christianity best suited to their needs: a more extreme Protestantism under Edward VI, a return to Catholicism under Mary I, and a moderate Protestantism under Elizabeth. The English found themselves changing from one religion to another as a new monarch gained control of the throne. Failure to do so had potentially dire consequences, including death by burning at the stake. As Thomas Cahill wittily remarked in his book on the Reformation, "Why should men be incinerated for adhering to beliefs that so recently had been required of them?"[231]

The Uniformity Act of 1559 revised the Book of Common Prayer. Other revisions occurred in 1662 when the book was used in the American colonies.[232] The English church became the Anglican Church that initially took root in the American colonies. Today's Episcopalian church has its roots in the Anglican Church and is part of the same Worldwide Anglican Communion.

The English Renaissance also began during Henry's reign. A revolutionary period that began at the end of the fifteenth century and lasted until the seventeenth century, the Renaissance is considered a rebirth of art and culture and includes architectural, scientific, artistic, and literary achievements. Most notable in England were the plays performed in the theaters. William Shakespeare, arguably one of the greatest poets/playwrights, created his celebrated plays during this period and into the reign of James I. One play, *The Tempest,* dealt with a shipwreck of the *Sea Venture* that was bringing colonists to Jamestown, Virginia, in the United States. The ship ran aground off the shore of Bermuda at Gate's Bay. Considering this location lay far from Shakespeare's home, the breath and subject matter of Shakespeare's work led some to question whether he actually wrote all of the plays. Others believe that since his works focus more on conversation than location, it is likely that he did.

During the Tudor reign, England expanded its land holdings in areas other than France. English settlers had owned land in Ireland since 1169; however, England became fearful that its arch enemy, France, might seize control of the island and so used a variety of incentives to gain the loyalty of Irish chieftains. Elizabeth I went so far as to establish plantations in Munster and Ulster and suppress the resulting uprisings in protest. Present day problems between the two countries are probably rooted in tensions caused by these events during the Tudor rule.[233]

Exploration of America also began during this period and Sir Walter Raleigh stood out as one of the explorers who had a major impact in such exploration. He acquired interest in America from his half brother, Sir Humphrey Gilbert, another explorer, who is associated with the founding of Newfoundland.[234] Raleigh established the first English colony in the America. Located at what is now Roanoke, Virginia, it soon became known as the "lost colony" when its English settlers mysteriously disappeared. He left a mark on one state by naming it Virginia after Elizabeth I, the Virgin Queen. Many years later, Raleigh, North Carolina, took its name from the explorer who, though certainly exceptional, apparently didn't introduce the potato to Ireland or tobacco to Virginia as legend has it.

Raleigh did make use of the queen's desire to settle parts of Ireland by acquiring large tracts of land in the province of Munster. He also used his influence to help his maternal cousins, William and John Chapman, also known as Champernowne, acquire land in County Kerry.

Stuart Rule
1603-1649 (Part 1)

James I, King James Bible, Expansion in the New World, The Pilgrims and the Mayflower Compact, The Jamestown Settlement, The competing roles of the King and Parliament, Macbeth and James I, Religion and Charles I

Self-importance has led to the downfall of many leaders who refuse to accept reality and lack leadership skills to compensate for their self-aggrandizement. Both King James I and his son Charles I relied heavily on their own sense of importance and could not understand that the winds of change had blown away from notion of absolute monarchy.

When the Stuarts came to power, the Crown still had the right to name its successor. Before Queen Elizabeth died, she named James VI of Scotland as her successor. It may seem odd that she waited so long; however, James was the son of her cousin, Mary. As most people know, the two cousins did not have a loving relationship.

Immediately upon accession to the throne, James VI of Scotland became James I of England. Since his reign in Scotland had been fairly successful—including by moderating Calvinism's introduction into Scotland and by thwarting assassination attempts—James believed that he would have comparable control over England and the English. He failed to understand the differences between the two countries and what the monarch's power entailed, but he was soon met with conflict that centered on religion and another one that centered on the role of monarchy. They would prove to be problems he could not easily resolve to his satisfaction.

A significant group of Puritans (i.e., Protestants who wanted to purify or cleanse the English church of its "popish" rituals and beliefs) hoped that King James I would be more partial to their religious beliefs since

Calvinism (i.e., the Presbyterian church) had strong adherents in Scotland where James had lived. The Puritans pushed for the abolition of episcopacy (i.e. church hierarchy) but James feared such a move might lead to the end of the monarchy. Acknowledging that fear, he sometimes remarked, "No bishop. No king."[235] He rejected calls for change. At the beginning of his reign, he did practice tolerance towards the Puritans; however, he bewildered many by also pressing for all of his subjects to adhere to the Church of England.

James did not ignore all of the requests made by the Puritans. He ordered a revision to the bible. Published in 1611, the King James Bible, as it later became known, would last for centuries though many would not understand its relationship to James I. It remains an important part of his legacy.

But religion played the dominant role in his reign together with conflicts with Parliament. Troubled by resistance to other forms of religion, religious groups left Britain to form colonies in America during James' reign. The Pilgrims, who did not acquire their name until the nineteenth century, first headed to the Netherlands, a country more tolerant of other religions. Called Separatists, they did not consider themselves under the umbrella of the Church of England. They preferred separation from the church. After several years in the Netherlands, though, they found themselves unable to fashion the life that they desired. They came from an agricultural background and possessed few skills of any other kind. Kept out of guilds held open to native workers only, the separatists had to make their living by various low level paying jobs, which held them back from advancing economically. Subservience to the laws and customs of another country also hampered the group from living as Englishmen, something they did not reject when they rejected the Church of England. Needing a change, they decided that America provided the best opportunity.

To get the help they needed, the Separatists contacted the Virginia Company in England to get the necessary patent for land in America. James I had given the Virginia Company a charter in 1606 to colonize what is now the United States in hopes of competing with Spain, a Catholic country, and increasing prospects for trade. One of the founding members of the company, Edwin Sandys, whose descendant would one day marry Diana, the daughter of Winston Churchill in 1935, viewed the separatists' request as an opportunity for England to establish a foothold in the New World.[236] As he held no animosity toward their difference in religious belief, he pushed for approval of their journey and succeeded in doing so. Told that the emigrants planned to make their living, at least in part, by cod fishing, King James I allegedly responded positively. After all, he supposedly said, the apostles were fishermen. In reality, the separatists did not take the correct type of fishing gear with them, so cod fishing never became a major source of financial sustenance.

Along with a group of people from Plymouth, England, approximately 35 Pilgrims, as they were subsequently called, boarded the *Mayflower*. They attempted to use two ships but the condition of one ship made it impossible. While it wasn't their desire to do so, those individuals who agreed to finish the journey all piled onto the *Mayflower*. In addition to the crew, other travelers included people who had the requisite skills to help ensure the survival of the group in the New World. In some histories, they are labeled "The Strangers," since they came from other locations and did not have personal connections to the religious body of travelers. In 1620, the tired and sickly passengers, many of whom suffered from scurvy, landed on what is now referred to as First Encounter Beach in Cape Cod. After a very unpleasant introduction to some Indians who were not at all happy to learn the unexpected visitors had stolen their buried corn seed, the passengers on the ship landed for the second time in what is now Plymouth, Massachusetts, a location outside the boundary of their patent, where they formed the first settlement in New England.

Since their legitimacy appeared questionable due to their location, the Separatists and other members of the group found it necessary to work together and find agreement on their plans before debarking. Realizing that they needed to establish some form of government, they wrote the Mayflower Compact while still on board the ship. The document became the first set of rules for self-governance in the New World. It contributed to a successful attempt at a democratic form of government, which the colonists eventually adopted. The group also agreed to name John Carver as its first governor.

Earlier, in 1607, the Jamestown Settlement, named for the king and sponsored by the Virginia Company, gave the English its first settlement in the New World. Previously, the Spaniards had more presence due to their explorations following the voyager Christopher Columbus.

Edwin Sandys, who had assisted the Jamestown settlers and the Pilgrims, served as a leading Parliamentarian and critic of James I. He rejected the divine right of kings and favored a constitutional monarchy. He was also against monopolies and in favor of free trade. His many exploits made him an intriguing personality, so much so that Duncan and Diana Sandys in the twentieth century named one of their daughters Edwina in memory of him.[237]

In 1604, Sandys' Committee in Parliament wrote the "Form of Apology and Satisfaction" that is considered a rebuke of James I's belief in an absolute monarchy. While a number of different issues are discussed in the document, the ones of most importance deal with Parliamentary privileges, particularly as they relate to "freedom of election, freedom from arrest for persons elected, and freedom of speech." Nothing became of their "declaration" immediately; however, it symbolized a change in what Parliament perceived as their basic rights.[238] Over the course of the seventeenth century, Parliament would prevail over the Crown.

James did not change his concept of the monarchy to suit Sandys or his colleagues. A firm believer in absolute monarchy (absolute rule by one person) and the divine right of kings (meaning a monarch's power came from God), James' stance often put him at odds with the largely Puritan and Puritan sympathetic Parliament, which also was critical of his spending habits. As often happened in Britain, religion and money created many problems for a king. Already at odds with the king over their respective roles, Parliament chafed at providing more money to a king who did not respect their authority and spent money with seeming abandon. In response to many of their quarrels, James I sometimes dismissed Parliament until further money problems forced him to call it back in session; his son, Charles I, followed a similar pattern but with unfortunate consequences for him

During James I's reign, two civil wars took place largely due to the actions of James I. He did not win either of them.

Luckily for James, he escaped the fate that befell his mother, Mary Queen of Scots, and his son, King Charles I. The beginning and end of his reign ended in the same place. News of Elizabeth I's death reached him while James remained dressed in his bedclothes. Years later, he died in his bed.[239]

From a literary standpoint, fans of Shakespeare can thank James I for the play *Macbeth,* which Shakespeare wrote to please his patron. Perceptive viewers can spot compliments to the king splashed throughout the play. Other references such as "two-fold balls and treble scepters" refer to historical events, in this instance, to the double coronation in both Scotland and England. The biblical and witchcraft imagery in the play are also thought to be an effort to please the king who had a passion for scripture and an interest in witchcraft.[240]

King Charles I served as king of England from 1625 until his execution in 1649. Religion became dominant themes of his reign but he lacked his father's diplomatic skills in dealing with the varieties of religious belief in countries that he controlled and he did not know when compromise with Parliament was more in his interest than confrontation.

Scotland was heavily Presbyterian at the beginning of Charles' reign. Catholicism had a strong hold in Ireland. The Church of England, which supported the king, still had proponents, particularly among some of the English nobility. Even a shrewd politician would have difficulty managing the opposing beliefs.

Although he had a Catholic wife, Charles fell clearly in the camp of those people adhering to the Church of England. He found it difficult to compromise his beliefs, so he did not.

Like his father before him, Charles I believed his authority came from the divine right of kings. Parliament eventually issued the Petition of Right, a document designed to prove that the king was not above the law.[241] The Petition promoted the rights of liberty for subjects in England, and in the longer run for citizens of the United States. Charles I accepted it with the intention of ultimately ignoring it. He miscalculated the power of Parliament.

Oliver Cromwell rose to power and ultimately helped decide the fate of Charles I. Refusing to compromise, Charles I paid the ultimate price for adhering to his beliefs. He was beheaded in 1649 after being found guilty of treason, which was a new definition of the word. Originally referred to as opposition to one's king—now it was in opposition to one's country.

Interregnum Rule
1649-1660

Puritans in America, Effect of Interregnum in America, Puritan London

The Interregnum period is the period between the end of the reign of King Charles I and the restoration of his son, Charles II, as king. Prior to the Interregnum, Puritan elements began appearing in large numbers in parts of Upper and Lower Norfolk Counties as well as Nansemond County, Virginia. A church built at Sewell's Point on land owned by one Henry Sewell had a Puritan bent. One of its ministers, Reverend Thomas Harrison, had formally been a minister for none other than Virginia Governor Berkeley; however, once he became responsible for the church on Sewell's Point, Harrison changed his affiliation and became a Puritan minister who refused to use the Book of Common Prayer as required by the Anglican Church. That stance and other religious issues enraged the governor; Harrison ultimately had to leave his congregation.[242]

Both Henry Sewell and his wife died around 1644 and their only son, Henry II, was sent to Holland and then England in 1649 for education as a merchant. That year, 1649, marked the beginning of the Interregnum period in England, so it did not seem a coincidence that Henry's relatives thought it necessary to send him back to his father's native land at that time. Henry lived in England during this period of great religious change until 1660, when he returned to America and lived near former neighbors who had immigrated with other Puritans to Anne Arundel County, Maryland, from Virginia beginning in 1650. The year 1660 was the last year of the Interregnum period in England.[243]

The reason for Sewell's eventual relocation to Maryland is easily explainable. Virginia maintained close ties to England. The governor considered the Anglican Church the one true church and did all he could to rid his state of Puritans. During the Interregnum period, a new governor took over from the old one. While the colony no longer seemed disposed to cleanse itself of Puritans, the attitude toward Puritans did not change to a welcoming one. Meanwhile, Maryland, originally part of the Virginia colony, became a separate colony when Charles I awarded a charter to Lord Baltimore, a Catholic. After his father's death, Cecil Calvert, the new Lord Baltimore, and a Catholic, had no qualms about inducing Puritans to move to his colony. Indeed, he welcomed the move. In addition to needing more settlers, he wanted to maintain the status of the Catholic Church by showing tolerance to other faiths, particularly the Puritan religion. He supposedly found it extremely helpful in proving his concerns for Puritans during the Interregnum period in England.

During the Interregnum, Oliver Cromwell had both led the victorious Parliamentary army and came to rule much like a king. He experimented with several forms of government. Two of them failed. The Commonwealth under Parliament control ended when Cromwell dissolved Parliament. Cromwell then attempted to hold control through the use of the military officers. That too failed. At the end of his power and before his death, the government became a protectorate under the authority of a constitution. Cromwell consistently declined offers to take control as king, since the Interregnum period represented the end of rule by a king or queen.

In terms of trade, the Navigation Acts increased both the colonies' and England's ability to make money by the sale of tobacco and other crops by prohibiting the use of non-English ships (primarily Dutch) to transport goods.[244]

The Puritans flourished during this period and other religions became more accepted. Cromwell tried to stamp out Catholicism but tolerated other religions, including Judaism. John Milton, the great Puritan poet who wrote *Paradise Lost* married his third wife at St. Mary the Virgin, Aldermanbury.[245] Due to his proficiency in Latin, he received an appointment as a Latin secretary to the Council of the Commonwealth. His job involved the translation of political Latin documents transmitted between foreign powers into English. During the Interregnum, he famously opposed Archbishop Laud (who was executed in 1645) and supported freedom to divorce, freedom of speech, and freedom of the press, believing that the people of England had the right to depose kings who acted as tyrants. At the funeral for Oliver Cromwell, John Milton walked behind the casket together with two other poets, Andrew Marvell, who joined Milton as Latin secretary, and John Dryden. A statue in Milton's memory is in Westminster Abbey.

During the period of "Puritan London," as it is sometimes called, the Church of St. Mary the Virgin gained notoriety. Located in what was then a wealthy area of town, membership included many former mayors, councilmen, aldermen, assessors, and people of substance. Author Tai Liu referred to it as a "strong Puritan parish with Puritan ministers" that included Edmund Calamy, a Presbyterian Puritan. According to Liu, "Calamy rose rapidly to eminence in the Revolutionary period and on the national scene where he had eminence unequal to anyone. His salary topped the salary of all other ministers in London. At his house, the strategy and actions of the London Puritans were planned."[246]

Calamy had an extremely large following at the Church of St. Mary, so much so that among his congregants sat worshippers from parishes outside his church boundaries. Numerous carriages congested nearby streets. Calamy opposed the execution of Charles I. Like many other people, he grew frustrated with the revolutionary government and helped negotiate the return of Charles II, for whom he eventually served as a chaplain. The site of the damage caused by the Great Fire of London in 1666, particularly the destruction of his church, had a grievous effect on Calamy, who was shocked by what he saw. He died shortly afterward. He was buried where the pulpit of St. Mary, the Virgin once stood.

The Restoration Period (Stuart Reign—Part 2) (1660-1685)

A Quaker helps Charles II escape to France, the Restoration, Quakers in England and the United States, Regicides, The Black Death and Great Fire, Events in the Colonies, Rifts with Parliament, Habeas Corpus, Change in theatrical productions, Rise of the Churchill men, James II

Charles II knew he needed to make a hasty retreat after the Battle of Worcester in 1651 when he attempted to regain the throne. His journey to freedom took him to a number of locations where he hid from his enemies. At one time, he took refuge in the top of an oak tree to escape his pursuers, who evidently didn't think to look upward. When he reached the English Channel, he still feared capture and possible execution. Luckily, someone introduced him to three Quaker sailors who promised to take him from Shoreham on the *Surprise* to safety in France. After crossing the Channel, one of the valiant Quakers, Richard Carver, carried Charles on his shoulders through the waves to dry land and safety.[247]

Twenty years later, the same Quaker once again met the king when he presented himself before Charles II to ask for the release of some Quakers held captive by the English. The precise number is debatable. His efforts failed at first but on meeting the king a second time, he had the good luck to persuade him to release and pardon many of them, including the writer John Bunyon, author of *Pilgrim's Progress,* who actually opposed the Quakers but ended up imprisoned with them due to his preaching as a nonconformist minister.[248] The episode marked a strange turn of events for some hapless victims of religious intolerance.

Charles II did attempt to stop the effects of penal laws on Catholic and Protestant dissenters by issuing the Declaration of Indulgence, a declaration that provided more tolerance to nonconformists, Catholics and other dissenters by suspending enforcement of the penal code that punished them; however, the actions of Parliament made the Act virtually worthless.

While Charles II preferred tolerance, the Quakers remained a religious group that Parliament and Governor Berkeley of Virginia continued to abhor. Founded by George Fox in England in 1650, the Quakers supposedly got their name from the way they "trembled at the word of the Lord." Despite Parliament's actions, the king acted in a more tolerant fashion. In 1681, Charles II gave William Penn a land grant for Pennsylvania to satisfy a debt he owed to Penn's father. Named after the elder Penn, Pennsylvania became a Quaker colony, though Penn ensured that Pennsylvania also became a haven for religious dissenters. He believed firmly in religious tolerance.

Virginia, like England, practiced intolerance toward Quakers. Their religious views were considered heretical and the colony's religious establishment had little tolerance for viewpoints that challenged its authority. Governor Berkeley of Virginia asked Captain William Carver and other members of the House of Burgesses to begin the prosecution of Quakers. Despite the order, Carver and others did not seem to make wholehearted attempts to do so at first. Elizabeth Harris, a popular follower of George Fox, the first Quaker missionary and supposed founder of American Quakerism, later suffered expulsion from Virginia and traveled to the Puritan territory of Anne Arundel in Maryland, where she married the widowed John Warner, the father-in-law of the same Henry Sewell who had once lived in Virginia.[249]

In addition to religious groups, Charles II showed remarkable tolerance to the regicides responsible for his father's death, although he seemed to agree to their being pursued. A few captured members of the group lost their lives in response to the outcry of the public. Hanging seemed too easy for most of the general public who clamored for a more serious punishment than death for the killing of their king. Most regicides were hanged and quartered. A few unlucky ones had to witness the butchery of their fellow victims.

A few regicides escaped to America. They found protection in various locations until the threat of imminent discovery forced them to move to yet another location. At one point, Protestant Major-Generals Goffe and Whalley received refuge in the house of Puritan Micah Tomkins for two years in Milford, Connecticut, perhaps due to Reverend John Davenport's intervention, until they seemed in danger of discovery.[250] They managed to avoid capture throughout their escape in America, something that Charles II probably preferred to their torture.

Also impacted by the Restoration, land ownership was in jeopardy. The people of what is now Connecticut realized that they had no legal basis for the land on which they lived and worked. Many of the inhabitants had left the Massachusetts Bay Colony due to some differences in the practice of their Puritan beliefs and a quest for more land. They settled in various areas, such as Milford, Windsor, Hartford, Wethersfield, and New Haven, each with a minister who preached to their liking.[251] Although they were outside the boundaries of an English charter, they loved the independence of self-government. With the Restoration came fears that the independence might be removed since the king and England were no longer friends of the Puritans. They also feared backlash for adhering to self-government without the permission from the king. A small delegation headed by John Winthrop Jr. left for London to meet with the king to secure a charter that would grant them independence.[252]

When Winthrop first met with King Charles II, he found Charles unimpressed by the request and unwilling to grant it. At a second meeting, Winthrop gave the king a ring that Charles I had given to his grandfather, Adam. Winthrop stated that he gave the ring to show his esteem for and loyalty to the king. That action seemed to melt the resistance to the charter for the ring once belonged to Charles I.[253] The 1662 Charter for Connecticut granted legal authority to the newly designated Connecticut, confirmed its constitution, which was similar in many respects to the principles of the subsequent United States Constitution, and defined its boundaries. In exchange, Connecticut agreed to give the king one-fifth of all the gold and silver mined within its borders.[254] New Haven and other smaller locations that were swept into the boundaries did not express joy at the development for they hoped to keep their independence, though such thinking proved impractical given the political changes in England.

During Charles II's reign, a number of major events occurred. The Black Death, thought to be the Bubonic Plague, struck England several times, killing a substantial number of people each time. It probably originated in China in the early fourteenth century, but spread in London due to overcrowding and the presence of rats on ships traveling from port to port. Their fleas spread the disease though the filth in the city and river didn't help. Londoners learned too late that poor hygiene facilitated disease. The last major plague occurred in 1665 when it killed approximately 100,000 people in London, including 105 in the parish of St. Mary the Virgin, Aldermanbury. Although the effects on the population proved severe, the population grew and recovered after the plague ended.[255]

Samuel Pepys' diary documented what it was like to live in London during the plague. Apparently, he survived by having some trait that provided immunity. Other residents were not as lucky and became trapped in their homes when one occupant fell ill with the deadly plague. Heavy coats, beaked masks, herbs, and chemicals often employed to avoid the plague and diminish the smell did not always meet with success; however, residents were anxious to try anything that might save them. Plague pits used to bury the dead became commonplace.

After the many problems related to the plague, a new catastrophe happened in the form of the Great Fire of London, which burned four-fifths of the city within the Roman walls in 1666. Since wood frame buildings and narrow streets were the norm, they proved easy prey for the rapidly moving fire that started in a bakery on Pudding Lane in September of that year.[256] Fearful of another war, many residents believed an invasion had occurred. Frightened, people became alarmed that more than a terrible fire was happening. So much panic and chaos erupted that King Charles II actively helped in trying to contain the fire and manage the chaos.

A major disaster, the fire demolished most civic buildings, St. Paul's Cathedral, and all of St. Mary the Virgin, Aldermanbury, with the exception of 24 stair steps, built in the twelfth century, which led to the crypt.[257] It had the positive effect of ridding the city of wood-frame buildings and overcrowded conditions that led to the plague and other diseases. After a period of debate and planning, Sir Christopher Wren received the charge to restore many of the churches destroyed in the fire. His designs, including the design of the London skyline, put a new face on London, which included the Church of St. Mary.

Other major events occurred in the colonies. King Philip's War in New England, 1676-77, marked the last major effort by the Indian tribes to drive out the English colonists. At approximately the same time, Virginia's Bacon's Rebellion, often thought of as the precursor to the American Revolution, marked the first time that the colony of Virginia attempted to overthrow an English governor. The rebels failed and several, including Captain William Carver, the only English seaman to become involved, were hanged as a result of their actions. Since London had experienced several catastrophes, they did not actively interfere with the events in America, but Governor Berkeley was recalled not long after the rebellion ended. He died in England in 1677.

From a legal perspective, King Charles II's constant difficulties with Parliament led to the passage of the Habeas Corpus Act ("a writ requiring a person under arrest to be brought before a judge or into court, especially to secure the person's release unless lawful grounds are shown for their detention") previously found in the Magna Carta, which prevented unlawful or arbitrary imprisonment.[258] Passed in 1679, the Act is considered a safeguard of individual liberty. It gave more authority to the court or a judge to examine the facts of a case and ensure the liberties of an individual and stemmed from the growing power of Parliament over the role of the king in government. It granted the same liberties in America.

Changes in art and literature resulted from a lack of Puritan control. Authors and artists had more freedom to work. Certainly, the scandalous personal life of Charles II played a part in the tolerance; however, most people were eager to enjoy a more liberated lifestyle, if not to the extent of sexual freedom.

International relations produced several wars involving Holland and France. The king turned traitor by accepting money from France to not take certain actions against the French. His continued problems with Parliament made him reluctant to call them to convene for such purposes. He made a risky move, but Charles II still managed to keep his head and survive. One settlement that occurred as a result of the various military fights transferred control of New Amsterdam to the English government, which named it New York in honor of the king's brother, the Duke of York. A short interruption of English rule occurred when the Netherlands temporarily gained control.[259]

The king's reign also marked the rise of the Churchill men. Sir Winston Churchill, a Cavalier, was the son of Sir John Churchill of Dorset and Sarah Winston, daughter of Sir Henry Winston. Winston attended Oxford but left before graduating due to the Civil War where he served as a captain on the side of the Royalists. He played tennis with Charles II and courted the same mistress, who, as some state, gave birth to Winston's baby.[260]

The legitimate son of Sir Winston Churchill, John Churchill, was the son of a Royalist and the grandson of a Roundhead. He became the

First Duke of Marlborough and the hero of his descendant, former Prime Minister Winston Churchill and the first owner of Blenheim, the location of Churchill's birth.

During the reign of James II, John Churchill became a member of the peerage. His association with James began when he served as a page. Loyal to the king, Churchill joined the army and led troops to stave off a series of rebellions. His bravery and leadership skills drove him to prominence. When William of Orange seemed to gather great support, Churchill quickly assessed a change in the wind and switched his political allegiance to William. His loyalty earned him the designation of Earl of Marlborough after William died and Queen Anne took the throne.

Thanks to Rupert, the cousin of Charles II, John Churchill became the governor of Hudson's Bay Company (HBC) and shared heavily in its profits. On one occasion, he and the other head shareholders received a 50% payout. Still in existence today, the HBC became a major force in the colonization of Canada. At the time of Churchill's involvement, the fur trade occupied most of its business. To his credit, he protected the interest of HBC by arranging for marines and Navy ships to provide security. When others challenged the legality of the company charter, the issue went to Parliament, which confirmed it. The town of Churchill, MB, in Manitoba, Canada is named for Lord Churchill, the first Duke of Marlborough.[261]

In addition to the many other problems, fear of succession occurred due to worry that Charles might convert to Catholicism and that his successor might change the religious direction of the Anglican country. In the end, Charles II did convert on his deathbed, and his brother, James Duke of York, succeeded him.

By this time, England was holding fast to its Anglican ways and remained skeptical that a Catholic king would continue to tolerate Protestantism.

Nerves were rattled when Louis XIV of France, a long-time opponent of Protestantism, revoked the Edict of Nantes (1685) that had guaranteed the rights of Protestants to worship as they pleased. Many feared that James, with his Catholic leanings, might try to make Catholicism the religion of England; after all, James had issued a Declaration of Indulgence that suspended the Penal Laws against the Catholics.

During his short reign, James II tried to consolidate the American colonies and began demanding their charters. Connecticut refused. Afraid that the birth of James' son might prolong the papist reign, the English began encouraging a willing William of Orange, a Protestant and the grandson of Charles I, to seize the Crown. William had married his cousin, Mary, who was the daughter of James I. Responding to the pleas, William invaded England, quickly wrestling it away from James, his father-in-law. The age known as the Glorious Revolution had begun.[262] Not wanting a fight in England, James chose flight. As he sailed away from London, James managed to throw the Great Seal into the muddy waters of the Thames.[263]

Explaining the reason for James' flight required some diplomacy and negotiation between Whigs and the Tories (the names of the political parties recently formed). The Whigs supported the Magna Carta in its statement that "rulers must obey the law and that legitimate authority comes from the people." The Tories cited their belief that "people have no right to rebel against a government because they disagree with it." Their compromise with respect to the king's departure was that he "broke the original contract between king and people, abdicating it and leaving it vacant."[264]

Support for James appeared in Scotland and Ireland, but James did not regain his Crown. The Battle of the Boyne in Ireland ended in defeat for James whose army was outnumbered by that of the Protestant William. Some later pushed for James as a candidate for sainthood but the Pope thought otherwise. He ordered the bells to be rung in

Rome after learning of James' defeat at the Battle of the Boyne. Each year on July 12, the Orange Order celebrates the victory that assured the ascendancy of Protestants in Ireland. It also marks the defeat of the Catholics who had desperately wanted to regain their land more than James had hoped to regain his throne.[265]

The Great Fires of London (1666) and Chicago (1871)

When Americans think of great fires that almost destroyed a major city, the Great Fire of Chicago in 1871 is what probably first comes to mind. The conflagration destroyed thousands of homes and a large part of the city. It shocked people throughout the country, as wiping out such a large part of a city by fire seemed unimaginable. Shock also filled London, one of the largest cities in Europe, when the Great Fire burned buildings in 1666. Both fires started after a long, hot, and dry summer with little rain. Wind contributed to the spread of both fires. In preparation for the winter, Chicago homes typically had a great deal of fuel, which helped fan the flames. Warehouses in London had combustible and flammable material. London had no fire engines or firemen. Most buildings in both cities were built of wood. In London, narrow streets and tight clearances between structures spelled disaster. How did the Chicago fire compare to the Great Fire of London?[266]

Chicago	**London**
Square Miles Affected: 3.24	Square Miles Affected: .68
Structures Destroyed: 17,000	Residences Destroyed: 13,000
People Killed: 324	People Killed: 9 Known
Homeless: 100,000	Livery Halls Burned: 43
Cause: Undetermined	Churches Burned: 87 out of 109
Time to Recover: 7-20 years	Cause: Fire In a bakery
	Time to Recover: 50 years

Rebuilding in London used more stone than wood. Rebuilding in Chicago accommodated a population that almost doubled to 1 million almost 20 years later. The number of people killed in both cities could not be accurately determined, since some bodies were incinerated and some people drowned.

After the Chicago fire, the United Kingdom made a donation of 8,000 books to the City of Chicago "as a mark of sympathy now, and a keepsake and a token of true brotherly kindness forever." Even Queen Victoria donated a book—one on her husband. Queen Elizabeth donated one on Buckingham Palace on the 100th anniversary of the fire. As a result of the initial donation, the city established the first public library system in 1873.[267]

The Glorious Revolution and the Stuart Rule (Part 3)

1688-1689 & 1689-1702

William and Mary College, Coronation, English Bill of Rights, Declaration of Independence, Diminution of monarchy control, Churchill connections

Most Americans have heard of the College of William and Mary but many may not associate it with the Glorious Revolution. It is in fact the second oldest institution of higher learning in the United States. The original plans pre-date Harvard and go back to 1618 but the charter for William and Mary was not actually signed until King William III and Queen Mary II of England did so on February 8, 1693. While it has a building known as the Sir Christopher Wren Building, evidence that Wren designed it is tenuous at best. In 1724, a mathematics professor attested to the fact that it was "modeled by Sir Christopher Wren," thereby opening the debates that have surrounded its origin ever since.[268] Ironically, fires damaged it on three occasions, causing it to be rebuilt inside the original walls and leading some to remember the Great Fire of London in 1666.

The coronation of William III and Mary II is unusual in some respects. First, it is a coronation of a double monarchy (two people rather than one person), though William quickly took over as the leader. Second, it is the coronation of a person of Dutch ancestry, unusual when remembering the recent wars between the two countries. Third, it is marked by the oath that each of the monarchs took shortly after their coronation to swear that they would obey the rules of Parliament.[269]

The English Bill of Rights (1689) specifically delineates the various ways in which the late King James II endeavored to "subvert and extirpate the protestant religion and the laws and liberties" of England. No longer willing to endure the constant battle of wills between Parliament and Crown, Parliament decided to limit the rights of the monarchs at the onset of the reign of William and Mary. The Bill of Rights provided for the "rights of petition, free debate in Parliament, freedom of election, trial by jury, the right to bear arms and the frequency of Parliament."[270]

Though the Declaration of Independence in America took much of its language and style from the document, both documents resulted in different types of governments. America has a form of checks and balances evidenced by the different roles of Congress, the Executive Office, and the Supreme Court. England has a Parliamentary Constitutional government that gives that body most of the rights formerly possessed by the king. In today's world, such a government is one in which the head (now prime minister) is a person representing the political party that has the largest representation in Parliament. The assent of both monarchs to this change in the late seventeenth century is sometimes known as 'The Bloodless Revolution," but more commonly as "The Glorious Revolution."

Two bills enacted shortly after the Bill of Rights included the 1689 Toleration Act that promoted religious toleration and the 1694 Triennial Act that prevented the monarch from dissolving Parliament and required parliamentary elections every three years.[271]

Both the English Bill of Rights and the American Declaration of Independence contained a listing of the many cases of abuse that the king was guilty of as he governed his people. The American Constitution, which was meant to flow from the Declaration of Independence, lists the Bill of Rights that give many of the same rights found in the English Bill of Rights. These rights relate to such subjects as freedom of religion, speech, press, assembly, and petition, the quartering of troops, the right to a jury trial, and the elimination of excessive bail amounts, fines, and cruel and unusual punishment.

Thus, while the forms of government took different paths, their founding documents for a new type of government asserted similar basic rights.

Neither William nor Mary seemed to object to the diminution of their rights. They seemed relieved to just be the monarchs. Throughout his reign, William failed to receive much love from his subjects who thought of him as a more cold and stoic figure with a sour disposition. To be fair, they did not welcome him with great love but with a sense of expediency. On the plus side, William's Calvinist views prevented him from strictly enforcing religious restrictions though he had no trouble in objecting to people as individuals.

One of the people with whom he expressed reservations was John Churchill. The two men had many ups and downs despite Churchill's wife being the best friend of Mary's sister, Anne. Disagreements notwithstanding, Churchill was a loyal general. He excelled at defending England and the ruling monarch.

When William died in 1702, his sister-in-law, Anne, became queen, for Mary had died years prior to William's death. The Churchills probably thought it a good fortune for them. It was and it wasn't. They would eventually have a falling out with Queen Anne.

Queen Anne (Stuart Rule, Part 4)
1702-1714

Queen Anne, Marlborough, Blenheim, The War of Succession, The union of Scotland and England, and The new power of Britain

The character of Queen Anne is something still debated today. On the one hand, there is the characterization by Lady Marlborough, once a close friend, who later sought to disparage her in writing. On the other hand are historians who give her credit for intelligence and strong action.

Poor health followed Queen Anne for most of her reign, a physical problem that led others to believe they could control her. Anne opposed such interventions and that led to her eventual disassociation with Lady Marlborough. It also created problems in her associations with the two powerful political parties, the Tories and the Whigs, the latter of which the Marlboroughs supported. Winston Churchill wrote that "the age of Anne is rightly regarded as the greatest manifestation of the power of England which had till then been known."[272] The close association of Queen Anne and Lady Marlborough in the first five years of Anne's reign may have been the reason for that declarative remark. Nevertheless, Churchill got it right.

John Churchill, the Duke of Marlborough, performed brilliantly and heroically as head of the British Army. During the War of the Spanish Succession, which lasted throughout most of Anne's reign, he successfully defeated the French at Blenheim (the English name for Blindheim, a village in Bavaria, Germany). In gratitude, the Queen gave him the gift of the Royal Manor of Woodstock. She promised to pay for the building of a palace, which became Blenheim. The terms of the cash offer seemed vague, resulting in disputes on the size of the building and the cost. Lady Marlborough, a woman who knew her own mind, wanted Sir Christopher Wren to design the new palace but she deferred to her husband, who settled on a less talented and somewhat dubious architect, John Vanbrugh, a fellow member of the Kit Kat Club (an eighteenth century political and literary London club that usually advocated for Whig objectives), who apparently could not keep the budget under control and would not accede to Lady Marlborough's demands. He resigned before the building was finished. Vanbrugh's assistant, Nicholas Hawksmoor, assisted Christopher Wren in redesigning churches after the Great Fire. Both worked on St. Paul's Cathedral and Hawksmoor designed six other churches by himself.[273]

The War of the Spanish Succession (1701-14) of which the Battle of Blenheim was a highlight, came about due to the concern of England, Holland, Austria, and other smaller entities in their coalition over who would succeed Charles II of Spain. Their concern was with the European balance of power, a balance that they did not want to be disturbed by France. Well-founded, their fears stemmed from Charles II's decision to have the grandson of Louis XIV of France succeed him. If that happened, France and the Bourbon dynasty would control most of western Europe. England, in particular, did not want that to happen.

War in Europe also spilled over to the American colonies. France, together with Spain, fought Britain for control of land. Different Indian tribes cast allegiance with each side. The war in the colonies caused a great deal of bloodshed and destruction. The French and Indians razed the towns of Deerfield and Haverhill, Massachusetts. The British and Indians massacred inhabitants and destroyed most of St. Augustine along with 32 missions in Florida. The Spaniards insisted the attack's motivation was to kill Catholics. The British also successfully attacked parts of Nova Scotia.

The wars ended when both sides wearied of war, financially and as nations. The Treaty of Utrecht ended the War of Spanish Succession, which was the war in Europe, and the Queen Anne's War in the colonies. The Indians, who lost a great deal of land, were not included in the settlement talks.[274] France agreed to recognize Queen Anne as queen and a Hanoverian successor (Protestant, with Hanover being a state in Germany). By terms of the settlement, a Bourbon king became King of Spain but the two Crowns of France and Spain could not be joined in union.[275] Queen Anne's War was actually the second of three such wars. The first two began due to war in Europe. The last started in the colonies. In Europe, the Treaty of Utrecht put Hudson's Bay, Newfoundland, Nova Scotia, Minorca and Gibraltar under British control.[276]

France and Spain were, by treaty, prohibited from uniting their countries under one king. The union, not universally appealing to either country, helped England keep better control over its "back door" (i.e. Scotland), something the increasingly powerful nation wanted to do. It also wanted to avoid having two kings on the same island, one for Scotland and one for England. Daniel Defoe, the author of *Robinson Crusoe,* served as a spy.[277] He wrote many pamphlets promoting the union. For Scotland, the union provided much-needed funds while allowing the country to keep its Scottish Kirk (Presbyterian Church), its own system of laws, its schools, and burghs. Scotland, which experienced severe economic hardship, received a guarantee of access to colonial markets. The union meant that the next ruler would be Hanoverian.

After the union of Scotland and England, a new national flag was created. Known as the Union Jack, the flag conjoined the cross of St. George (England and Wales) with the cross of St. Andrew (Scotland) to symbolize the birth of Great Britain. Following the Act of Union in 1800 between Britain and Ireland, the United Kingdom was fully established; the cross of St. Patrick (Ireland) was added to round out the Union Jack, although following Brexit this may likely change.

For a country beset by troubles over religious concerns, it seems curious that the English so willingly let Scotland keep their national church. Political expediency trumps many other things.

Queen Anne, pregnant 16 to 18 times, depending on the source of information, had no living child to succeed her when she died in 1714. Without children to succeed her, the issues of succession and union with Scotland became urgent in the years prior to her death.[278]

It is amazing and a testament to her determination and sense of duty that Anne endured so much physical and emotional pain, while also ruling Britain. Despite long and protracted wars in Europe and the American colonies, Britain emerged with a major naval presence, a feat that catapulted Britain into an even higher standing in Europe. The War of Succession expanded Britain's territories outside the boundaries of England. Gibraltar proved an invaluable asset in controlling access to the Mediterranean. Britain's territories in North America increased, while the territories of Spain and France diminished in size. This new power balance would eventually make it easier for the colonies to achieve independence.

Hanoverian Rule
1714-1837

Act of Settlement, George I, Robert Walpole, George II, The French and Indian War, George III, Taxation without Representation, The Declaration of Rights, The Declaration of Independence, The American Revolution, The US Constitution, The Treaty of Paris, Slave reparations

Most Americans today are somewhat knowledgeable about succession to the throne in Britain. For example, they probably have heard that Prince Harry is unlikely to ever become king, since he is sixth in line to the throne. In 1714, King George I of Hanover, the second cousin of Queen Anne, succeeded to the throne of Britain. He was 52nd in line for the throne. Religion made all the difference.

The Act of Settlement of 1701 was passed to reinforce the English Bill of Rights, approved by William and Mary. English Protestants were concerned about the future royal succession, as William and Mary were childless. Anne, who followed them onto the throne, also had no living children. The Act ensured that the person who would succeed to the throne after Anne's passing, or any other sovereign, would be a Protestant, though more than 50 Catholics stood in line when Anne died. The union of the two countries under the title of Great Britain included an agreement to abide by the Act of 1707.[279]

Hanover at the time was not very important politically, or in any other sense. But George was Protestant. Not many, if any, of the retinue of people he brought from Hanover spoke English and George was not Catholic. Despite the influx of diversity that would probably occur with a monarch from another country, Britain did not want to take the chance of having another king who would pull the country toward Catholicism nor did it want a monarch likely to challenge the authority of Parliament at every turn.

In some ways, George I was an egalitarian. He had two mistresses whom he rotated every other night for his pleasure. One was fat. The other was thin. They were popularly known as The Elephant and The Maypole. On the other hand, his abusive behavior toward his wife seemed excessive in relation to her perceived offense. George I had no qualms in having extramarital affairs. When his lonely wife dared to have an affair, the suspected Swedish partner suddenly disappeared while unsubstantiated rumors that he was chopped up and placed beneath her bedchamber floorboards or thrown in a river were circulated. George I, the not so great husband, divorced his wife and had her imprisoned in Ahlden House near Celle until she died.[280]

The Whig party, which was more strongly Anglican—or High Church—and was more supportive of the Crown than the Whigs (with a minority of them favoring a return to the Stuarts), saw their power diminish. The influence of Parliament continued to grow under George I, further reducing the power of the king. {Queen Anne was the last British monarch to veto an act of Parliament.} One of Parliament's new powers included the right to approve a monarch. As Parliament approved his accession, George I was not an absolute monarch. Further, he absolutely did not have a huge fan following. Riots broke out in protest to his succession. Jacobites, who supported the return of the Stuarts to the throne in the person of James The Pretender (i.e. the son of James II, the 'Old Pretender," who had died in 1701) supported the exiled Stuart king and protested vehemently. Prime Minister Robert Walpole, the first prime minister, held most of the strings of power at the beginning of George's reign and did his best to calm the country.

Walpole promoted a policy of salutary neglect to give the American colonies freedom to run their own affairs in an effort to encourage their success. Trade benefited Britain as well as the colonies, so Walpole wanted to make sure that the colonies excelled in trade. While the concept worked well for the colonies, Britain would come to the realization that a change was needed after the colonial French and Indian wars. The cost of war required revenue from additional sources.[281]

Walpole also pursued a policy of peace, which ended up being costly and burdensome in a multitude of other ways. He preferred negotiation and compromise to warfare; as he was fond of saying, "Let sleeping dogs lie." He had great trouble realizing that war might ever be necessary.

The reign of George I wasn't especially memorable. He never seemed to acclimate to English life and ways, preferring Hanover—he made several visits there during his reign—a fact that did not endear him to the British people, even as near the end of his life, he finally took an English mistress. He died in his beloved Hanover in 1727 and was buried there. His son, George II, succeeded him.

Like his father, George II did not grow up in England but he took the trouble to learn English, albeit with a heavy accent, which helped to narrow the gap of his unpopularity from being a foreign-born monarch. {George II was the last British monarch to be born in another country.}

George II had an early life punctuated by conflicts with his father. They reconciled before his father's death but his life with his prime ministers was frequently mired in conflict. Things did not run smoothly, particularly since Parliament had the political advantage.

Although he did not prefer to have Walpole continue as his prime minister, George found himself in a situation that he could not control. Walpole continued as prime minister as did his strategy for avoiding war. Unfortunately, Parliament had other ideas that did not include compromise to prevent war. Britain found itself involved in the War of Jenkins' Ear in 1739, a conflict between Spain and Britain about trade in South America, and the War of Austrian Succession (King George's War in America) in 1744.[282] The War of Jenkins' Ear took its name from a British sea captain whose ear, supposedly cut off by members of the Spanish Coast Guard who decided to search his ship, became a symbol of British pride after it was brought before the House of Commons. People could not believe the arrogance of the Spaniards who would do such a repugnant act, especially to an Englishman.[283] The parties involved in the war, including France, eventually settled their disputes and Britain increased its naval superiority, though it came at a cost as all wars do.

Prime Minister Walpole was eventually outmaneuvered and replaced by Prime Minister Pelham. The wars of the period involved both France and Britain, which made strategic alliances with other European countries. George II seemed most interested in defending Hanover, his native land, much to the disgust of the British people. He actually fought in some battles and was the last monarch to risk his life on the battlefield.[284] His fierce determination to protect Hanover at all costs seemed to energize him.

George II died in 1760 unable to finish another war started during his reign. His grandson, George III, succeeded him. The Seven Years' War, as it was called in Britain, or the French and Indian War as it was called in the American colonies, would have a profound impact on colonial America and contribute to the coming of the American Revolution.

In North America, the French had built forts to the west of British settlements making it difficult for the colonists to move westward, with or without the king's permission. Westward expansion proved particularly difficult in the Ohio Valley where the border was fluid in the minds of American colonists. To their dismay, the French thought otherwise and French troops tried to halt all expansion into what they considered as their territory.

Britain, which controlled thirteen colonies, feared that France might take more deliberate action to harm its colonies or encroach onto their lands. In reality, Britain had expansion plans of its own that France could block. France had territory to the north in Canada as well as the West. Geographically, its territory exceeded that of Britain. Spain also controlled a large amount of land farther west and in Florida. The thirteen colonies included states now in the United States but geographically the states were much smaller than they are now. Economically, the colonies were much more developed and they had a much larger population, but encroachment by Spain and France seemed a real possibility. Britain thought France might try to expand from Canada in the north to New Orleans in the south. Alarmed at the prospect, Britain decided immediate action had to be taken. That meant convincing American colonists to help thwart the French by arming themselves and agreeing to fight them in a joint effort. Colonists also saw the threat and agreed to help. They began to form militias, a popular idea that spread rapidly and expanded into the early nineteenth century, when militias exercised in parades between military engagements, thus providing a social outlet for those who joined them.[285]

Americans often think of the eighteenth century as a time when British rule forced the colonists to fight for liberty and justice due to the actions of a mad, tyrant king. The English Privy Council tried to clamp down on the colonies after 1760; however, this proved difficult given the variety of governments and local laws established in each colony. The navigation laws imposed by Britain to manage trade by favoring Britain is one example of a failed attempt to totally control colonial trade. The colonies accepted the laws but found ways to circumvent them.[286]

During the French and Indian War; however, the British took another tactic. They tried to instill a sense of unity and military competence throughout all the colonies. When the war ended, Britain greatly expanded the scope of its colonial territory.

Britain acquired the French territory east of the Mississippi (from the Mississippi to the Appalachian Mountains), including Baton Rouge and the French land holdings in Canada. They also received the right to navigate the Mississippi. Florida, previously a Spanish possession, went to Britain. At that time, parts of Louisiana, Mississippi and Alabama were included in Florida, though France had given large parts of Louisiana to Spain prior to the ratification of the Treaty of Paris. From a religious perspective, Britain agreed to tolerate the large Roman Catholic population of former French territories, particularly Canada, for fear of starting yet another war. William Pitt the Elder, the Prime Minister who directed the French and Indian War with superb military genius, denounced the treaty before Parliament; however, Parliament ratified it. Blocked from moving west of the Mississippi, colonists eager for expansion often disregarded the prohibition.[287]

Without Britain's assistance, the American colonies faced an impossible task of expanding and achieving independence. The United States could have become a territory held by one or more of the three different countries. The French and Indian War helped put an end to that possibility. But there was a consequence for Britain in taking this direction. Before the war, the majority of American colonists still considered themselves British. After the war, they gained more confidence in their ability to defend themselves and work together, independent of Britain. The dynamics began to change.

One dynamic had to do with Britain's attitude toward the colonies. In the age of salutary neglect, which existed prior to 1760, the American colonies had the tacit permission to practice self-government and freedom of religion, though restrictions in a given locality might have forced people to move to other localities. Britain passed laws that applied to the colonies, but they did not provide adequate oversight to ensure that they were followed. Prime Minister Walpole believed that this laissez-faire attitude helped both the colonies and Britain.

During the years of salutary neglect, Britain also did not stop American colonies from establishing their own local laws, even though there seemed to be no consistency in the forms of representative government or the laws from colony to colony. By law, colonies had restriction on their freedom. In practice, the colonies had more freedom than Britain liked. The colonists also had much more freedom of religion than people in Britain, as one colony might favor one form of observance over another. As Britain began to clamp down on the colonies, it found that both the experience of self-government and the freedom to practice religion created major obstacles in its desire for greater control. The colonies tried at first to obtain representation in British government. Even though they sent petitions to Parliament and boycotted the purchase of British products to protest the lack of representation, their efforts were in vain.[288] As those in power in Britain determined, all members of Parliament represented all subjects wherever they might reside; after all, many towns and ports of the country did not elect members to Parliament, so why, they asked rhetorically should

Americans? Britain did not want to lose any part of Parliamentary control to the American colonies.

Parliament's continued obstinacy and its creation of new laws to collect more revenue to pay for the expensive Seven Years' War sealed the deal for revolution. From 1765-70, Parliament passed several acts in an attempt to increase revenue. The Sugar Act (1765), the Stamp Act (1766), and the Quartering Act (1766) all contained provisions to extract more money from the colonies. The predictable outcry resulted in the repeal of the Sugar and Stamp Acts in 1767; however, Parliament passed the Townshend Acts in 1767.

Different from the other forms of taxation, the Townshend Acts, named for Charles Townshend, cabinet member, did not tax the colonies directly. It taxed them indirectly by placing taxes on the products that the colonies could not make themselves. A second boycott occurred. Colonists still saw these acts as burdensome taxes without representation. Parliament's actions ignited their fury. Britain realized it had to make some changes, so in 1770, it decided to repeal the Townshend Acts with one exception—tea.

Parliament thought the colonies could still claim a major victory but Parliament would retain its right to tax the colonies. Although tea did not become the national drink of England until after the Revolutionary War when William Pitt, the Younger, engineered low duties for its import, Brits (even colonial ones) still had a hankering for their tea. That meant that Parliament erred when it attempted to keep the tea tax. Colonial anger did not erupt immediately, as they did not want to forgo drinking tea. But as they thought about it, perhaps while drinking tea, their fury grew.[289] The British had constructed the new law in such a way that the British East India Company, the biggest importer of tea and a company nearing bankruptcy, could eliminate the middleman, i.e., the American merchant. The company, badly hurt by the Financial Crisis of 1772, needed a monopoly of the colonial tea market to avoid bankruptcy. Cutting out the colonial middleman and taxing tea only added insult to injury in the eyes of the colonists.[290]

At the end of 1773, the American colonies decided to play tit for tat. In Boston, some colonists secretly boarded three of the East Indian Company ships under the cover of darkness, dressed as American Indians. Instead of stealing it, they threw the tea overboard. {According to the ditty of the time: "We made a plaguey mess of tea/In one of the biggest dishes/I mean we steeped it in the sea/And treated all the fishes."} Parliament now took its turn to become incensed. The colonists had the audacity to destroy British goods, an action that could not be condoned. While it had tried to appease the colonists by revoking previous harsh taxes, Parliament now reacted harshly. We could say that if the ship had been a bridge, it would have been a bridge too far. Parliament wanted to find a way to impose a punishment that would prevent the colonies from trying to defy them in the future.

Depending on one's perspective, Parliament's retaliatory action could be called the Coercive Acts (British) or the Intolerable Acts (colonies). They could have been dubbed the Fire Acts since they ignited a war.

The colonies now had an issue that almost every colonist could support: the need to make changes in the level of British control. The time had come for the colonies to unite and construct their own demands and act collectively. The First Continental Congress formed. While unity seemed simple enough, different interpretations of what the word meant occurred. The process of resolving the differences reflected the birthing pains for potential independence. Georgia would not even attend the Congress for fear of losing British support in its war with the Creek and Cherokee Indians on the Georgia border.[291]

The first Continental Congress created a list of Rights and Grievances (known as The Declaration of Rights), which members of that body presented to King George III. Members of the congress asked for respect and for the type of treatment afforded to all Englishmen born in England. In turn, they offered allegiance and subordination subject to representation in Parliament. They objected to taxation without representation. Among other things, they also objected to saving British money by quartering soldiers and insisted on the right to trial by jury.[292] They planned to boycott British goods unless they received redress for their grievances. To that end, they set a date for a second congress to follow up on the progress of their petition and to discuss what further action might be needed.

King George III refused to consider the demands of the colonists. Before a second Congress could be convened, the "shots heard round the world" were fired at the Battle of Concord, Massachusetts on April 19, 1775. The battle is remembered as the spark that started the American Revolutionary War.

The fight for independence took several years. During those years, the Declaration of Independence was published (1776). "Life, liberty and the pursuit of happiness" became words that were deeply embedded in the psyche of most Americans. The writings of two English-born political philosophers, John Locke and Thomas Paine, heavily influenced the document. Locke, the son of a Puritan, believed that a legitimate government is based on the consent of the governed, not the divine right of kings or absolute monarchy. According to him, people had the right to join together in a revolution to overthrow a government that does not guarantee political and civil rights. Thomas Paine, the son of a Quaker, wrote political documents that influenced the American Revolution and the French Revolution. *Common Sense* argued for independence from Britain and helped the patriot cause by convincing colonists to take up arms against Britain.

Paine's influence played a major part in steering Americans away from the notion that they were Britons, which was the way that many people viewed themselves at the time. "Europe, not England, is the parent country," he wrote. His enthusiasm for independence made him lash out at the tendency to think of the fraternal relationship between Britain and America for "every day wears out the little remains of kindred between us and them."[293] He wanted a decentralized Republican government with a charter similar to the Magna Carta. He famously wrote, "In America, the law is King … and there ought to be no other."[294] Memorialized in New Rochelle, New York, Paine can be viewed in a wax form at his museum at the end of Paine Avenue where a more modern-day communicator, Bob Smith (Buffalo Bob) once lived. Despite the popularity of television media, the written words of Paine have a wider reach and remain popular. They continue to inspire people who still remember his words and acknowledge their contribution to the Declaration of Independence.

Finalized in 1783, the Great American Divorce did not end the relationship between the new United States of America and Britain. It opened up the opportunity for a new relationship. As the years progressed, the two countries would have major ups and downs, including the War of 1812; however, they still maintained a special relationship as history discloses.

Approved in 1781, the Articles of Confederation became the first governing document of the new United States. Ratified in 1788, the Constitution changed the governing of the country. Although some similarities with the Articles of Confederation existed, profound differences predominated. Since that time, a number of challenges have been made to the constitutionality of various laws, and the Constitution is used to determine whether legal changes are needed. Various amendments provide protections not included in the first Constitution.

It is important to remember the influence of the English Bill of Rights (1689). While the two documents differ, both of them protect the rights and property of individuals and both were put into place by actions that did not include killing off the ruling class as the revolution in France had.

James Madison, Thomas Jefferson, and George Mason all played a major part in ensuring that religious liberty became part of the Constitution and Bill of Rights. When George Washington went to Rhode Island in 1790, in part to promote the Bill of Rights, a group from a Jewish congregation gave him a letter that asked for his help in granting religious tolerance to citizens regardless of their form of worship. Washington responded in a letter. He gave them assurance that the government would not sanction bigotry and that "every one shall sit in safety under his own vine and fig tree, and there shall be none to make him afraid." The First Amendment was added to the Constitution in the following year.[295]

Another relationship was reflected in what is popularly known as Jay's Treaty, 1794-95. The French Revolution was still raging, but that did not seem to help relations between Britain and the United States. Much of their disharmony resulted from their trade imbalance and British naval actions that affected American commerce. Not everyone in America had warm feelings toward Britain. Memories of the American Revolution had not faded and Thomas Jefferson, a major force in American politics, much preferred France.

With tensions at the breaking point, Washington knew that something had to be done before a war ensued. He sent Alexander Hamilton and John Jay to negotiate a treaty that would avoid the possibility of war. Much to Jay's distress, Hamilton undercut him by promising that the United States would not join a neutral alliance that might jeopardize relations with Britain. Jay had no choice but to negotiate what he could without his one great bargaining chip. For that reason, Britain actually benefited from the treaty while Jay received an agreement that had already been made on the surrender of northwestern posts. Britain did agree to remove troops from the western frontier. The treaty did give the United States a most favored nation relationship on trade but blocked much of its access to the British West Indies due to the size of ships allowed access. Some agreement on the seizure of ships and goods became part of the treaty but the entire substance of the treaty proved unacceptable to most Americans.[296]

The Jay Treaty did have one unintended consequence. Worried about the United States' negotiations with Britain over trade, Spain negotiated more favorable terms with the United States over access to the Mississippi River.

Another treated negotiated in 1795, the Pinckney's Treaty, also related to boundaries. An agreement between Spain and the United States, the treaty set the southern border of the United States and further increased the international status and power of the United States, although some restrictions on trade remained intact.[297]

Most Americans are aware that Francis Scott Key wrote the song that would much later become the national anthem, *The Star-Spangled Banner,* after viewing the flag wave after a decisive victory over Britain at Fort McHenry during the War of 1812, which lasted until 1815. It was set to the tune of a well-known British drinking song, *The Anacreontic Song* or *To Anacreon in Heaven*. Key used the same tune for an earlier poem, "When the Warrior Returns,"[298] (much as, several years earlier, the tune for the French national anthem, *La Marseillaise*, was composed for another purpose.) The song's significance far exceeds the role it plays at the beginning of sporting events. For most Americans, it is an inspirational song that reminds us of our resiliency as a nation.

George III's reign also featured the Napoleonic Wars, which ended in 1815. Once again, the British battled with France, which affected the number of resources that could be used in relations with the United States. George IV succeeded his father in 1820 and later approved the Catholic Emancipation Act, which applied to Roman Catholics in both Britain and Ireland. Some restrictions had been lifted earlier but troubles in Ireland forced ratification, which allowed both Catholics in Ireland and Britain admission to Parliament. Daniel

O'Connell of Ireland helped bring the Act to fruition. The Act also loosened the control of the Church of England and allowed more religious diversity, something that had already occurred in the United States.

The Catholic Emancipation did something else. Gone were the days of James I when England feared rule by Catholics. The new act reflected a liberal change that recognized political expediency.[299] Before the Act, Catholics had to bear the brunt of huge restrictions on their ability to hold a seat in Parliament, inherit land, receive an education, and marry. Priests feared imprisonment.

A major change created by the Catholic Emancipation Act was parliamentary representation, which meant that parliamentary participation was no longer dependent on religion but economics. Members had to own property worth at least ten pounds, so the amount still hindered some Irish Catholic representation. It also split the Tory party.[300]

In the area of political and economic policy, George Canning, the brilliant Tory statesman, feared that Spain might try to retake its colonies in South America after the Napoleonic Wars. Britain traded heavily with those colonies and any interruption due to Spain's ambitions might harm the balance of power that the nation desired on the European Continent. By negotiating with France, Canning ensured that it would not interfere with the colonies. With one major power no longer a threat, he next called upon the United States to join Britain in a movement to bar Spain from further colonization in South America.[301]

The United States feared European intervention. Given these concerns, President Monroe may have taken the bait; however, John Adams dissuaded him by convincing him that the United States should go it alone. In 1827, Monroe announced before Congress the country's unilateral action, which became known as the Monroe Doctrine. Essentially, it freed, in writing only, the western hemisphere from further colonization by European parties. It contained a promise that the United States would not interfere with existing colonies and dependencies in South America. It also made it clear that the United States would never intervene in continental wars unless the rights of the United States were at stake. In reality, the doctrine had no teeth, as the United States was not a major player at that point and lacked the military resources to prevent what it warned the Europeans to keep from doing. Luckily, Britain had its back, since doing so protected the British interest in keeping the balance of power and good trade relations with South America.[302]

William IV succeeded his brother. During his reign, slavery was abolished throughout Britain. The Slavery Abolition Act of 1833 became a reality due to the efforts of the abolition movement. The end of slavery occurred a few decades prior to its abolishment in the United States, where a Civil War helped make abolition happen. In this case, England led the way, and America followed.[303]

But both countries attempted to provide reparations for owners of slaves. The British government gave millions of dollars to slave owners who lost their slave labor after the Act. Modern-day Britons are left to wonder why the money was not provided to slaves rather than the owners so that the slaves could more easily transition to lives as free people.[304]

During the Civil War, which occurred during Queen Victoria's reign, Abraham Lincoln attempted to follow Britain's lead by signing a bill in 1862 that would have allowed reparations in the amount of $300 per slave freed from slavery. Intended as a compromise position between slavery and outright emancipation, compensated emancipation did not sit well with the southern states. The bill failed; however, owners in the District of Columbia did receive compensation due to the presence of the federal government in that location. Approximately 900 owners freed their slaves and received $300 for each one. It is important to note that the "value" of many slaves greatly exceed that amount though it seems outrageous to put a price on the value of a human being.[305]

As the Hanoverian reign drew to a close, fear over succession became an issue. King William liked his niece Victoria but disapproved of her mother, the Duchess of Kent. In fact, he loathed her. At one point near the end of his reign, he stood in a crowded room near both of them and uttered, "I trust to God that my life may be spared for nine months longer. I should then have the satisfaction of leaving the exercise of the Royal authority to the personal authority of that young lady, heiress presumptive to the Crown, and not in the hands of a person now near me, who is surrounded by evil advisers and is herself incompetent to act with propriety in the situation in which she would be placed." To his credit, King William died shortly after Victoria reached her majority in 1837.[306] {Technically, the daughter of one of the sons of George III, Victoria was a Hanoverian; she remained so until she married Prince Albert, in 1840, whereupon, as a dutiful wife, she took his family name, Saxe-Coburg and Gotha. In 1917, in consideration of Britain having been at war with Germany, King George V proclaimed that the family name would henceforth be known as Windsor.}

Queen Victoria, Last of the Hanoverians
1837-1901

Emergence of Queen Victoria, Effect of Victorian age on social customs, Crimean War, Industrial Revolution and effect on the United States, Death of Victoria

Queen Victoria possessed an attribute that other Hanoverian monarchs did not. She was a woman and she proved that height, age, sex, and imperious behavior are not qualifications for a great leader. With a body less than five feet tall and a remarkable skill in negotiation, Victoria, who began her reign at the young age of 18, proved that a woman's place is not necessarily at home in the kitchen. In fact, her skills and abilities enabled her to become the second longest-reigning monarch of Great Britain. Only Queen Elizabeth II, another female monarch, has had a longer reign. But Victoria became the first to prove that a Queen could rule in a fast-changing world without creating unusual disturbances, including wars. She single-handedly saved the monarchy from extinction by proving its value once again.

During her reign, Victoria found that there were economic benefits associated with showcasing royalty. Many modern-day Americans are entranced by royal weddings. The royal weddings of Diana, Kate, and Meghan all captivated millions of people who, thanks to television, could view most of the gala from the vantage point of their own homes. Such ceremonies, while costly, still added millions to the coffers. In 1838, the wedding of Queen Victoria had a similar effect. The print media disclosed irresistible tidbits about the Queen. The insatiable thirst for knowledge turned into what the *Smithsonian* magazine labeled, Victoria Fever.[307] Fans of royalty wanted to know everything they could about the marriage. The ceremony itself had its share of missteps, though witnesses state that the Queen remained calm and survived everything in a most regal manner.[308]

Small as she was, Victoria had an influence on the social values of both Britain and America. After she dressed in white for her wedding, other women followed her lead until a white wedding dress became commonplace. Similarly, when she dressed in black after her husband died, many women also adopted that practice, though probably not for as long as Victoria did. Her values influenced British society as well as American society, which is not to say that all abided by them or approved of them. The Comstock Act of 1873 became a notorious consequence of aimlessly adhering to values without considering the ramifications. The Act banned the mailing of "obscene, lewd and lascivious" material, including information about birth control and contraceptives thus becoming one of the first laws to impact a women's right to control pregnancy in the United States.[309]

Some scholars and journalists say that Queen Victoria provided value in a way that transformed the monarchy. While she tried to be more involved politically, she perhaps exercised more power by acquiescing to demands that the role of the monarchy become more ceremonial in nature. Although her husband's role was subservient to hers, she allowed him to establish his own mark in the construction of the famous Crystal Palace.[310] Truly in love, she tried her best to serve as both queen and loyal wife. At times that meant her husband became more involved in Crown affairs than he would otherwise be. Some of that involvement may have been the result of her nine pregnancies. (Unusual for the time, all of her children survived into adulthood.)

Although she disdained wars, Victoria did control the reins of the monarchy during one of them. The Crimean War (1853-1856) pitted Britain, France, and the Turkish Ottomans against Russia for control of the Ottoman Empire. Given the historic bitter rivalry between Britain and France, the war made them strange "bedfellows." Austria sided with the allies and lost the protection of Russia.

Changes in medicine and technology that occurred during the war affected warfare in the United States. The use of the telegraph and synchronized watches would become more commonplace. For the first time, the press covered the war, and photographs were taken for dissemination to the public. Florence Nightingale's nursing led to major changes in medicinal care for soldiers. Tennyson wrote the famous poem, "The Charge of the Light Brigade" based on a battle that took place during The Crimean War.

Although Britain entered the war in hopes of achieving a balance of power in Europe, it ended up taking an isolationist stand after the end of the unpopular war. The United States maintained a friendly relationship with Russia during the war but did not interfere in its progress. Russia's loss sent it scrambling for funds to replace money spent on the costly war. It had calculated that ownership of Alaska lacked any perceived value as the fur trade had declined. It also decided (probably correctly) that Americans would one day overrun it and seize it anyway. As a result, Secretary of State William Seward managed to negotiate the purchase of Alaska for the bargain price of $7 million. The purchase would be labeled "Seward's Folly" until the remarkable nature of the deal was fully understood.[311]

When the former American colonies entered into their own Civil War, many thought that Britain would support the Confederates. Trade in cotton, key to Britain's textile trade, seemed essential to the British and to other global markets as well. In fact, Senator James H. Hammond of South Carolina made a speech in 1858 that included his remark that "old England would topple headlong and carry the whole civilized world with her, save the South. No, you dare not make war on cotton. No power on earth dares to make war upon it. Cotton is king."[312]

Britain, unfortunately, seemed determined to remain neutral though some conflicts with the North did occur. The North also tried to blockade ships carrying cotton, though the South thought that a decrease in cotton exports would draw Britain into the war. Instead, Britain and other markets found cotton sources from other countries, including India. When the war ended, the trade in cotton from the South never recovered from the damage inflicted by the war.

While the Industrial Revolution began in the eighteenth century, in Britain, it continued to grow into the nineteenth. It quickly changed the demographics throughout the country. The agriculture-based economy meant more people lived outside of the cities. With the growth of cities due to industry that made use of such natural resources as coal and iron, the population outside of the city shrank. While Britain led other countries at the beginning of the revolution, the United States by the fourth-quarter of the nineteenth century eventually caught up and surpassed it. By the end of the nineteenth century, the world would be struggling with problems with environmental and living conditions caused by the industrial revolution.

Aside from the changes wrought by the Industrial Revolution, changes in the political landscape of Europe also occurred. Queen Victoria received the nickname "Grandmother of Europe" due to the placement of her descendants in the European royal families.[313] One daughter married the head of the German Empire and her son, Victoria's grandson, became Kaiser Wilhelm II. One granddaughter became the wife of Nicholas II, the last Tsar of Russia. Both of the two latter men would play a major role in world unrest during the twentieth century.

A peaceful death claimed Queen Victoria's life in 1901. Her longtime trusted friend, Abdul Karim, was allowed the last look at her before her coffin was closed for good and placed in the Royal Mausoleum on the Frogmore Estate at Windsor Home Park, not far from Windsor Castle. He also received permission to walk in the funeral procession; however, only days later, he had to turn over all correspondence from the Queen and then leave the country. A lonely woman had finely found solace in the companionship of an Indian friend but race consciousness ripped it asunder after her death.[314]

King George V Reign
1910-1936

King George's character, Archduke Ferdinand, Causes of WWI, U-boats, Airpower, Enemy damage to St. Mary's Church, Meuse-Argonne Offensive, Churchill in the trenches, Economic conditions

Sadly, the oldest son of Edward VII died before he could succeed his father. The second son, George Frederick Edward Albert, acquired the throne though he never believed it likely. Dramatic changes occurred during his reign. Nothing would be the same when all was done.

Quite different from his father, George turned out to be a family man who proposed to his dead brother's fiancé at the insistence of his grandmother. His sense of duty and decency are characteristics that he passed on to his own grandchild, Queen Elizabeth II.

Despite his more relaxed demeanor, George had the unfortunate problem of leading a nation embroiled in a world war only four years into his reign. Tensions between Austria-Hungary and Serbia flared prior to the war. The assassination of Archduke Ferdinand of Austria by a Serb ignited the war, which may have happened anyway due to growing tensions and the buildup of the German military. Attitudes about war pre-1914 led nations to believe that armed attacks were good for a nation. The First World War, which many thought to be a short war and the "war to end all wars," proved to be anything but that. The duration and experience of the war changed attitudes about the beneficial effects of war.

The four main causes of World War I involved "militarism, alliances, imperialism, and nationalism."[315] Several treaties formed between 1839 and 1907 created alliances among countries. Fueled by fear of military expansion and aggressiveness, countries formed various alliances to protect their interests from unwanted moves by others. Although the Triple Entente, the alliance among France, Russia, and Britain, linked the three countries, it did not require that Britain enter the war due to another country's attack on other members of the alliance. Nevertheless, when Germany invaded Belgium, it violated the 1839 Treaty of London signed by both the United Kingdom and Germany. Bound by that treaty to defend the neutrality of Belgium, the United Kingdom entered the war.[316] In addition to the treaty, Britain also grew concerned about the impact of a major war on its ability to continue shipping and trade without interference, particularly by Germany. Economically, it depended on trade with its vast empire and its ability to ship safely on the open waters. Though Britain had the strongest navy, obstructions could present enormous problems.

The growth of nations and the formation of empires spread the war to colonial areas. That forced the relocation of precious resources to defend those areas. The growing rise of nationalism in Serbia, in particular, sparked tensions with Austria-Hungary that eventually launched the world into war.

Austria-Hungary, Romania and Germany formed the Central Powers in opposition to the Triple Entente. The Ottoman Empire soon joined the alliance. Over the course of the war, more countries entered the war, most of them on the side of the Allies.

Although the British had the greatest naval power, Germany had undersea boats or U-boats (the "U" designated an abbreviated Anglicized version of the German word unterseeboot), which played a large role in the war and had the unintended consequence of causing the United States to enter the war. The United States had wanted to remain neutral and trade with both Germany and Britain but the torpedoing of the *Lusitania* passenger liner in 1915 with 128 Americans on board provoked anger and began to change public opinion about Germany. Many cities, including St. Louis, began changing German-named streets in 1918. Berlin Avenue became Pershing Avenue. Although Germany agreed to make changes in the way it approached and attacked ships after the *Lusitania* disaster, it eventually strayed from that agreement. The Germans sank more US ships. That fact along with the discovery by Britain of a potential German-Mexican alliance, as revealed in a telegram from German Foreign Minister Arthur Zimmerman to the German Minister to Mexico, made the US change its stance on neutrality and enter the war.[317]

Airpower became significant in 1916 and grew in importance in 1917, but the technology had not yet reached the level of significance it had in the Second World War. Other technological changes affected the production of guns and chemicals. The howitzer saw major action and chemical warfare did horrific damage. Large numbers of soldiers suffered from exposure to gas. All of these changes created more problems in trench warfare.

The Church of St. Mary was damaged during one of the few Zeppelin raids in London. Bystanders remembered the scary event that damaged but did not destroy the church. Repairs enabled congregants to continue use of the church after the war ended.[318]

The United States entered the war in the spring of 1917. It thrilled Churchill to have the support of the Americans in the war effort. Astonished that the Germans even considered pulling the Americans into the War, he remained grateful that they had.[319]

At first, a relatively small number of American men (approximately 120,000) fought in 1917. Later, in 1918, another 80,000 more men served in the National Guard.[320] Approximately 500,000 men served under Pershing at St. Mihiel.[321] Approximately one million Americans and French soldiers assisting them served at the Meuse-Argonne Offensive. By the end of the war, over four million Americans had served in the military and over one million served in combat zones in Europe. African Americans generally served in quartermaster labor units. Two hundred thousand African American men served and performed construction work, including building roads and digging trenches, probably due to discriminatory attitudes and because the United States Army was not integrated until a few years after the end of World War II.[322]

Despite the addition of so many Americans for the war effort, some Britons voiced their anger in song, including one named, "I Want to Go Home."[323] Churchill did not possess the same anger, as he understood that the sheer magnitude of additional soldiers would help win the war.

General John J. Pershing, a native Missourian, served as Commander-in-Chief of the American Armies that formed the American Expeditionary

Force (AEF).[324] During the summer of 1918, approximately 10,000 troops from America began arriving each day. Most went to the Western front where other Allies, including the British forces, had soldiers. Pershing wanted to support the Allies in the fighting but did not want the American forces split to reinforce British and French troops. He preferred that they fight separately under his command.

Fighting separately did not make the fighting easier. One soldier's story that illustrates the horrific conditions during World War I is that of Thomas M. Chapman, a young member of the AEF, First Army, 89th Division, 354th Infantry, Company M, which fought on the Western Front under Pershing. Chapman's regiment fought in France on the Western front. They first fought at two sectors in Toul and St. Mihiel before moving onto their involvement in the Meuse-Argonne Offensive, the largest campaign of the war that proved significant in ending the war. Victory came at a price. Over 26,000 men died in the 89th Division and another 120,000 men appeared on the list of men wounded.[325]

Company M captured the Bois de Barricourt. For their efforts, they spent days in slimy funk holes, which were not the trenches but small areas scraped out of the side of a trench and covered with a waterproof sheet. Funk holes were considered dangerous and the men were later banned from using them to sleep. The men had worn out their shoe leather on stress-filled hikes. The days were not typically sunny but dreary. Fog, rain, and mud described the environment on most days and that made soldiers depressed and miserable. The wounded had it even worse since there were no blankets or overcoats to shield them from the horrible environment.[326]

Machine gun fire continued at a fierce pace, frazzling the nerves of those who could still fight. A shortage of food, particularly warm food, existed due to problems with supply lines. Some members of the division suffered gassing, which occurred with regular frequency during the beginning of the offensive. Machine gun fire from air raids left many soldiers hunched over in terror in their foxholes. The terrain included a dense forest that created an "extremely strong natural fortress." Enemy snipers perched in trees shot at soldiers who came into their individual sight. During one of the division's first movements forward, air cover did not approach a level that provided good artillery support. Nevertheless, the troops followed orders to move forward using whatever they could to provide coverage. They resorted to using pocket electric flashlights to light the way. That particular movement did not last long but other advances followed it.[327]

When the troops arrived at the Meuse River, some took a bridge that the 315th Engineers built to replace one destroyed by the Germans. Others swam across the river to capture German soldiers. They managed to successfully cut the effectiveness of the railway, which formed the basis for German communication. When they had taken the Heights of Barricourt, General Foch exclaimed, "The War is over!" His prediction proved correct. The force of the attack persuaded the Germans to halt their fire. When the smoke cleared, one conciliatory German commander asked the Americans for permission to bury their dead and tend to their wounded.[328]

Churchill also fought in the trenches on the Western Front for a period of time. Blamed for the disaster in the Dardanelles, he was excluded from the War Coalition Government and resigned as First Lord of the Admiralty. On January 5, 1916, he took command as Battalion Chief of the 6th Battalion Royal Scots Fusiliers. "He showed up in the trenches with a phenomenal array of extras, from hampers of wine to an improbably large bathtub. But he shared and won the men over." During his five months in the trenches, he learned to appreciate the danger and horrible conditions under which the fighting men suffered while he continued to write his wife to send him some of the more elusive provisions, such as "sardines, chocolate, potted meat, clothes, and a big bath towel."[329]

Knowing how interested the Germans might be in his position, Churchill took pains to hide most of his activities from them. He supposedly used a French helmet to disguise himself from the Allies.[330] Though he narrowly missed being killed on separate occasions, Churchill learned to communicate well with the troops. He trained them and helped them deal with their situation by learning to protect themselves as best they could. He never ducked when bullets or shells passed nearby, telling his men that "Its no damn use ducking, the bullet has gone a long way past by now."[331] Churchill's resolve, bravery, and determination were all characteristics admired by his men and his experience on the Western front would help him strategize larger conflicts with a better understanding of front line conditions.

Before the war, he dealt with the American Charles Schwab, Chairman of Bethlehem Steel, on manufacturing Royal Naval submarines. Schwab had personally witnessed the sinking of a vessel by the Germans. Happy to help, he did so in way that avoided the US stance on neutrality. He ordered that the manufacturing be done in Canada to avoid a conflict with American neutrality; however, George Sylvester Viereck, the German editor of the American pro-Germany and pro-Austria-Hungary publication, *The Fatherland,* delivered a harsh written rebuke of his efforts.[332]

A prominent Jewish American, Bernard Baruch, would become a major supporter of the relocation of the Church of St. Mary in memory of Churchill and spent a great deal of time corresponding with him prior to their actual meeting. During the war, he served as a member of the US War Industries Board. He and Churchill became great personal friends, with Churchill often staying at Baruch's home when he came to the United States.

When the war ended in 1918, the face of Europe, Russia, and many of the other countries involved in the war changed—"a drizzle of empires, falling through the air."[333] The Austro-Hungary Empire, the

Russian Empire, the German Empire, and the Ottoman Empire no longer existed. The Russian Revolution had a huge impact on the end of the Romanov dynasty. The "new" countries of Austria, Hungary, Czechoslovakia, and Yugoslavia replaced Austria-Hungary. Turkey emerged from the Ottoman Empire but without the surrounding territories that had previously been part of its empire. The country of Poland made its reappearance while Finland separated from Russia. The Baltic states of Estonia, Latvia, and Lithuania gained independence. Romania increased in size. Ethnic and cultural identities did not necessarily correspond to the new borders established at the end of the war, which created numerous conflicts and even bigger issues in the coming years. In fact, the problems became some of the issues that led to World War II. The Treaty of Versailles (1919) also helped start World War II due to its severe terms, insisted upon by France, which endured the most suffering from battles fought in their country, and the fact that Germany was denied a role in the negotiating process. Germany's resistance to its terms never wavered but intensified over time.

Estimates of men and women killed or injured vary depending on the source. The United States reported a total number of 8.5 million military personnel killed on both sides, with 21 million wounded out of a total number of 65 million soldiers. The report did not show all countries nor did it list civilian casualties, which included people who were near the fighting or who died from hunger and disease related to the war. It also did not include people missing in action, people with emotional problems, and, possibly, those individuals who were gassed. The number of casualties and percentage of casualties per total population mobilized per country was also high. Russian had over 9 million casualties, which amounted to 76.3% of their total mobilized forces. Britain suffered over 3 million casualties, France suffered over 6 million casualties, and the United States suffered over 323,000 casualties.[334] Given the large number of men dead or wounded, the war also affected women who had hoped for marriage and children after the war.

Socially, more women in Britain and the United States entered the workplace during the war to support their families and industries that lost men to the war. American blacks fought in the war but they were sent to fight separately under the French, showing that racism had not officially ended. Medically, the influenza pandemic, 1918-19, struck and affected millions of people around the world. The presence of so many soldiers seemed to hasten its spread in locations where it first started, making it an unintended consequence of war. The flu showed rather harshly that war has horrific consequences beyond the fighting.

After the war, US President Woodrow Wilson pushed for the formation of the League of Nations, even as he negotiated the Treaty of Versailles. While other members of the Big Four—Britain, France, and Italy—agreed, the United States Congress did not. Part of the failure had to do with bad blood between Senator Henry Cabot Lodge and Wilson but Wilson had suffered a stroke after his grueling circuit of speech giving aimed at getting people to accept the idea, which he believed could stop future wars. In the end, frail and in poor health, he advised Congress to reject his ideas rather than vote for a concept revised beyond his liking. A disappointed Churchill thought that the refusal of the US Senate to vote for entry into the League of Nations hurt the chances of a security system that the league could offer all nations.[335]

Despite his misgivings about Wilson, Churchill made trips to the United States on several occasions to either market his books or speak on world issues. The year 1932 was a particularly big year for him. His daughter Diana wed. He made speeches in many cities in America. And, then a car nearly killed him as he crossed a street in New York City while looking for Bernard Baruch's house. Churchill wrote an article about his travails and descriptively entitled it, "How it Feels to be Run Down by an Automobile." He found an able interlocutor by the name of Mario Edward Cantasano, a former chauffeur and the man who accidentally hit him. The hapless man, well spoken and horrified by the accident, heard that his "victim" was Winston Churchill. As Mario said, it was "ten o'clock at night, and {nobody} would expect to find a British statesman running across the street."

In his article, Churchill admitted his guilt. The British, he told Cantasano, are used to people driving on the other side of the street and so he disembarked from the vehicle as he did in England and looked at the wrong side of the street in error (as untold numbers of Americans have when in Britain). Churchill's daughter invited Mario to tea where she and Winston assured him that they cast no blame. When he left, Mario said, "I like him very much. I do not think I could have run over anybody I would have liked any better. So, after all, maybe it was fortunate for me it was Mr. Churchill I damaged and not some other person I mightn't have liked." Churchill suffered a scalp wound and two cracked ribs.[336]

That same month, the Washington DC, *Evening Star,* published a story on Churchill's recent talk on the "World Economic Crisis." Churchill balked at the idea of having an international air police at the disposal of the League of Nations. He didn't think that the British taxpayers would support the idea of using an airplane that they built for use by League of Nations to run errands. He also discussed difficulties nations felt due to the worldwide depression, the depreciation of money, and the likely end to the payment of reparations by debtor nations. And he made a point that both the United States and Britain were in agreement over the need for any nation to trade wherever they like without handicap.[337]

The Depression had severely hurt countries worldwide, making it difficult for old debts to be repaid. Its effect on the economic health of nations was another reason that Churchill believed that Britain and the United States should look to each other for help. However, as the United States State Department noted, the US had become more isolationist during the years of the Great Depression. Both Britain and the US went off the gold standard in the early thirties due to economic conditions. At the time, the US held the most gold; however, Roosevelt closed all the banks for a period after there was a run on them. When they reopened, they would no longer redeem dollars for gold.[338] Preferring to focus on their own internal needs, the US did not intervene when Japan and Germany began promising economic relief and promoting expansion. The Japanese seized northeast China in 1931, Italy invaded Ethiopia in 1935, and Germany expanded its territory in Eastern Europe. Concentrating on its own problems, the US again did not intervene. The fall of France caused the president to reconsider America's isolationist policy but an intervention did not occur.[339]

In Europe, things did not fare much better. World War I had devastated countries and the worldwide depression made daily life worse. Countries did not wish to return to a world war scenario and most did not have the financial or other resources to do so. Germany thought differently. Bogged down by an impossible debt and tight restrictions imposed by the Treaty of Versailles, it also had a populace that suffered from the effects of World War I and the economic depression. Germany believed that it could change things by using quick and aggressive moves aimed at consolidating the Aryan race. It quickly changed to just expansion. When it failed to abide by the terms of the Treaty of Versailles and expanded its army, built up munitions, and expanded into other areas, Germany found no resistance among nations outside the country initially targeted for expansion of German colonists in the name of Lebensraum (living space).[340] The world thought that a policy of appeasement would peacefully end Hitler's plans.

George V died on January 20, 1936. His oldest son, Edward Albert Christian George Andrew Patrick David, became King Edward VIII.

King Edward VIII Reign
January 20, 1936 – December 11, 1936

Abdication

Having fallen in love with an American divorcee, Wallis Simpson, Edward's reign did not last a year. At the time, the Church of England would not allow such a match, nor would the public accept it. A popular king before his abdication, Edward's star fell when he abdicated to marry the twice-divorced American and continued to fall after newspapers reported their trip to Nazi Germany in 1937. Shockwaves filled the air. Edward was given the title, Duke of Windsor. Winston Churchill, the only notable politician to support him, actually grew angry over the abdication as evidenced by letters that came to light in 2001 but are still classified as top secret.[341] Supposedly, the letters also verify the pro-Nazi sympathies of the Duke and Duchess of Windsor, though some historians continue to argue that they had no such sympathies.

George VI Reign
December 11, 1936 – February 6, 1952

Neville Chamberlain, Dunkirk, Appeal to the United States, FDR denounces Mussolini and prepares people for war, Lend-lease, *Finest Hour* speech, Battle of Britain, The Blitz, The Atlantic Charter, Pearl Harbor, US enters the war against Germany, End of the war, Nuremberg Trials[342]

After his brother abdicated the throne, Albert Frederick Arthur George Saxe-Coburg-Gotha, succeeded him and became King George VI.

The abdication shocked the world, particularly since it occurred in such unsettling times. Churchill's support of King Edward III cost his reputation dearly. The new king had to quickly come up to speed in the new, difficult circumstances.

British Prime Minister Neville Chamberlain practiced a policy of appeasement, with which most of his countrymen agreed. He met with Hitler on three occasions to try to maintain peace and believed that Hitler would put a halt to most of its expansionist plans. Chamberlain's eagerness to accept Hitler at face value had much to do with his assessment of his country's resources at the time. Britain, he thought, did not have the military might to stop Germany and the probable death toll would be too much for the country to handle if it tried. He agreed to Germany's plans for Czechoslovakia, which then housed many Germans, since "the quarrel {was} in a far away country, between people of whom we know nothing." His justification to the British people amounted to a declaration that they would now have "peace for our time."[343]

But the Germans continued advance, the tide of public opinion changed in 1939, and Chamberlain resigned as prime minister in early 1940. Churchill replaced him. Chamberlain died about six months later. Suffering from colon cancer, his illness may have affected his judgment. For some time, Churchill, and probably many others, had expressed concern about Germany's growing militaristic approach. Churchill could see the ramifications of it but could not gain support from the majority of the people with whom he shared power. World War II started but the United States did not immediately participate. Still fearful of "entangling alliances and protracted war," Americans wanted to concentrate on dealing with problems at home.[344]

During 1940, Churchill made several speeches in which he made reference to the United States. He tried to reassure the British people that the United States had their back but he also wanted Americans to understand their importance to the war effort. The evacuation of British soldiers from Dunkirk in 1940 seemed miraculous given the number of men involved and the fear that the Germans might kill them before a rescue could be made. Luckily, Germany made serious errors and the rescue proved successful.

On March 4, 1940, Churchill spoke before the House of Commons in part to determine the response to what had happened. Still trying to get the United States to enter the war, his speech also served as an appeal for its help. The last portion of the speech is the most famous. It also closes with the hope of rescue by the United States.

> Even though large tracts of Europe and many old and famous States have fallen or may fall into the grip of the Gestapo and all the odious apparatus of Nazi rule, we shall not flag or fail. We shall go on to the end, we shall fight in France, we shall fight on the seas and oceans, we shall fight with growing confidence and growing strength in the air, we shall defend our Island, whatever the cost may be, we shall fight on the beaches, we shall fight on the landing grounds, we shall fight in the fields and in the streets, we shall fight in the hills; we shall never surrender, and even if, which I do not for a moment believe, this Island or a large part of it were subjugated and starving, then our Empire beyond the seas, armed and guarded by the British Fleet, would carry on the struggle, until, in God's good time, the New World, with all its power and might, steps forth to the rescue and the liberation of the old.

On May 26, 1940, President Franklin Roosevelt delivered a speech in which he tried to prepare Americans for the possibility of war. The president understood that at some point the United States could no longer remain neutral. The threat to democracy demanded intervention. Hampered by isolationists, Roosevelt needed to start changing attitudes about the possibility of war. Only Congress could declare war but isolationists had a hold on congress. The next month, he gave another speech in Virginia wherein he denounced Mussolini and emphasized that the isolationist track no longer suited the country. The United States needed to start furnishing material to the Allies and ramp up production to make the country ready for war.[345]

Churchill, knowing how important the United States could be in the war effort, persisted in trying to strengthen a bond with the president. In his response to his pleas for help during the Battle of Britain, Roosevelt sent "surplus" military equipment to Churchill. By law, Britain had to pay for the help Roosevelt offered. On September 2, 1940, Roosevelt signed the Destroyers-for-Bases Agreement whereby 50 US naval destroyers were given to Britain in exchange for the use of naval and air bases located in eight British possessions. These bases included ones at Newfoundland, Bermuda, and locations on the Avalon Peninsula. The United States certified that the destroyers were not needed for the defense of the country; in truth, they were not in prime condition. The US, as a neutral country, had to be careful about the help given to a country involved in a war. In return for the destroyers, the US received 99-year leases at the sites, free of charge.[346]

When Churchill told Roosevelt that the cash demands for other purchases could no longer be supported, Roosevelt came up with a new program—the Lend-Lease Program signed into law by Roosevelt on March 11, 1941, after Congress had approved legislation to authorize it. Under that program, the United States supplied war materials under lend or lease provisions. The program provided a provision for reciprocal aid under the Mutual Aid Agreement, which reduced the cost of Britain's war debt. Much of the reciprocal aid related to the provision of supplies to the US while in the European Theater. Mutually beneficial, it reduced the cost of shipping such supplies from the United States. Intended as a means to defend Britain whose "interests were vital to the US," it was a war program only and officially ended on Victory in Japan Day.[347]

On June 18, 1940, Churchill gave his famous *Finest Hour* speech during which he prepared his countrymen for the forthcoming war. By this time, the British people had heard about the evacuation of several hundred thousand soldiers from Dunkirk—perhaps the largest evacuation in military history. They had just heard that France had fallen to the invading Germans. Britain seemed to "stand alone." In an attempt to raise spirits, Winston prepared a speech that acknowledged to past problems but shined a light on a dark time. He wanted people to be prepared for war but to also take heart that the United States and others would be providing needed supplies. If failure happened, he said, it would also affect the United States, a thought that he hoped motivated people to fight on and "never surrender." These following passages are taken from that speech.

> Hitler can bring under his despotic control the industries of the countries he has conquered, this will add greatly to his already vast armament output. On the other hand, this will not happen immediately, and we are now assured of immense, continuous and increasing support in supplies and munitions of all kinds from the United States; and especially of aeroplanes and pilots from the Dominions and across the oceans coming from regions, which are beyond the reach of enemy bombers …
>
> What General Weygand called the Battle of France is over. I expect that the Battle of Britain is about to begin. Upon this battle depends the survival of Christian civilization. Upon it depends our own British life, and the long continuity of our institutions and our Empire. The whole fury and might of the enemy must very soon be turned on us. Hitler knows that he will have to break us in this island or lose the war. If we can stand up to him, all Europe may be free and the life of the world

> may move forward into broad, sunlit uplands. But if we fail, then the whole world, including the United States, including all that we have known and cared for, will sink into the abyss of a new Dark Age made more sinister, and perhaps more protracted, by the lights of perverted science. Let us therefore brace ourselves to our duties, and so bear ourselves that, if the British Empire and its Commonwealth last for a thousand years, men will still say, "This was their finest hour."

On August 17 of that same year, Churchill spoke to the House of Commons about the airplane pilots who so heroically were fighting in the Battle of Britain. His famous line, "Never in the field of human conflict was so much owed by so many to so few" inspired many. Once again he inserted America into his speech by telling of the upcoming resources that they were producing to help Britain wage a war. Blessed with an outstanding ability to communicate his message, Churchill inspired the British people, and he did so in a positive way. He knew how to massage the English language, arrange it in almost poetic form, and deliver it with remarkable intonation. Edward R. Murrow, the American broadcast journalist, coined the following description of Churchill's facile use of the English language, "Churchill mobilized the English language and sent it into battle." John F. Kennedy later used his words without attribution when he conferred honorary citizenship on Churchill.[348]

Churchill's style of speaking contrasts sharply with that of Adolph Hitler but both men show the importance of speech and style in influencing others. Churchill repeatedly expressed his belief in their common goals of the US and Britain and their ability to help each other.

> Some months ago we came to the conclusion that the interests of the United States and of the British Empire both required that the United States should have facilities

for the naval and air defence of the Western hemisphere against the attack of a Nazi power which might have acquired temporary but lengthy control of a large part of Western Europe and its formidable resources.

We had therefore decided spontaneously, and without being asked or offered any inducement, to inform the Government of the United States that we would be glad to place such defence facilities at their disposal by leasing suitable sites in our transatlantic possessions for their greater security against the unmeasured dangers of the future.

The principle of association of interests for common purposes between Great Britain and the United States had developed even before the war. Various agreements had been reached about certain small islands in the Pacific Ocean, which had become important as air fuelling points. In all this line of thought we found ourselves in very close harmony with the Government of Canada.

Presently we learned that anxiety was also felt in the United States about the air and naval defence of their Atlantic seaboard, and President Roosevelt has recently made it clear that he would like to discuss with us, and with the Dominion of Canada and with Newfoundland, the development of American naval and air facilities in Newfoundland and in the West Indies. There is, of course, no question of any transference of sovereignty—that has never been suggested—or of any action being taken, without the consent or against the wishes of the various Colonies concerned, but for our part, His Majesty's Government are entirely willing to

> accord defence facilities to the United States on a 99 years' leasehold basis, and we feel sure that our interests no less than theirs, and the interests of the Colonies themselves and of Canada and Newfoundland will be served thereby.
>
> These are important steps. Undoubtedly this process means that these two great organisations of the English-speaking democracies, the British Empire and the United States, will have to be somewhat mixed up together in some of their affairs for mutual and general advantage.
>
> For my own part, looking out upon the future, I do not view the process with any misgivings. I could not stop it if I wished; no one can stop it. Like the Mississippi, it just keeps rolling along. Let it roll. Let it roll on full flood, inexorable, irresistible, benignant, to broader lands and better days.

The Blitz of England by Nazi warplanes began in September 1940 and lasted through May of 1941. Previously, German warplanes had engaged with the British Royal Air Force (RAF) in the Battle of Britain from July-September 1940. The Germans intended to invade England but failed to overwhelm the RAF. They did inflict heavy damage. Then, from September of the same year until May of 1941, the Blitz was underway. Germans began bombing London and other cities during night raids. During this period of bombing the Church of St. Mary the Virgin, Aldermanbury received devastating damage. Only the twenty four steps, the walls, interior columns, and tower survived. Many other churches also received some damage, including St. Paul's Cathedral.[349]

Churchill and Roosevelt wrote to each other many times during the course of the war in Europe. They met for the first time in secret on board the ship, the *HMS Prince of Wales*, on August 14, 1941, off the coast of Newfoundland, Canada. Churchill so enjoyed the meeting that he spoke about it in a radio broadcast on August 24, 1941.[350]

> … this meeting was bound to be important because of the enormous forces, at present only partially mobilized, but steadily mobilizing, which are at the disposal of the two major groupings of the human family, the British Empire and the United States, who, fortunately for the progress of mankind, happen to speak the same language and very largely think the same thoughts, or anyhow, think a lot of the same thoughts.
>
> The meeting was, therefore, symbolic. That is its prime importance. It symbolizes, in a form and manner, which everyone can understand in every land and in every clime, the deep underlying unities, which stir and, at decisive moments, rule the English-speaking peoples throughout the world. Would it be presumptuous for me to say that it symbolizes something even more majestic, namely, the marshaling of the good forces of the world against the evil forces which are now so formidable and triumphant and which have cast their cruel spell over the whole of Europe and a large part of Asia?

The *Atlantic Charter*, a joint declaration between the United States and Britain rather than a treaty, came about due to that meeting. The Charter included principles that reflected "their hopes for a better future of the world." The following three principles would become issues in forming a settlement after the war.

> First, their countries seek no aggrandizement, territorial or other;

> Second, they desire to see no territorial changes that do not accord with the freely expressed wishes of the peoples concerned;
>
> Third, they respect the right of all peoples to choose the form of government under which they will live; and they wish to see sovereign rights and self-government restored to those who have been forcibly deprived of them.

Roosevelt and Churchill focused on freedom and the right of self-government, both of which are threads found in the history of Britain. Roosevelt pushed for the references to self-government, which foretold the break-up of the British Empire, an empire that was anathema to the United States. In fact, the war would help change the character of the Empire. Aside from their very different views on the British Empire, the Atlantic Charter does reference shared values, a commonality that Churchill always believed they had.[351]

Freedoms mentioned in the charter included those expressed by Roosevelt previously. Norman Rockwell, so impressed by the concept, painted four pictures that symbolized them. The United States used prints of the painting in its successful war bond drives.[352]

Although their two countries periodically collaborated, the major milestones in the war temporarily diverted attention to other issues. The Imperial Japanese Navy Air Service attacked the US Naval Base at Pearl Harbor on December 7, 1941. This resounding act launched the United States into World War II. Hundreds of Japanese fighter planes caused horrific damage to America's naval fleet. The fighter planes destroyed or damaged twenty American naval vessels, including eight battleships, and 300 airplanes. More than 2,400 American died in the attack and another 1,000 were injured. Though relations between Japan and America had not been good, the surprise attack shocked all Americans. Roosevelt asked Congress to declare war. Germany declared war on the United States on December 11, 1941, in response to the attack on Pearl Harbor though it did not have any treaty that required it to do so. Hitler inexplicably ignored the issue of having yet another country to fight in the war.[353]

When Churchill learned of the attack, relief spread over his body. He "slept the sleep of the saved and thankful" that night."[354] At last, the US would provide help in defeating Germany. In an address before the US Congress in late December 1941, he linked the two countries by asking a rhetorical question of the Japanese, "Who do they think we are?"

Just six weeks after the United States entered the European Theater, the Eighth Army Air Corps (Army Air Force) activated the 8th Bomber Command. Brigadier General Ira C. Eaker was assigned the Command Headquarters in England. The 306th Bombardment Group became the first operational bombardment group in the command. Stationed at the former Royal Air Force Base (RAF) in Thurleigh, England, from September 1942 until December 25, 1945, the group also completed the first 300 missions over Occupied Europe and Nazi Germany. In doing so, they suffered enormous casualties. Airmen were fond of repeating the slogan {that} "fly(ing) in the Eighth Air Force then was like holding a ticket to a funeral—your own."[355]

Alfred C. Villagran, only 19 when he started as a B-17 radio operator, flew 33 of those missions over northern France and Germany. After his first mission aborted, his crew received an assignment to bomb Munich, an extraordinary assignment for a first bombing. Once his airplane flew over Munich, flak or ground anti-aircraft fire, began filling the sky. According to Villagran, the allies lost more planes to flak in World War II than to enemy fighter planes. When some flak finally hit his plane on his first bombing mission, it knocked out the two engines on each side of the cabin. The closeness of the engines to the cabin generally placed a plane in danger of fire. On this occasion, the loss of two engines put the plane into a spin, from which it is generally extremely difficult, if not impossible, to recover. Encountering more flak during the descent, time was of the essence. Somehow, the pilot pulled the plane out of the spin and turned the plane in the direction of Britain.[356]

Unfortunately, six German fighters started firing at the plane. Soon the German planes began lowering their landing gear as a signal to the Americans that they wanted the plane to land in Germany. Their sights were on the plane that they hoped to recover and use in a deceptive move against other American airplanes. Villagran and his fellow crewmembers had no intention of surrendering their plane. Not doing so put them in tremendous danger.

The crew had one unfilled spot on the plane that day. The vacant spot was the crewmember assigned to the tail gun. Villagran, the radio operator, had to quickly fill the spot and begin firing at the German aircraft. He was shorter than the other possible replacement. After one of his guns became jammed, another crewmember gave him a gun.[357]

The flight back to England took five hours and the chances of doing so successfully seemed dim. Without the two additional engines, the plane was severely disadvantaged. Somehow the Americans made it to the English Channel with three German fighters still on their tail but at that moment the Germans decided it was time to shoot down the American plane. Out of nowhere, a B-29 plane came to the rescue. The rescue pilot's presence was a fluke but his aim was spot on. He downed two fighters and, according to another crewmember, Villagran downed the third. After that, the crewmembers threw everything out of the plane that they could in hopes of securing a safe landing with less weight at the nearest RAF airfield. Land they did but a third engine fell off in the process and created a loud noise. The engine's loss could have destroyed the ship. But it didn't.[358]

United States Army Air Force photo courtesy of Al Villagran. Jimmy Doolittle stands on the right.

Exhausted by their ordeal and still anxious, the crewmembers put their belongings in quarters provided by the English. They could not be flown to the home base until the next morning. Still in their flight suits and wanting to stretch their legs, the crew visited a shop in the town. They decided to help Villagran buy a handkerchief he needed. The cashier in the store balked at the idea, since Al had no ration cards. After much back and forth bickering, the visibly upset clerk asked them, "Don't you know there is a war going on?" The absurd question broke the tension and enabled the warriors to find laughter in the chaos and terrible stress of what had happened. They left the store laughing and went to the nearest pub to enjoy a relaxing drink. The next day, they returned to the air on yet another assignment from the former RAF airbase.[359]

While still stationed at the airbase, the men of the "Mighty Eighth" received a visit from then Princess Elizabeth (now Queen Elizabeth II) and her parents, King George VI and Queen Mary. The three members of royalty stood in front of a plane named for Elizabeth. Elizabeth christened the plane, the "Rose of York." Information on the event or the photo of the event made its way into the hands of enemy combatants. Although the plane had flown 62 successful missions it became a target to the Germans who seemed to relish targeting certain planes. It was damaged by enemy fire on February 3, 1945, on a bombing mission over Berlin. Nine crew members and a BBC reporter, Guy Byam, lost their lives.[360]

Survivors of the air battles, like soldiers in all battles, learned to move forward in their lives having survived horrific circumstances. Years later, Al and some of his friends from the Mighty Eighth helped raise awareness of the Church of St. Mary the Virgin, Aldermanbury. A television show recorded their selection of a winner for a free wedding at the Church of St. Mary. The occasion marked the end of a wonderful annual dinner of the veterans. The chosen couple later decided not to get married but their declination did not affect the good times had in choosing the winner. In 2019, a grateful France awarded Al Villagran the Legion of Honor at the St. Louis Soldiers Memorial. He accepted it in memory of his fellow crewmembers.[361]

During the war, the two countries worked independently but also shared a great deal, including the airfields in England. Intelligence, war supplies, and strategy are examples of the sharing, which also included battlefield operations. Not always in lockstep, they still communicated and tried to work out their different opinions and goals. Their joint effort led to a successful conclusion.

Churchill, Roosevelt, and Stalin, also known as the Big Three, met at Yalta in Crimea, Ukraine, from February 4-11, 1945, to begin discussions of the post-war world before the conflict actually ended. Roosevelt's demeanor had changed noticeably. He seemed to be suffering from some sort of serious affliction but his death two months later surprised the other two men. Roosevelt's illness probably had some effect on his negotiations but he believed that he could trust Stalin, whom he called "Uncle Joe." He underestimated Stalin's character.[362]

With enormous losses to its homeland and its people, Russia wanted to receive more than just war reparations. It cast its eyes on territory currently held and had no intention of allowing the free elections desired by both Britain and the United States. Churchill did not want to see the territorial ambitions of Germany transferred to Russia and tried hard to create a better balance of power. Roosevelt's actions stifled his attempts. Called back to England for elections, Churchill suddenly found himself voted out of office and unable to influence further changes.

Another conference held in Potsdam in July of 1945 saw a change in leadership. Roosevelt had died and Churchill's bid to remain in power had failed at the voting booths. As the new person representing the

United States, Harry Truman had a tough time getting his demands met.[363] He failed to limit the dollar amount of reparations that Germany owed and he failed to prevent communism from taking hold in Poland. It is doubtful that he could have succeeded given the circumstances. The face of Europe was starting to change dramatically.

Russia annexed the Baltic countries (Estonia, Latvia, and Lithuania). Finland ceded some territory to Russia. The Allies divided Germany and Austria into four parts. Over the following years, some of the borders and alignments changed; however, Russia gained a great deal of territory at the end of World War II.

Casualties for all countries are estimated differently but Russia's losses far exceeded the loss of life of the combined losses of both the United Kingdom and the United States. It is not difficult to understand Russia's desire to take more territory except when viewed through the lens of democracy and the belief that nations have the right to self-government.

After the war, the Nuremberg Trials decided on the fate of some of the Nazi leaders responsible for war atrocities. Churchill did not want trials but he did want leaders to be executed or turned over to Allies who would imprison them. Roosevelt believed that his country wanted to see trials and Stalin thought trials served up good propaganda. Churchill did not want the trials to be a show or to cause future problems in dealing with world leaders. The trials did not go smoothly. With so many countries involved, language proved a huge barrier. The law also proved difficult because countries adhered to different laws.[364]

When the trials concluded, word spread with the results. Churchill supposedly commented to Lord Ismay, "It shows that if you get into a war, it is supremely important to win it. You and I would be in a pretty pickle if we had lost."[365]

A voice from that time in Nuremberg came from Stanley Tilles, a young soldier in the United States Army, who received a voluntary assignment to coordinate the arrangements for executions at Nuremberg. Jewish by birth, Stanley was not especially observant. Still, he believed his religion affected the assignments to him.[366] He agreed to participate at Nuremberg since the Army promised his discharge after the executions. He suspected the quality of his remaining time might be poor if he refused. Present at all the executions, but not the executioner; he confirmed that all the deaths took place in the normal amount of time allotted for deaths by hanging. He made an important assertion since some people claimed the Germans were deliberately executed in a cruel way.[367]

Forced to watch all of the executions and listen to the prisoners' final words made Tilles wonder whether repeated murders at the hands of the Nazis somehow made them immune to the horror of what they were doing. Tilles tried to detach himself from the executions but sometimes found it impossible. The task of watching people die was not an easy one. With the executions finally complete, the Army cremated the bodies and flew the ashes over Berlin where they were scattered and "became dust in the wind." The disposition of their bodies was humane and eliminated the possibility of their graves being desecrated. It was the direct opposite of the cruelty that they imposed on their victims.[368]

PART THREE

Special Relationship: Christopher Wren's Church

St. Mary's in ruins after bombing during the Blitz of London in 1940. Photo courtesy of America's National Churchill Museum.

CHAPTER 16

London in the Aftermath of War

The aftermath of war brings the sweet taste of victory and the sour taste of reality. London had changed. Churches, homes, and businesses had been bombed, some beyond repair. Loved ones did not always return from war. They gave the ultimate sacrifice only to have their families sacrifice without them. Women who depended on jobs for their livelihoods often had to return home when the previous occupant of a workplace returned from war. Children who had spent the war years in the country returned home to find, at times, difficult reunions with parents. Shortages of food, clothing, and other essential items made day-to-day living difficult. The smell of burnt buildings lingered in the air. Dirt and dust became constant companions. Damaged homes provided less than quality heating during the cold winter months. Men and women who found it easy to maintain a stiff upper lip during the war years suddenly found it more difficult in the lean years following the war.

Even the government found the years difficult. The country was literally bankrupt and depended on an almost $4 billion loan from the United States to keep operating. Frustrating the officials even more, the interest rate on the loan made the repayment even more difficult. Socialist programs increased under the new Labor government but funds to operate them remained elusive.

Adding to these problems, the demographics also changed. People could no longer tolerate the crowded conditions in a city with so many charred remains. Both jobs and new housing on the outskirts of London seemed more attractive. As time progressed, former city residents would realize that relocation brought another set of problems; however, the movement of people out of the city, coupled with economic woes, greatly impacted the city's decisions about rehabilitating war-damaged churches in London. City planning also changed. More commercial establishments and industrial plants seemed destined for London. That meant a reduction in residential homes, and membership in city churches.[369]

Decisions on the repair of city churches had to be made. As governments often do when faced with crises, officials formed a committee to review the situation and make decisions. Another committee dealt with the potential need to reorganize parishes and reduce the number of churches to the number actually needed to support the population. The latter committee soon decided to merge parishes in the city and build 50 new churches outside of London. In that way, the diocese could redistribute ever-tightening, available resources. Churches targeted for destruction would sometimes have their sites sold so that new sites could be bought for other parishes. Overall, the desire to keep Wren sites for use as a city amenity seemed to have some bearing on decision-making.[370]

Christopher Wren churches received particular attention by the first committee. Committee members hoped to spare Wren churches not destroyed or irreparably damaged; however, assessments had to be made. Values were attached to all churches though spiritual values seemed missing. Part of the reason appeared to be the liberal bent of the post-war church in an era when the population appeared more conservative. That change reduced church membership.[371]

The churches, even the ones designed by Wren after the Great Fire in London, had varied designs. St. Mary's was on the smaller side with features that appeared plainer in design. It also had been largely destroyed by enemy incendiary devices. The church did not seem like a good candidate for rehabilitation. Further, it had been modified sometime after Wren's redesign and included Victorian elements that did not mesh with its original Baroque design. More likely candidates for restoration were the churches that had received little damage, churches with certain valuable or important features, churches with strong parishes or patrons, and churches that could be easily repaired.[372]

Both the Diocese commission and committee evaluated the church of St. Mary Aldermanbury as one of secondary architecture, presumably due to its less elaborate exterior design, and slated it for demolition and sale. Mrs. Robert Henrey, a novelist and member of the congregation, played a part in its eventual disposition.[373]

The final decision on many of the churches had to be delayed for economic reasons. The city did not have the money to restore all of them. For that reason, the Church of St. Mary the Virgin, Aldermanbury still stood in its rather inglorious and disheveled state when *Life* magazine decided to write a photographic piece on Christopher Wren war-damaged churches in London in July 1961. Both the delay and the article proved propitious for Westminster College.

Drawing of ruined St. Mary's by Patrick Horsbrugh, gift by Horsbrugh to America's National Churchill Museum. Photo courtesy of Steve Stinson.

CHAPTER 17

An Unexpected Suggestion

When *Life* magazine published its retrospective of famed British architect, Christopher Wren, on June 2, 1961, Westminster College was holding its annual college commencement ceremony. Attending was a representative from the English-Speaking Union (ESU) chapter in St. Louis, Missouri. He came with an unexpected suggestion.

Founded in 1918 by Sir Evelyn Wrench, the Union's mission in the United States is to ensure better relationships by providing opportunities for people to personally share information with one another. The Union tries to link people across the world to ensure that they communicate and understand each other in a friendly and improved way to help maintain peace in the world. Over the years, the Union has provided, among other things, scholarships to individuals attending Black colleges, language facilitation to accelerate the integration of immigrants into American society, education to improve language skills, and debating skills to improve communication. Its founder believed that peace in the world could be achieved by the "unity and purpose of the English-speaking democracies."[374]

All of that sounds like something Churchill would have said. In fact, he heartily approved of the organization and served as its chairman in Britain while the organizaiton was still in its infancy. He chaired it from 1921-1925 and obviously carried its sentiments into his *Sinews of Peace (Iron Curtain)* speech.

The ESU chapter's representative spoke on behalf of all its members. After some internal discussion, the chapter thought that Westminster College should develop a permanent memorial to honor Churchill and his prescient speech; however, they thought the memorial should be more than a plaque.[375] Given the importance of the speech, the chapter members thought the memorial should reflect that importance and possibly appear monumental.

Immediately, the college agreed. Sitting in on the meeting, Patrick Horsbrugh, a British born architect, quickly joined those in favor of the project. Introduced to the college by Emmett and Ruth Layton, landscape architects who worked on college projects, Horsbrugh would become a valuable addition as a consultant to Westminster. A well-respected architect and planner, he had invaluable skills that eventually landed him jobs at the University of Texas and the University of Notre Dame. He had already served as a visiting professor at Harvard and was currently a professor of architecture at the University of Nebraska. Horsbrugh had a deep respect for preserving heritage buildings. He once said, "Little by little, a nation can lose its historic references and can descend into a coast-to-coast monotony of reliefless suburban confusion."[376] His interest in the church had to do with its British heritage and historical significance.

The group at the Westminster meeting first thought of dedicating a sundial in Churchill's memory but after a short discussion, that choice seemed unremarkable at best.[377] President Davidson of Westminster College turned to Horsbrugh since he knew a great deal about English history and architecture. What did he think? Horsbrugh was not a person who liked the limelight. In fact, one newspaper published a photo of him and Horsbrugh reacted by calling the paper and accusing it of invading his privacy.[378] Some people may have wondered if he would respond.

A stroke of luck or some divine act placed Horsbrugh at Westminster at that very moment. Horsbrugh had a creative plan that fit nicely with Westminster's goal. As he started to speak, everyone listened carefully. He reminded everyone that the school was in the process of planning a replacement for its college chapel. Frederick Sternberg, an architect, had been hired for that purpose. Westminster could combine both goals into one project. The recently published *Life* article included photographs of churches designed by Christopher Wren. One of those churches was the Church of St. Mary the Virgin, Aldermanbury. As Horsbrugh explained, many churches in London sustained damage during the Blitz in World War II. The city still hadn't come to a decision on the fate of all of them. Why not try to relocate one of them to Fulton? A British heritage church would make a wonderful memorial to Winston Churchill who had both a British father and an American mother. If they could secure a Wren church for their purpose, that would be even better.[379]

Stunned by his recommendation, the others in the room took less than a minute to agree. A great idea! Let's do it. The plucky college began yet another unrealistic, improbable, unfeasible, yet highly successful project that would gain worldwide attention.

Soon Horsbrugh boarded a plane bound for London.

Esley Hamilton, former St. Louis County Preservation historian, makes a speech on the history of St. Mary the Virgin. Photo by Casey Buckman, courtesy of Westminster College.

CHAPTER 18

Checking All the Boxes

As Patrick Horsbrugh prepared to leave for London to begin his exploration of churches for possible relocation to Westminster College, his parting words to the college president included positive and negative assessments of the possible outcome. On the one hand, he believed that relocation costs probably fell within the realm of possibility. Building relocations were not uncommon, so the technology and transportation issues had precedents. On the other hand, Horsbrugh emphasized that a number of potential arguments, including "legal, ecclesiastical, civic, architectural, and sentimental ones,"[380] had to be addressed to the satisfaction of the British people.

Many Britons considered historic buildings artwork and a law forbidding their relocation from England had been passed. The relocation of Agecroft Hall, a fifteenth century Tudor manor house in Lancashire, England, to Richmond, Virginia, had resulted in public outcry in 1926. Considered a landmark building, its removal without proper notice shocked people. Even the House of Commons became involved. The owners delivered the knockout punch when they also ended up moving a bed that held historic value in the minds of the British people. In the end, the absence of legal constraints allowed the sales of both house and bed to happen. But the English people vowed, "Never again."[381]

On the positive side, the relocation of Agecroft Hall occurred without major incident. Even the stained glass windows made the voyage intact. Now on the Historic Register, the building's new home is in Richmond, Virginia, on the James River where it is a popular tourist attraction.[382]

Somehow, Horsbrugh had to change public thinking by convincing people that a war-damaged church destined for destruction could see happier days across the pond.

With many approvals needed (107 people were contacted), coordination of the entire project could not be fast-tracked and it would take Churchillian communication skills to accomplish the goal. Horsbrugh had the connections, the skill, the knowledge, and the personality traits required to coordinate the project. Westminster picked the right man for the job.

Westminster College's Standards for Church Selection[383]

Size:

- Large enough to serve as a College Chapel and for a variety of special ceremonies.
- The size must fit with the surrounding character of the campus.

Remaining fabric:

- Preference is given to one destroyed by fire rather than one heavily damaged by bombing due to the condition of the stone.
- The remaining fabric must represent more than half of the original structure.
- The historic aura of the church must be considered in the calculation of the economic value to warrant relocation and rebuilding.

Simplicity of plan:

- The foundation of the church should be regular in its plan to make it easier to rebuild
- The plan of the church must allow it to stand-alone.
- The church must be assessed to avoid issues related to irregular foundations, immense size, and London site conditions to ensure that the visible and hidden aspects of the church are suitable for the new location.
- The church must have balanced access to aisle and naves to meet ceremonial requirements and a logical flow of people in and out of the church.

Architectural character:

- Quality must be obvious and beyond dispute.
- The reconstructed church must be in a central college location and command its site.
- The church must not look out of place in its new location.
- The church should weave the old structure into the newer architectural landscape of the college campus.
- The church must have relevance to the American landscape just as it does to the British landscape.
- Preference should be given to a church that has some semblance of similarity to the simple, white-painted, timber churches with west towers and belfries that stood in New England.
- The church should stir powerful emotions.
- The provision of interior fittings to replace those damaged or removed by the bombing must be of quality material similar to British workmanship but should not place impossible demands on craftsmanship.
- The plan of the church should encourage the assembly of items that are similar in style to original ones, e.g., altar, reredos, organ, and organ case.

The Church of St. Mary the Virgin, Aldermanbury

Timeline

12th century: Church is initially built

1666: The Great Fire of London destroys all but 24 steps to the crypt area

1672: Christopher Wren designs and oversees the construction of a new, rebuilt church

1915: Zeppelin airships' incendiary devices damage the church

1940: Bombings during the Blitz of London destroy a large portion of the church

1946: Churchill gives his prescient *Sinews of Peace (Iron Curtain)* Speech

1961: *Life* magazine publishes an article on London churches damaged during the Blitz of London in 1940

1961: St. Louis Branch of the English-Speaking Union recommend that a significant tangible reminder of Churchill's visit be constructed

1961: Architect Patrick Horsbrugh recommends relocating and rebuilding a London church damaged in the Blitz in honor of Winston Churchill and his speech at Westminster

1961: The search begins and the Church of St. Mary the Virgin, Aldermanbury is selected

1962: Feasibility planning for completing the project begins and committees established

1962: Churchill calls it an "imaginative concept"

1963: Movement gains steam from congressional resolution declaring Winston Churchill an honorary citizen

1964: The Diocese of London gifts the church to Westminster for use as a college campus and tribute to Winston Churchill, who made his celebrated speech at the college

1964: President Truman participates in the Groundbreaking Ceremony

1965: Contract is let for the rebuilding of the church

1965/66: Westminster receives stones and organizes them for reassembly

1966: The Lord Bishop of London places and dedicates the foundation stone

1966: The outer shell of the church rebuilt

1969: The completed church is dedicated

2019: Major preservation work begins

Interior of the relocated church with church Mander Organ. Photo by Casey Buckman, courtesy of Westminster College.

CHAPTER 19

Negotiating the Relocation

When the Russians heard about Westminster's plan, they immediately had a satire published in *Pravda* on December 26, 1962. Entitled, *The Stones Are Groaning,* the article compared the relocation to the hypothetical relocation of St. Paul's Cathedral. It took exception to the supposed "sale" of a church to the United States, though the church was a gift. The article also implied that England needed the money though it refused to sell the bodies of the famous people buried beneath the church. Supposedly, the new owner, Westminster College, would replace the celebrity bodies remaining in England with new American ones. The author of the article gave suggestions for replacements.

Then the article referenced the "notorious" speech given at Westminster in Fulton. It said the speech "legalized the role of England as a junior partner to the United States." According to *Pravda*, it was the beginning of the "sell-out of England." For some reason, the article also implied that the Chicago slaughterhouse people were involved. The writer may not have understood geography or he just liked implying that the entire relocation was comparable to a slaughterhouse arrangement that could make St. Paul's its next lamb. Reporters interviewed people in Fulton, who sounded confused and amused by the article. They believed that Westminster did the right thing if the Russians believed the stones were groaning at the thought of a church relocation.[384]

As Horsbrugh warned, the negotiation process took a great deal of time and effort to complete. Countless offices and people required meetings to discuss Westminster's proposal. He had to explain that the college was not seeking just a monument to memorialize Winston Churchill; it was seeking an edifice that would portray the ideals for which he and both countries stood. In some way, it had to symbolize both countries, the United States and Britain, two countries that shared those ideals. Furthermore, it had to symbolize the "courage, steadfastness in the face of adversity, and the splendor" of the tireless effort to hold fast to those ideals in opposition to tyranny. That last symbol, "defiance of tyranny," seemed the most important.

Horsbrugh began his inquiry by writing a letter to the Chairman of the Georgian Group, an organization responsible for protecting buildings of Wren's era. Horsbrugh asked if any Wren churches had questionable retention issues. He found that there were indeed churches in that category and his letter was forwarded to the Council for the Care of Churches for further response. The council, which dealt with analyses of the condition, ecclesiastical need, and future of churches, identified a number of churches, including the Church of St. Mary the Virgin, Aldermanbury. Just as Horsbrugh surmised, he learned that consideration would be given to the various issues he had discussed with the college. In other words, he needed to prepare his argument to rebut such concerns.

Prior to these discussions, Horsbrugh visited the 21 churches on the list he received from the council and began an inspection of their condition and their likely fit with the campus of Westminster. Two people helped him with those inspections.

Christopher Wren had done a spectacular job of changing the London skyline with his redesigns of churches damaged by incendiary devices;

however, one of his most important skills had to do with the siting of churches. A congested city, London had buildings with very little space around them. Redesigns and restorations had to squeeze churches into small spaces that disguised their true size and full appearance.[385] On the other hand, the new site on the Westminster campus would be open. The church would be seen in all its glory, though some siting issues would be needed to ensure it could fit on a more rolling hill as opposed to flat ground.

Transportation of building stones and refurbishment of the present site also complicated discussions. Nobody wanted the land in London scarred by the removal of a church building. Restoring the site to one that could be put to a use, preferably as a park, was essential. Too much had been destroyed by enemy action. Westminster had to help restore the city, not add to its problems. The concerns and emotions of the British people also had to be considered, since all damaged churches represented the "hours of darkness and terror and of flame and death" during the Blitz.[386] A church selection should not result in negative backlash from the public.

To ensure that all considerations would be dealt with in an appropriate way, Horsbrugh met with the city planner, Dr. Thomas Sharp, C.B.E., and past president of the Town Planning Institute. Sharp had a good understanding of what he termed the "consequences of subtraction from the urban scene." Horsbrugh also thought it important to include Architect William Whitfield, who had experience in restoring churches, in the discussions.

St. Mary the Virgin appeared to have the best characteristics for relocation. Its architectural design seemed similar to that of many churches built during the seventeenth century in the United States. It did not have an overbearing or unwieldy design and it did not have an overly large appearance. So, it seemed like a church that could fit into a city that, at the time, had a semi-rural appearance. But removing it required careful thought. Only five minutes from the illustrious St. Paul's Cathedral, it would be missed.[387] It could not be plucked from its surroundings without consideration of the resulting appearance of the site.

Although the church seemed small, its size seemed appropriate for its continued use on a college campus. An architect who had helped with the rebuilding of the House of Commons advised that its size contained "the essential quality of intimacy and sense of occasion that could not exist if it was larger in size."[388] The interior plan also allowed the type of movement necessary for the type of functions envisioned in the church by Westminster College.

Although the church had undergone a series of unfortunate incidents, e.g., fire in the Great Fire of London, damage by zeppelins in World War I, and damage by German incendiary bombs in World War II, its exterior fabric and interior columns remained intact. Further, the 12th-century stairs that once led to the crypt area still remained. The bombing heavily damaged the fine woodwork that Wren designed and the interior property, except for the columns. But the group decided that the destruction provided the opportunity to use an existing pool of talented craftsmen to reproduce that work in the new building. That talent could breathe new life into the building. And, luckily, donations from other churches seemed likely.

Within most of Wren's churches, the team found evidence of his artistry and creativity. The "joinery, gold leaf designs, glasswork, plasterwork, and rich interiors gave his church energy."[389] The team believed such energy could be recreated if the church could be relocated to Fulton. Architect Marshall Sisson, selected on the recommendation of Horsbrugh, would be responsible for the work that needed the expertise of a British architect familiar in the restoration of British heritage churches. Sisson's background helped him make decisions on the best way to dismantle the church and rebuild it at Westminster

College. Horsbrugh believed he had exactly the right credentials for the job.[390]

Still, a long list of issues required solutions. Concern over "real estate values, street improvements, parochial and ecclesiastical requirements," and practical amenities had to be addressed to ensure that a balanced environment existed for all who remained and worked in the area.[391] The city that released the church into the hands of the Americans could not be harmed by their precious gift.

Finally, the decision to create a garden-like park setting on the former site in London, with some small evidence of the ruins, seemed agreeable to all concerned. The scrollwork mentioned in the *Life* article and so appreciated by the British people would remain in London.

But the ultimate decision-maker had to be the person memorialized by the sculpture. Westminster College President Davidson and Patrick Horsbrugh met with Winston Churchill to explain the project. It delighted him. He formally wrote his agreement with the "imaginative concept."[392] With that decision reached, the process still needed approval from the Church of St. Vedast, the Church of England, Parliament, and the City Council. Then the process of deconstruction and transportation across the pond would begin.

Mary Soames, Churhchill's daughter, is greeted by Dave Stinson as she arrives for the unveiling of the rebuilt church. Photo courtesy of Steve Stinson.

CHAPTER 20

The Genius of Christopher Wren (1632-1723)

In recognition of his birthday, Google Doodle developed a doodle honoring Christopher Wren in 2014. Only shown in the United Kingdom, it included a compass and ruler, instruments signifying his mathematical expertise. Today, some architects may have lost sight of the genius of Christopher Wren. Modern structures are having their day but Wren is still one of the most famous London architects. His redesigns of churches heavily damaged by the Great Fire of London in 1666 that swept through the city changed the London skyline. His work on St. Paul's Cathedral consumed most of his adult career; however, the breadth of his body of work is extraordinary.

Some geniuses possess splendid communication and leadership skills, just as Winston Churchill had. Other geniuses have extraordinary creative and artistic talents and communicate message through their work, just as Christopher Wren did.

Born on October 20, 1632, in East Knoyle, Wiltshire, Christopher Wren learned about churches at an early age. His father was a clergyman. Coincidentally, he attended a school named Westminster, a leading British, academic institution, prior to entering Oxford University where he earned both a bachelor's degree and a master's degree. Today, one of his churches now sits on the campus of a college named Westminster in memory of an individual who knew all about the other Westminster School in London.[393]

Wren's family supported the monarchy. His uncle, Matthew, also a clergyman, spent several years in the Tower of London, probably due to his Royalist leanings. Wren became more interested in education than politics. At university, Wren studied astronomy but he had a broad interest in mathematics and science. He loved to build things and he loved to conduct science experiments. When he left Wadham College, Oxford, upon graduation, he filled his time with science and drawing. He found it difficult to focus on just one project. His mind filled with possibilities that he wanted to explore.[394]

The age of Wren included renowned scientists and mathematicians such as Edmund Halley (Halley's comet), Sir Isaac Newton, and Blaise Pascal, the French mathematician. Among these notable contemporaries, Christopher Wren stood out for his genius in mathematics, particularly geometry.[395]

Wren's thirst for knowledge and his diversity of interests eventually drew him to architecture and building, which gave him an outlet for his creativeness and inventiveness and a use for his expertise in geometry. Building models, which he loved to do, was an important way to express architectural design. Though he lacked an architectural degree, he excelled in his architectural designs and he understood construction.[396]

Prior to Wren, people heralded Inigo Jones' reputation as an architect. Jones was the Surveyor of Works for the King. The portico he designed on St. Paul's Cathedral is considered one of his best works, though the Great Fire of London destroyed it. When Jones died in 1652, his passing left a void in architectural leadership that Wren was poised to fill.[397]

Visiting Paris in 1665 to learn more about architecture gave Wren the opportunity to escape the plague that swept through London, sickening and killing many people. Bernini, the sculptor-architect, who was in Paris designing the Louvre's east front, impressed him and instilled in him a love of the grandeur of Italian Baroque. The architectural domes that he found in Paris also inspired Wren. Together, these two inspirations became part of Wren's architectural genius.[398]

As it turned out, a major conflagration gave Wren the opportunity to unleash his genius on a large scale. Just prior to the Great Fire, Wren had completed a design for the dome of St. Paul's; however, St. Paul's and a large part of London lay in ruin after the Great Fire. Wren prepared a plan for rebuilding the city, but the magnitude of the devastation and other problems in starting restoration work prevented its acceptance. The following year, a rebuilding act allowed for a certain amount of rebuilding but only on a limited basis.[399]

In 1669, the King's Surveyor of Works died. Wren succeeded him in the position. He held that position for fifty years. While working on the rebuilding projects, Wren also served on a rebuilding commission that drafted the Rebuilding Act of 1667. It "forbade half-timbered buildings and any new buildings were to be almost standardized and built of brick and stone to the satisfaction of building inspectors."[400]

After a second rebuilding act was approved in 1670, the city was able to rebuild several of the churches lost by raising funds from a tax on coal. Since Wren worked for the king and not the City of London, he did not immediately become involved in the rebuilding. In all, the Great Fire destroyed almost 90 churches. Fifty-one of them were rebuilt. Finally, Wren became the Commissioner for Rebuilding the City of London, including the churches. Though other architects were sometimes involved, Wren approved the design of every church including St. Mary the Virgin, Aldermanbury. Documents in possession of America's National Churchill Museum verify Wren's involvement in the design and construction of the Church of St. Mary the Virgin, Aldermanbury, the only Wren church in the United States. Robert Hooke, the architect, assisted him.[401]

Since so many buildings were destroyed in the Great Fire, architecture in England had a rebirth thanks to Wren's designs. The use of wooden structures, much of them destroyed in the Great Fire, was discarded in favor of stone and brick. Wren planned to widen the streets to put more distance between buildings, but that plan never materialized into action due to a lack of funds and the resistance of some owners to accomplish it.[402]

According to his son, many people thought that redesigning the city should include highlighting its beauty and magnificence by making the buildings more regular, the businesses and streets more accessible, the public spaces better organized, and the wharf area more open. Wren thought that there should be large Piazzas, consolidation of public halls, improved alignment of streets, and a larger and spacious wharf on the bank of the river. He wanted all of the redesigned churches to be designed in a way that permitted the best opportunity for "capacity and hearing." He also wanted all the malodorous, noisy, and fire producing businesses to be located outside of the city center. He had a number of other ideas that completed his plan.[403]

What stood in the way of completing his plan? Money, of course, played a part, but people had other practical considerations. Rebuilding according to Wren's plan meant moving some of the buildings. The re-located buildings wouldn't be far from their original location; however, straightening streets and sidewalks meant some reconfiguration of buildings. People's lives had been greatly altered by the fire. They were not in the mood to have their homes and businesses altered, even if the alterations did not mean huge changes. Their lives had been changed. They had had enough change. They also distrusted city officials and loathed to turn over their properties lest they never get them back. Unable to make the changes he wanted did not make Wren's job easier. Forced to deal with unalterable constraints, he had to devise creative ways to fit the redesigned churches into the existing space.[404]

Wren began designing churches in English baroque, which is a dramatic style that shows movement, decoration and, some say, the power of the church and of royalty. Its more classical components were similar to the style of early seventeenth-century churches in colonial America. That tie between the United States and British religious architecture is a symbol of the special relationship that the two countries had and provided some of the impetus for selecting a Wren church for relocation to Westminster College in Fulton, Missouri.

The design and use of steeples marked much of Wren's work and their architecture "demonstrated his unparalleled architectural assurance." The dramatic change in the London skyline due to the many churches he re-designed and had built was remarkable. The skyline lent interest and provided some unity to the overall design of all the churches. Achieving what he did required more than just architectural skill. He had good negotiation skills for dealing with the parish churches. That mattered even though he did have the support of the king.[405]

Having an almost blank canvas to rebuild gave Wren many opportunities to use his creative genius. His work on the churches was similar to a poet's work or a composer's work. Each part of the church fit nicely with the other parts of the church or with other churches to dramatically change the skyline. Wren skillfully found ways to design them despite their locations in cramped and difficult spaces.

Unfortunately, many years after his death, a number of churches were destroyed. Some were lost due to war, some to the economy, and some to changing demographics that reduced the need for churches. Most losses were met with public outcry. Sadly, some churches that remained lost their previous interior compositions and key components of the

Wren design. Today, fewer than half of the churches that Wren saved still remain intact and used for religious purposes.

Wren's genius can also be attributed to his scientific and mathematical genius and his willingness to try new approaches to design. He understood that using the best material and the best craftsmen available are essential to a successful outcome when rebuilding a church. His knowledge of architecture and construction helped him find those people. When reviewing all of his churches, many consider St. Paul's Cathedral as Wren's best design work, although the final product did not agree with the approved design. It took 35 years to complete the construction work.

While serving as the chief architect of St. Paul's and other City churches, Wren designed several projects for Whitehall Palace but they were ultimately destroyed by yet another fire in 1698. Wren also served as the chief architect for the joint sovereigns, William and Mary, who commissioned him to work at Kensington Palace and Hampton Court. Greenwich Hospital was the last Wren design. His works show a great deal of his expertise in geometry. Geometrical shapes, including circles, ovals, and squares, are all included in his works to enhance the designs he created.

Other architects drew inspiration from Wren's work, particularly with respect to spires and domes. The dome of the US Capitol in Washington DC is but one example. His design of St. Paul's and other City churches in London, as well as his transformation of London's skyline, remain his crowning achievements for which he will always be remembered and hailed as one of the greatest architects in British history.

The melding of the genius of his work with the memory of the genius of Winston Churchill on the campus of Westminster College in Fulton, Missouri, highlights the special relationship that brought the two great countries together on the project and entwines the genius of both men in a monumental memorial.

CHAPTER 21

St. Mary the Virgin, Aldermanbury

A handsome building, the Church of St. Mary the Virgin, Aldermanbury is an excellent symbol of the darkest days of Britain and the indomitable spirit of its people. It portrays the very essence of survival and rebirth, as well as the ever-present desire to overcome adversity and tyranny and achieve the freedoms won by charting a course to democracy, even when the country was rocked by invasion, war, and numerous challenges to hard-fought rights. The church history yields the history of Britain from Roman times until the church's transport across the ocean to America. It then entwines the history of Britain with that of the United States in a monumental memorial to Winston Churchill, who became a citizen of both countries.

Built along the Roman wall in London, the church connects the city at its very beginning when it was known as Londinium. Although some documentation exists to show it was built in the 12th-century, the exact date is unknown. However, it is clear that it began at a time of Christian growth in London.

Pope Nicholas IV developed a list of ecclesiastical property subject to taxation in England and Wales during the period 1291-1292. In that listing entitled, *Taxatio Nicholai Ecclesiastica,* the church is mentioned as S. Marie de Althemaneber. During its possession by Elsing Priory,

Included with permission from the artist, Rachael A. Peden.

a curate served the church. After it no longer remained in the priory's possession, it became known as a rectory. Eventually, it was given in trust to the parishioners, who then elected their rector, subject to approval by the bishop.[406] Sir Wilham Englefield, who was mayor of London in 1429 and in 1437, built the steeple and gave the church new bells.[407]

According to Godfrey Thompson, a librarian at the Guildhall in London, St. Mary's was Roman Catholic until the Reformation. The original structure was added to and then replaced in 1497. The church fell under the auspices of the Church of England about 1539.[408]

St. Mary's rode the wave of changes in the religious landscape of Britain after the dissolution of King Henry VIII's first marriage and the Interregnum period when the Puritan religion held sway. With the revered clergyman, Edmond Calamy as its minister, the church became a popular site for visitors who crowded the streets with their carriages in an attempt to hear Calamy's sermons.[409] The church became a symbol of religious freedom, one of the many rights of man eventually won by the British people. With wealthy and important parishioners, the church reached its zenith in importance during the Interregnum era. Crypts below the church filled with bodies of former illustrious members, including former politicians and the two men responsible for Shakespeare's first folio.[410]

In 1570, an organ was placed in the church. John Howe built it. The organ's life span would be relatively short given the catastrophic event that beset London in the seventeenth-century.

When London experienced the plague in the seventeenth century, the church did not escape the ravages the epidemic wrought. During the period of July-November, 1665, a total of 115 burials occurred in the parish. A small parish, the church experienced similar percentages of deaths as the churches that were built farther from the wharf area, the site where rats first invaded. Particularly hard hit, pregnant women and women in childbirth typically had lost the benefit of midwives, many of whom died in the plague. Other people, not wishing to expose themselves to the unseen enemy, did not want to help them.[411]

Just as Londoners began to experience some relief at the end of the plague, a new tragedy struck. Samuel Pepys, the famous diarist, remembers being awakened by a member of his household. Peering out the window, he saw a fire "on the backside of Mark Lane." The fire did not immediately impress him as "the great" fire it came to be called. Further, smoke was not uncommon and remained a problem due to the furnaces in the city. He returned to his bed and fell asleep.[412]

At the time of the fire, the city within the walls of Cripplegate, including the church of St. Mary, looked almost the same as it did in Shakespeare's time when he lived close to the church. The walls of the fort, still very high, ran a course of two miles in length.[413] Medieval in construction, the structures crowded together on streets that narrowly divided the structures on either side of them. Since most had wood construction, they could be viewed as the fire's best friends. Still, the city itself appeared picturesque before the fire if one erased any fears for its unsafe condition and the sight of muddy and unsanitary streets without sidewalks to buttress them with added space in front of buildings.

The city was a city of "bells and spires" and many churches, including St. Paul's Cathedral, lay in the path of the expanding fire. Beneath them lay the smaller buildings, commercial, and residential. Luckily, the fire struck at nighttime, when large crowds of people that filled its streets during the day were still asleep.[414]

King Charles II had warned aldermen of the potential for fire and a few religious groups foretold of its coming. Supposedly, opposing voices to the government made veiled threats of possible damage. Nothing was done to prepare or prevent what became an inevitable disaster.[415] The fire came and conquered all in its path.

The rebuilding of London post-fire eliminated most of the unsanitary conditions that had fueled the fire and spread disease. The plague did not return to the refurbished city. Christopher Wren gained fame for his work in revitalizing the churches and London's skyline. A new church rose from the ashes of the old church, almost completely destroyed save 24 steps leading to the small crypt area below it.

Another horrific blow to the church occurred in 1915 when Germany, the first country to use aerial bombings during World War I, sent Zeppelin airships (shaped like long cigars and filled with gas) into the London sky. A three-ton bomb exploded near St. Paul's Cathedral as reported by the *Manchester Guardian* below.

> The next area of serious damage was round about Wood Street and Aldermanbury, just north of Cheapside. In Wood Street one of the great textile houses, Ward, Sturt, and Co. was fired by an incendiary bomb. It was completely cleaned out, the fire burning with a tremendous blaze for several hours. A stone's throw away in Love lane the very large silk warehouse of Bridge and Co. was also destroyed by fire. At the end of Love Lane is Aldermanbury, the old church of St. Mary the Virgin, standing in a small open space at the junction of the two streets. A tall block of offices overlooking the churchyard was struck by an explosive bomb, which exploded on the coping of the roof and rained down blocks of masonry into the street, wrecking the premises. The force of this explosion was such that every window in Aldermanbury was smashed. A feather warehouse was struck, and so tremendous was the force of the explosion that feathers were driven into

> the solid wall. At one place the lead was stripped from a roof and driven into the air, remaining curled into big balls over the telegraph wires and hanging down over the street.[416]

School children were asked to write about the bombing that took place. The following excerpts are by two children who attended Princeton Street School in Bedford Row.

> I then ran in and put on my boots and dared not strike a light as all the lights in the street were out except one. We then walked to East St., but {there} was no firemen there, as they had to attend to a bigger fire. We then went to see what this bigger fire was. It happened to be the National Penny bank. The fire soon spread and three shops were alight before the firemen arrived. The flames were terrible. A fireman named Green saved seventeen people. He went up again but {there} were no more people left and {he} was cut off from retreat. The poor man was at the top of the house. To save himself from being burnt to death he jumped to the ground and died a few days later.
> By J. Marriage[417]

> All of a sudden, I was awakened by a reverberating roar, like (the sound of) lions when they are hungry. I leapt out of bed like a slice of greased lightning and slipped into my clothes. I then heard a sound like a tattoo on a kettle-drum. I looked out of a window and saw a searchlight flitting about. Someone shouts, "Put your lights out" and I obeyed. My mother and sisters were in the parlour. I went downstairs and looking up I saw an elongated shape not unlike a cigar and of a silver grey in colour. There were little splashes of flame around it

> but none appeared to hit it. After a while I thought I'd like to have a look at a gun.
> By I. McHenry[418]

Though not as heavily damaged as in the Great Fire, the Church of St. Mary required work to repair the damage. Once again, it survived a seemingly hopeless situation only to rise again.

World War II brought more destruction. On December 29, 1940, the church took a direct hit during one of the Luftwaffe's heaviest air blitzes of the war. Only the bare, stone walls (the fabric of the building), 12 interior Corinthian columns, the tower, and the original twenty-four 12th-century steps remained.

The *London Times* reported the following information on December 31, 1940.

> The church St. Mary the Virgin, Aldermanbury was more conspicuous than many others in the city because of its spacious churchyard, in which stands a monument of unusual interest erected to John Hemmings and Henry Condell, who were fellow actors with Shakespeare. Both lived in the parish and were buried there. Another link with the past was the marriage at St. Mary's of the poet Milton with Katherine Woodcock, his second wife, in 1656. Wren re-erected the church on its old site after the Great Fire, and throughout the interior retained a correct idea of the architect's scheme of window lighting.

On the same day, in another article, *The London Times* carried another report about Winston Churchill. Accompanied by his wife, Clementine, he visited the area in which St. Mary's formerly stood intact and made a two-hour walking tour of the streets. As they passed along, the *Times* reported that they were greeted with cheers at which Churchill smiled and lifted his hat. His words made a lasting memory for those people who heard him speak that day. The "old and the new" references Britain and the United States.

> This monstrous product of former wrongs and shame has resolved to try to break our famous Island race by process of indiscriminate slaughter and destruction.
>
> What he has done is to kindle a fire in British hearts, which will glow long after the traces of the conflagration he has caused in London have been removed.
>
> He has lighted a fire which will burn with a steady and consuming flame until the last vestiges of Nazi tyranny have been burnt out of Europe, and until the Old World—and the New—can join hands to rebuild the temples of man's freedom and man's honour, upon foundations which will not be soon or easily be overthrown.

John Colville wrote in his diary that eight Christopher Wren churches sustained serious damage on December 29, 1940. He consoled himself that he and his mother toured the churches before the war began.[419]

Mrs. Robert (Madeleine) Henrey, a Parisian and member of the church congregation, fought hard for the repair of the church after the war. She later recommended that it be transported to the United States where it could be brought back to life. A prolific author, she wrote a book about the Aldermanbury district in 1958. In it, she describes the state of the church, which she hoped would be rebuilt.

The condition of the Church of St. Mary the Virgin, Aldermanbury after the Blitz created a great deal of stress for Mrs. Henrey. While the foliage around the ruined church appeared beautiful, the church, itself, appeared abandoned. She worried that it would never be rebuilt and felt "impotent and aggrieved" by the situation. Even the landscaping appeared to have lost its"leafy delight." While she loved the church, she despaired that it appeared so "utterly despised and neglected."[420]

Realizing the desperate condition of the church, the Diocese of London gave the church to Westminster College on January 14, 1964. Pamela Bennetts, the deputy secretary of the London Diocesan Fund wrote the following terms of the gift.

> On the 14th January, 1964, by a supplementary Reorganization Scheme, made under the Reorganization Areas Measure, 1944, the Diocese of London was empowered to arrange for the demolition and transfer to the United States of America the remains of the Church of St. Mary, Aldermanbury, in the City of London.
>
> The remains of the church were a gift, and were given in order that they might be re-erected and restored on the campus of Westminster College, Fulton, Missouri, for use as a College Chapel, and as a tribute to Sir Winston Churchill, who made his celebrated Iron Curtain speech at Fulton.[421]

Relocated to its present site on the campus of Westminster College in Fulton, Missouri, the church is freed from the dirt of the ages and the unfavorable "modern improvements." It now stands restored to its original purity of design, a monumental memorial to Winston Churchill, and the special relationship of the two countries that worked together to make the relocation possible.

Douglas Fairbanks Jr. collaborated with David Stinson to help raise a great deal of money to make the relocation of the church possible. Photo courtesy of Vera Fairbanks.

CHAPTER 22

The Swashbuckling Churchillian

Every nonprofit fundraiser needs a Douglas Fairbanks Jr., that is, a dapper, sophisticated, handsome, charismatic, persuasive, influential, well-spoken individual with a large number of famous and important friends who is willing to work pro bono with little to no recognition to raise funds and meet the goals of an organization that is meaningful to him and the friends he inspires. Very few organizations can find one. Finding Douglas Fairbanks Jr. was not difficult. But it was pure happenstance.

Born to one of the most famous actors of his time, Douglas Fairbanks Jr. greeted the world with panache. Even in his youth, he had style, personality, and verve. So much so, that he captured the attention of none other than Joan Crawford, whom he married at the age of 19. Active in social and political circles, his friends included A-list celebrities, foreign politicians, and members of prestigious families. His magnetism attracted many to his flame that shone brightly and extended beyond his theatrical and movie performances.

Unknown to many people, one of his greatest achievements dealt with his participation in fundraising for the relocation of the English heritage building, St. Mary the Virgin, Aldermanbury, to its present site on the campus of Westminster College in Fulton,

Missouri. The backdrop for that story requires some knowledge of Fairbanks Jr., the man.

While critics often said that Fairbanks Junior did not command the same presence as his famous father on stage or in the movies, the son actually eclipsed the father in real life. A Navy man in World War II, the young man learned the art of military deception while assigned to Lord Mountbatten's Commando staff in the United Kingdom. He used that skill well in other military operations. Fairbanks had such a good relationship with Mountbatten that he made him godfather to his three daughters and dedicated a book to him.[422]

His awards included the United States Navy's Legion of Merit with the bronze V (for valor), the Italian War Cross for Military Valor, the French Legion d'Honneur, the Croix de Guerre with palm, the British Distinguished Service Cross, and the Silver Star. The Brazilian government awarded him the National Order of the Southern Cross (officer grade). After the war, the German government awarded him the Federal Cross of Merit for his contribution to the relief of the needy in occupied Germany. Although he entered the war with trepidation, he emerged as a hero.[423]

Unwilling to sit idly, Douglas seized every opportunity and attacked life with gusto. He pursued an acting career before and after his military service and even worked with his father on the movie, *The Return of Zorro,* where he honed his very own swashbuckling skills.

The actor's involvement in the church fundraising project began with a brief stint on a game show. The vice president of the college and talented project manager, Dave Stinson, a handsome and equally personable man, made a fundraising trip to Manhattan where he was approached on the street by a recruiter for the game show, "Password." As fate would have it, Fairbanks ended up appearing as his partner on the show. The two men failed miserably on the game show, but decided to make amends by going on a Manhattan club crawl. That event led to a lifelong friendship.[424]

As Stinson's son, Steve, said, "Fairbank's involvement in the project put a gleam and sparkle on the project. Today, we would say he made it hip … when Fairbanks came to Fulton, the champagne flowed. He also brought elegant dresses for mom."[425]

Fairbanks helped make the rededication of the church in 1969 as part of the Churchill Museum and Library a success. Vitally interested in the project, Fairbanks coordinated invitations to members of the Churchill family, Mountbatten, and other notable and wealthy people. His engaging personality convinced them to participate. He enlarged the scope of donors tremendously via his connections in Hollywood, London, and New York. He found the sculptor, Franta Belsky, who did the sculpture of Churchill standing outside the church. His celebrity made the sculpture possible. Dave Stinson relished the protocol and fundraising advice Fairbanks gave him. They made a good fundraising team. Additionally, Fairbanks' friendship with Mountbatten allowed him to serve as a go-between between Mountbatten and the college. Using his show biz talents, Fairbanks served as the Master of Ceremonies for the large and successful fundraising dinner for celebrities and journalists that took place in New York. Not content to sit on the sidelines, his energetic approach to the project led him to check in frequently on its progress and offer outstanding advice as the need arose.[426]

Why was the project so important to both Fairbanks and the college? First, it seemed critical to address the impact of the *Sinews of Peace (Iron Curtain)* speech and highlight its importance to freedom and the need to oppose tyranny to prevent another war. Second, it cemented the long-standing relationship between the two countries. Fairbanks, who had houses in both countries, fought with men in both countries, and had many friends in both countries, believed that the relationship

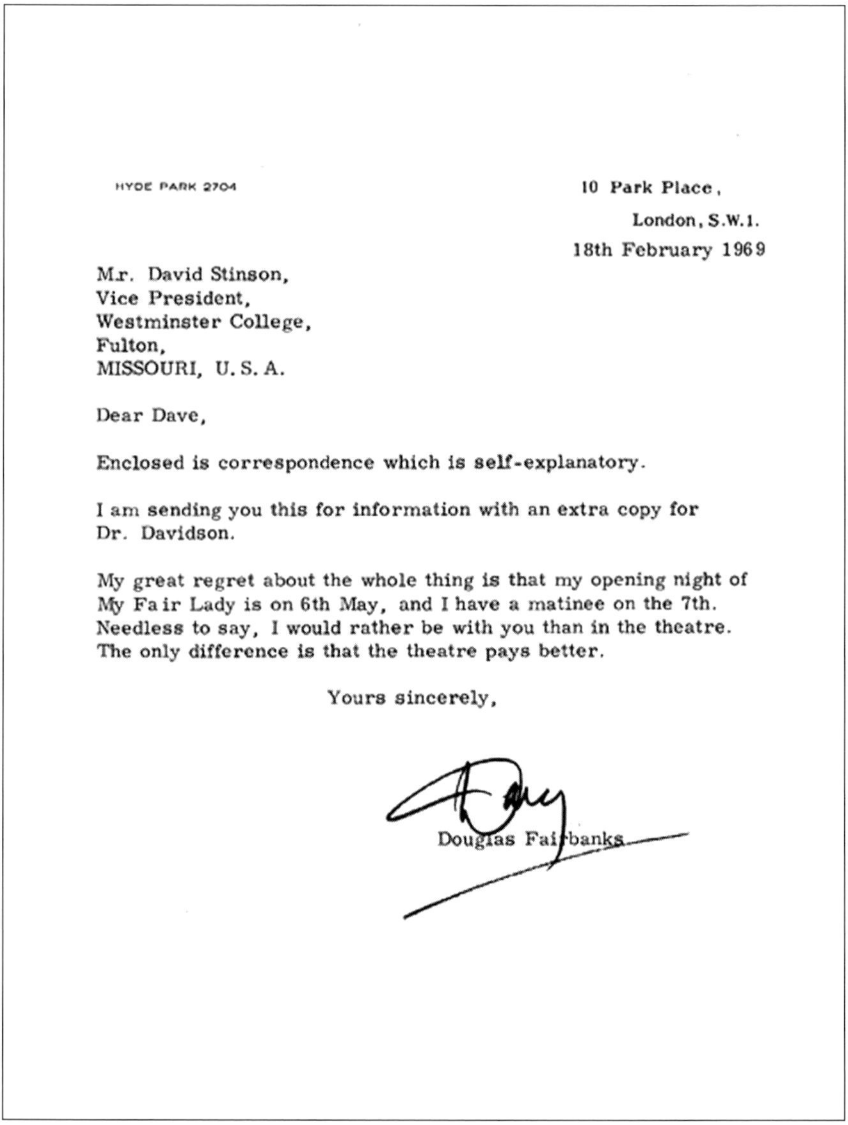

HYDE PARK 2704

10 Park Place,
London, S.W.1.
18th February 1969

Mr. David Stinson,
Vice President,
Westminster College,
Fulton,
MISSOURI, U.S.A.

Dear Dave,

Enclosed is correspondence which is self-explanatory.

I am sending you this for information with an extra copy for Dr. Davidson.

My great regret about the whole thing is that my opening night of My Fair Lady is on 6th May, and I have a matinee on the 7th. Needless to say, I would rather be with you than in the theatre. The only difference is that the theatre pays better.

Yours sincerely,

Douglas Fairbanks

Letter courtesy Steve Stinson.

between the two countries strengthened their joint ability to secure and maintain world peace in a nonbelligerent way that avoids the catastrophe of war.

The project also combined two important factors, a particular need, and a particular purpose. The removal of a Christopher Wren church destined for destruction, and a church that had lost most of its congregation in its post-war setting, seemed a perfect way to set it free of its former constraints and achieve rebirth in a new location that shared the same democratic ideals as the former one. Second, it served the additional purpose of symbolizing the success that can be achieved when both the United States and Britain work jointly to achieve a goal that benefits not just them but the world at large.

Churchill called it "an imaginative concept." Fairbanks thought of it as a way to once again work together with England for a common purpose. He undoubtedly delighted in honoring both Churchill and the genius of Christopher Wren. The idea took hold and the monumental task of relocating the church achieved its goal. Unfortunately, Fairbank's performance in a play prevented him from attending the re-hallowing of the church.[427] As they say in the theater, "The show must go on."

In recognition of his efforts, Fairbanks was named one of America's National Churchill Museum's first "fellows", an honorary designation given to those people who bring unique skills and talents that further the mission of the organization. His contributions will be long remembered.[428]

The crowd at the church reveal uses all available space, including rooftops to catch a glimpse of the parade. Photo courtesy of America's National Churchill Museum.

CHAPTER 23

Helping Hands

Even when a dynamic person leads the team, the fundraising project requires the assistance of a number of well-known people and inspirational leaders who support the cause and communicate its message.

Four presidents, current and former, supported the project. Both Dwight Eisenhower and Harry Truman had worked with Winston Churchill and admired his strength, vision, courage, and leadership. When Churchill died, Eisenhower wrote a farewell speech that school officials included in the church dedication ceremony. The following remarks are an excerpt of that speech that was also broadcast as Churchill's coffin was carried up the Thames by launch. When Eisenhower made them on that day in London, he worried that he might choke on his words. Eisenhower had also suffered a stroke years earlier and stress made his speech difficult.[429]

> Winston Churchill was Britain—he was the embodiment of British defiance to threat, her courage in adversity, her calmness in danger, her moderation in success. Among the Allies his name was spoken with respect, admiration, and affection.[430]

Truman had brought Churchill to his home state where he provided him with a worldwide stage for communicating his warning about the threat of communism and tyranny. He allowed him to speak the words that presaged the Cold War. As the project of rebuilding began, he shoveled the first dirt in preparation for the rebuilding. Poor health prevented his further participation.

John F. Kennedy had loved Churchill, though his father had more isolationist beliefs during World War II. He thought that the memorial was a splendid idea.

> It will tie together powerful events—the 17th century, 1940, and the Blitz, the Iron Curtain address, and the extraordinary and powerful influence on the free world of Sir Winston Churchill's public service.[431]

When Kennedy's short term ended, Lyndon Johnson took up the gauntlet and proclaimed the importance of the memorial.

> I am pleased and proud that you have had the foresight, imagination, and energy to undertake this project as a tribute to one of the outstanding statesman of our time. Sir Winston was a great national leader, a great world statesman, and, above all, a great human being.[432]

All of the presidents did their part to convince people of the importance of the relocation and rebuilding project. Kennedy went one step further. He gave Churchill exactly what he wanted—American citizenship. Kay Halle, arguably the Doyenne of Washington DC, helped make citizenship possible. Formerly engaged to Randolph Churchill, she spent a great deal of time at Chartwell and was a favorite of Winston Churchill. Her quest for citizenship for Winston began in 1957. In 1959, Kennedy did support the idea but thought it unconstitutional. Relentless, Kay made numerous other contacts to elicit support. Two resolutions were introduced on the matter but they did not produce the desired effect. Finally, the Department of Justice, in 1963, decreed it could be done in a constitutional way. A bill to grant citizenship finally made its way through the House and Senate and passed on April 2, 1963. Churchill accepted the honor in a letter dated four days later.[433]

When Churchill learned that Kennedy had decided to convey honorary citizenship to him, he brimmed with anticipation. It was the first time that a foreign national had received citizenship by action of a president. His response to Kennedy included the following remarks. He did not fail to stress the special relationship between the two countries.

> I am, as you know, half American by blood, and the story of my association with that mighty and benevolent nation goes back nearly ninety years to the day of my Father's marriage. In this century of storm and tragedy I contemplate with high satisfaction the constant factor of the interwoven and upward progress of our peoples. Our comradeship and our brotherhood in war were unexampled. We stood together, and because of that fact the free world now stands. Not has our partnership any exclusive nature: the Atlantic community is a dream that can well be fulfilled to the detriment of none and to the enduring benefit and honour of the great democracies.
>
> Mr. President, your action illuminates the theme of unity of the English-speaking peoples, to which I have devoted a large part of my life. I would ask you to accept yourself, and to convey to both Houses of Congress, and through them to the American people, my solemn and heartfelt thanks for this unique distinction, which will always be proudly remembered by my descendants.[434]

Committee members also helped with the fundraising effort. Henry Luce, whose magazine published in a serial format some of Churchill's histories, and St. Louisan Richard Hiller Amberg co-chaired the effort until the latter's death in 1967. As publisher of the *St. Louis Globe-Democrat,* a newspaper where his son would also work, Amberg had powerful media connections.. His wife was a good friend of a Churchill relative, Lady Sarah-Spencer Churchill. His son later became general manager of the *Washington Times.*

Charles Thomas, CEO of Monsanto, became the chairman of the Industrial Committee and coordinated with a wide range of executives to drum up support for the project. President Eisenhower had appointed him to serve as a civilian advisor on scientific matters for the National Security Planning Committee that he established.[435] Joyce Hall, who published some of Churchill's paintings on *Hallmark* cards and collected many of his paintings, was Campaign Co-Chair along with Henry R. Luce.

Other individuals who served as sponsors included:

From the United States

The Hon. Dean Rusk, Secretary of State

The Hon. David Bruce, US Ambassador to the Court of St. James

The Hon. John Hay Whitney, New York City

The Hon. Harry Darby, Kansas City, Kansas

Rt. Rev. Arthur Lichtenberger, Presiding Bishop, Protestant Episcopal Church in America

The Rev. Eugene Carson Blake, Stated Clerk (The United Presbyterian Church in the U.S.A.)

The Rev. John Rood Cunningham, representing the Presbyterian Church in the US

Bernard Baruch, New York City, 1870-1965

Morris L. Ernst, New York City

The Hon. W. Averell Harriman, New York

From the British Commonwealth

The Most Rev. and Rt. Hon. The Lord Archbishop of Canterbury
The Rt. Hon. Alec Douglas-Home
The Rt. Hon. The Earl Attlee
The Rt. Hon. The Earl of Avon
The Rt. Rev. and Rt. Hon. The Lord Bishop of London
The Rt. Hon. Vincent Massey
The Rt. Hon. Harold MacMillan
The Rt. Hon. Quinton Hogg
The Rt. Hon. Harold Wilson
Sir Patrick Dean

All of these people worked diligently to ensure that the Winston Churchill Memorial, as it was then called, was a "visible testimony to the days when Britain and her people stood alone against the forces of tyranny" and as a symbol of the heroic resistance led by war-time Prime Minister—Winston Churchill."

Stones awaiting the rebuild of the church. Photo courtesy of America's National Churchill Museum.

CHAPTER 24

Dismantling and Rebuilding the Church

When Karen Laine and Ben Napier, two HGTV home improvement stars, demolish a house, they always seem to rescue a piece of furniture and give it new life or they repurpose a wall or flooring into a beautiful new use, typically a piece of furniture. They are not just believers in recycling, they are people who respect and honor homes by bringing a part of the old building into the new one. Similarly, the people who worked on the relocation and rebuilding of the Church of St. Mary the Virgin, Aldermanbury, had great respect for the church. They wanted to be sure that they honored its past. Avoiding the limelight, they continued to put the church first. The church always served as the star of the show.

The rebuilding project had a successful start. To retain its historical significance, at least 51% of the church had to remain intact and be suitable for relocation. The church met that requirement. Though much of this chapter discusses some additional masonry and other elements, mainly dealing with the interior, doors, window, and new substructure, those items did not affect the historical integrity of the church. The finished product is the church rebuilt and reborn in a new location.

Work on dismantling the building did not take place until 1965. It took that long to receive permission from a multitude of organizations with a vested interest in the outcome. Even Parliament and the London City Council had to agree to its relocation. Belatedly, Sisson sought permission from St. Vedast alias Foster Church, which had accumulated congregations from about 13 other churches as a result of the reorganization of churches in London. The names of those churches are engraved on a plaque in the church. The rector gave his permission, to the delight of Westminster College.

Demolishing an entire building may not be easy but it is certainly easier than taking apart a building stone by stone, especially when the building is historic and almost 300 years old. Fred C. Sternberg, a St. Louisan, was overall manager. Marshall Sisson, a British architect from Godmanchester, England, provided project management and architectural guidance based on his expertise in British architecture and building restoration. His expertise proved invaluable as the church was disassembled in London and rebuilt on the campus of Westminster College in Fulton, Missouri.

Fred Sternberg, a past president of the St. Louis branch of the American Institute of Architects (AIA), had a distinguished career building homes and commercial buildings in St. Louis, Missouri.[436] He did excellent work in supervising the rebuilding of the church and translating Sisson's designs to the finished product. Both Patrick Horsbrugh and Emmett Layton, the landscape architect who did work at the college, recommended him.

Marshall Sisson, former treasurer for the Royal Academy of Art in Piccadilly from 1947 to 1965, also received a hearty recommendation from Horsbrugh. A modernist, he still loved the old Wren churches and jumped at the chance to be part of the project.[437] He previously served as a member of the Ancient Monuments Board for England, the Cathedrals Advisory Committee of England, and various committees of the National Trust for England. He also did work on buildings at Oxford, Cambridge, and Durham Universities. Importantly, he did reconstruction work on several churches, including the London churches of St. John the Evangelist, Westminster, St. Andrew-by-the-Wardrobe (Wren), and St. Katherine Key. He also did restoration work on a number of medieval churches, guildhalls, and historic homes in England. The combined expertise of both men and their contacts in each country helped make the project a success.[438]

Before disassembly, measurements had to be taken of the building so that Sternberg could prepare designs for reconstruction purposes. The medieval foundation did not lend itself to a completely rectangular or regular building, so the dimensions and the tower had to be adjusted. Further, the church on the Westminster campus had to meet current code requirements and accommodate new electrical and mechanical systems that had not been part of the building in London.[439]

Horsbrugh's involvement also proved beneficial. Dr. Davidson referred to him as a "magician" due to all the doors he opened for Westminster College. Davidson had made a trip to London to personally inspect the ruins and the works that Sisson had previously restored. When he first saw the latter ones and the degree to which they had been restored, his "heart leapt up." One of the restorations had been in worse shape than St. Mary the Virgin, Aldermanbury. He deemed the restorations magnificent and felt more confident than ever that the church on the Westminster campus in Fulton would be the same.[440]

While in London, Davidson met with Sir Evelyn Wrench, founder of the English-Speaking Union. He then met with members of both houses of Parliament, the Archbishop of Canterbury, the Bishop of London, the Lord Mayor, Montague Browne, Sir Winston Churchill's secretary, and many other individuals, all of whom had some degree of importance to the project.[441]

As workers disassembled the church in London, they made chalk markings with coded numbers on each stone to make sure that they could be reassembled in proper order.[442] The stones were then loaded into crates in order of their disassembly to ensure easy reassembly.

Since the church did not house original construction plans, which they could not find anywhere, the architects had to begin making plans by referencing old photographs of the building. They also looked at other Wren churches for references, including an 1848 drawing and the original building accounts.[443] Photogrammetry, the science of calculating measurements from photographs, enabled the architects to figure the measurements for the rebuilding of the church.[444] It measured 75 feet in length and 49 feet in width. The ceiling measured 38 feet high.[445]

The form on the original tracery in the belfry windows and in the large east window, as well as in the scrolls at the east end, were detected in the structure and used for rebuilding purposes. The form and detail of the roof and ceilings were more difficult to gauge since none of them remained. Sisson had to use measurements, engravings, photographs, and original building accounts to calculate their dimensions. Luckily, old photograph negatives were available.[446]

Medieval stone and brick rubble from the twelfth century church filled the inside the church walls in London, since Wren recycled material when possible. The rubble came from a number of churches in London before the Great Fire, not just the Church of St. Mary's. It had to be removed before the stones could be shipped; however, removing the rubble meant ensuring that no medieval fragments slipped in with the stones saved for shipment. Interesting pieces of carved stone that could not be shipped were given to the Guildhall Museum.[447] It is possible that some of the rubble may still exist in storage at St. Paul's Cathedral.[448] Also left behind were the Victorian embellishments added post-Wren. According to Sisson, they were "injudicious alterations."[449]

The sandstone bases of the columns could not be moved without damage and remain on the former church site as a monument to the church that once housed them. The thirteenth-century steps that led to the small crypt area were removed and crated, as was the bell tower sans bells and spire. Six of the Corinthian columns were also packed for shipment. The last two appeared too damaged for further use. Replacements columns similar to the original were made in St. Louis.[450]

Employees at Mander Organ, in England, made the seventeenth century reproduction organ in the loft area. The founder of the company, Noel Mander, worked as a firefighter in London during World War II. He became horribly upset when he heard the plaintive sounds of the old organ as the fire from the incendiary device began to lick its woodwork. He made it his personal mission to oversee the construction of the new organ and install it in the church on Westminster's campus. He also helped the college acquire priceless artifacts from other churches.

Particular care was taken to ensure that nothing received damage in London or in transport. Additional stones from the original quarry used in the seventeenth-century were added to the mix as well as stone facing from the contemporary Wren Church of St. Swithun on Canon Street, which had not been rebuilt. Some 700 tons of stone required transport in different stages via a shipping line that agreed to ship the stones free of charge in return for their use as ballast. They sometimes remained on hold for several months waiting for suitable ships for transport.

The first shipment of crates made their way by barge "from the city's financial district down the Thames to the Royal Victoria dock for loading in the *American Champion*, bound for Norfolk, Virginia" on February 18, 1966.[451] It cost approximately $200,000 to take the church apart and ship all of the stones.[452] The entire project was estimated to cost in the neighborhood of $1.5 million. Once in the United States, railroad coal cars shipped them via the Gulf, Mobile, and Ohio Railroad from Chicago, Illinois to Mexico, Missouri through St. Louis. From Mexico, Missouri, the stones were trucked to Fulton, Missouri.[453]

The blackened stones received a good scrubbing before their disassembly; however, the coal soot on the railroad coal cars blackened them once more and erased the chalk marks so diligently applied in London. At one point, Dave Stinson, the college vice president and manager of the project, had to take a train to one stop on the railroad line to "rescue" stones waylaid by workers in one of the railroad yards. He spread some money across some palms and everything was "back on track" so to speak. His close scrutiny and oversight of the project made him a valuable asset to the church team.

The Epple Construction Company in Columbia, Missouri, took charge of the actual church rebuilding. They thought it wouldn't be too complicated given the order prescribed by Marshall Sisson. They were in for a big surprise. According to John Epple, the company president, each crate was supposed to have specific numbered stones inside them. He had gone to London to ensure this process took place as intended. To his great surprise, the markings on the crates received did not match the markings of the stones they held. Apparently, a different worker from the one originally assigned the task of crating the stones took charge of the project. To fit the crates into the ships, the stones had been juggled from crate to crate.[454] The change in plans meant that putting the church back together was akin to completing a large puzzle with the puzzle pieces made of stone.

All of the stones had to be laid on the ground in some orderly fashion. There were so many of them that they stretched a great distance. Each stone was re-inspected and additional stones ordered from a St. Louis stone company to fill any gaps created by problems in transport. Sisson slightly altered the design on the west side of the church to include a large window for extra light. The window was an unnecessary element in the London church due to the proximity of other buildings that blocked the possibility of any light on the west side. Somehow, the skilled craftsmen and construction workers performed a miracle and made sure that all the puzzle pieces fit. They, like many of those people mentioned, are the unsung heroes of the project. All of their work was meant to replicate, to the extent possible, work done on the original church.

President Truman came to Westminster in 1966 to take part in the laying of the building cornerstone. The Lord Mayor of London was also on hand to participate and see Truman dig the first dirt with a shovel. Three stones of Portland limestone had been sent to the college for use in the ceremony.

The completed interior of the church has a remarkable display of works donated by a wide range of people from both Britain and the United States. No stained windows are found since Wren believed in the importance of clear light shining through windows. The new clear, handmade Cathedral glass windows are reproductions of the ones used by Wren. The interior columns "with boldly carved capitals retain all the original material" that could be salvaged. Those capitals deemed too damaged for re-use were replaced with cast stone reproductions.[455] The new pews are in the seventeenth–century design and seat 400 people. Woodwork is oak and the flooring beneath the pews is parquet. Bedford limestone flooring covers the rest of the church floor.[456]

The small altar is made of marble as are the two steps leading to the altar. The plastered ceilings reproduced the original Wren design rather than the Victorian ones installed before the church bombing. Sisson expressed his feelings of admiration for the local plasterers involved in the reproduction and installation. The medallions, flowers, and other designs in the ceiling work were made from original molds sent from London.[457]

The internal fittings are not exactly like the ones in the former church; however, they are characteristic of other churches redesigned in the

Interior of the church on the campus of Westminster. Photo courtesy of America's National Churchill Museum.

17th century. The former Victorian embellishments post-seventeenth-century were not reproduced, since Sisson deemed them unsatisfying adornments for the baroque church. The doorways to the two vestries contain the "beautifully carved Corinthian columns and pediments, which originally formed part of the altarpiece of the Wren church of St. Dionis Backchurch, destroyed in 1878." Carved by Grinling Gibbons, who worked for Wren, they are beautiful works of art. Gibbons also did carvings for St. Paul's Cathedral.[458]

Before closing his remarks in the college newspaper, Sisson also expressed his gratitude and admiration for the work of Frederick Sternberg and his associate, Pershing Myres.[459]

It would take almost three years to raise the necessary funds to complete the rebuilding, and furnish the interiors. Just as the original cost of the project exceeded the cost for Wren to rebuild the church in the seventeenth-century, the cost today is much, much higher (millions more) than the cost to rebuild in 1969. The grand unveiling of the rebuilt church took place in 1969.

When questioned, stonemason Eris Lytle indicated why people were so happy to work on the project.

> There were those who thought it was a foolish way to spend the money, but after it was completed they changed their tune. It was well worth doing because it was a once-in-a-lifetime deal. You will never do it again.

Current preservation work involves using material from national companies that produce quality work. Construction work meets present-day building codes. Interior work includes donated work from other English churches and reproductions made to copy the original works of art, including the chandeliers. Modern construction methods allow for better ways to meet construction problems that caused water intrusion issues in the past. Many of these issues resulted from trying to site the church with a new substructure in a hilly area. The old church stood on a flat surface with no usable substructure other than a location for crypts. The wonderful workers in the mid-twentieth century did a fantastic job of rebuilding the church. The new preservation work will ensure that the church is preserved for future generations.[460] When the old church interior is compared to the rebuilt one, the two interiors are very similar.

The following is an incomplete list of some of the contractors who worked on the project and furnishings donated to the church prior to its reveal in 1969 as well as contractors who have recently done work on the church to preserve it for many more years. The list shows that the project reached a wide assortment of men and women willing to support the effort. It includes churches in London, donors in St. Louis, and donors worldwide. The project took more than a village. It took an international cadre of Churchillians to complete the magnificent memorial. Everything was done to make it as close to the church that Wren designed as possible given the changed location of the building.

Placed on the National Register of Historic Places on March 16, 1972, the church memorializes a historically significant person, Winston Churchill. The exterior of the building is almost exactly as it was prior to World War II and is "typical of Wren's city churches." The interior reconstruction "has produced a spatial effect that is totally Wren for it exhibits a subtle attempt to centralize a longitudinal area, a factor characteristic of almost all Wren's later churches."[461]

A Guide to the Interior and Exterior of the Church[462]

Construction Company:
Epple Construction, Columbia, Missouri

Replacement Stones for the substructure (in Missouri):
– The Stone Center, 3200 Brannon Ave., St. Louis
– Alabama limestone (interior flooring in lieu of exterior stone) slightly grayer in appearance than the original stone
– Indiana limestone (base) grayish (Note: The substructure leading to the crypts did not exist on the original structure that was situated flat on the ground without a museum substructure.)

Replacement Stone to fill in any gaps (in London):
– Wandsworth Stonemasonry Works Limited from the Dorset Quarry
– Portland limestone

Original Portland Stone:
– Dorset Quarry
– New ashlar limestone blocks matching the historic stone were used to clad the elevation and repair areas damaged by the Blitz. Sisson identified areas on his drawings to indicate where stone needed replacement.

Master Stone Mason:
– Eris Lyttle, Jefferson City, MO, Epple Construction Company

Window Frames and Ornamental Metal:
– Architectural Bronze Studio Inc., 2600 Tenth Street, St. Louis

Window (Large one on the west side in the base of the tower):
– Keystone (i.e., the stone at the apex of the arch) of this window comes from the belfry of St. Swithun, Cannon Street. That church was not rebuilt. The remaining portion of the window replicates Wren's style.

Wood Paneling (Interior):
– Gravois Planing Mill, 3026 Juniata Avenue, St. Louis

Ceiling Decorative Plaster:
– Alfred Gass, St. Louis artisan

Ceiling Design:
– Marshall Sisson

Chandeliers:
– Reproductions of those designed by Christopher Wren.
Made in Cleveland, Ohio.

Windows (Cutting glass and fitting it to the frames):
– Jacoby Studios, 822 Wilmington Ave., St. Louis

Altar Furnishings:
– St. Matthews Presbyterian Church

Altar Table and Furnishings:
– Mr. J. C. Penney donated these objects. He came to the celebration of the church reveal in 1969.

Altarpiece and paneling, altar rails, vestry front, and lecterns:
– Marshall Sisson directed the construction of these reproduction items by Arthur Ayres (1902-1985), the famous woodcarver, in London. They were shipped to the United States. The central part of the altarpiece has the same characteristics as the design of seventeenth-century reredos (i.e., the ornamental screen covering the wall on the back of the altar) and what is known to have existed in St. Mary the Virgin, Aldermanbury, before the alterations that took place in 1843.

Communion Service:
– The communion service is made of seventeenth century sterling silver. It was a gift from the Rector and Churchwardens of St. Vedast alias Foster, London.

Altar Candlesticks:

– Made of seventeenth-century sterling silver, the candlesticks were a gift from the Westminster Catholic Cathedral of London.

Columns:

– The columns no longer support the roof. Christopher Wren designed the original ones and the few replacement ones are reproductions.

Spiral steps in Wren's Tower:

– Some of these steps were saved and shipped from London to the United States.

Glass:

– Blenko Glass, West Virginia

Vestry Doors and Entryway Carvings:

– The Corinthian columns and pediments originally were part of the Church St. Dionis Backchurch, London (destroyed by fire in 1878). Wren designed that church as well.

Tower Bells:

Five bronze bells (G, A, C, D, E) cast by Petit and Fritzen of Aarte-Rixtel, Holland. The bells are a memorial to Dr. W.B.A. McNutt.

Other Carvings:

– Done by Arthur Ayres in the Wren style.

Red, White, and Blue Church Kneelers:

– Organized by Mrs. Joseph A. Bascom of St. Louis, head of the American Tapestry Committee, the kneelers were gifts from many women. About 450 women in 38 states contributed, as well as a number of women from London. Mamie Eisenhower donated a beautiful kneeler now in the museum archives. Frances Stephens,

Associate for the Royal College of Art and a specialist in liturgical design, created the kneeler designs. The women in England did fundraising that included bake sales to pay for the material that they used and donated willingly to the project.

Chair Cushions and Communion Rail Kneelers:

– These gifts came from Stephen Lee, cousin of designer Derek Lee, Arthur H. Lee and Sons, Ltd., England. One needlepoint chair cushion bears the Churchill coat of arms. Another represents Churchill's title of Lord Warden of the Cinque Ports. The communion rail cushions reference Chartwell (Churchill's home), Churchill's love of painting, and the history books he wrote.

Vestments:

– The vestments were a gift of Mrs. Arthur Lee, London

Plaster Ornament Models of the Main Ceiling and Cornice:

– Designed by Marshall Sisson, made in London, and shipped to the United States.

Pulpit:

– A pulpit fall references Churchill's American citizenship. The Diocese of London donated the pulpit as a gift after 9/11. The carvings are done in the style of Grinling Gibbons (1648-1721), an English sculptor who did work at Windsor Castle, Hampton Court, St. Paul's Cathedral, and other London churches. Originally in Wren's All-Hallows-the-Great Church in Upper Thames, the pulpit relocated to St. Paul's Hammersmith in London after All-Hallows-the-Great was demolished in 1894. When St. Paul's Hammersmith underwent a renovation, the Diocese gifted it to Westminster College.

Organ:

– The organ is a thirty-eight-rank tracker instrument adopted from a seventeenth century design. Built by N.P. Mander Ltd., England.

It contains some pipes that are circa 1770. The newer pipes are 95 percent tin. The case was originally built in 1741 for Woolrich Parish Church, Kent, England. The crown and mitres are from the Church of St. Michael Paternoster Royal, London. The organ memorializes Philip T. Thurmond.

Organ Balcony, Seating, and Stairs:
– Designed by Marshall Sisson, the construction of these items took place under the supervision of the architect, Frederick Sternberg.

Chandeliers:
– Made N-L Lighting, Cleveland, Ohio

Bible:
– Printed on handmade paper, the bible is No. 193 of 200 copies made. Outer covers contain wood from the Old House of Commons where Sir Winston Churchill once served.

Other Donations:
– Many donors contributed money to purchase and install, if necessary, pews, windows, candelabras, prayer books, chairs, drapery, bells, library, books, medallions, ornamental plaster, sconces, landscape, doors, trees, columns and a variety of other items.

Wording of the Ten Commandments in the Interior:
– Taken from the seventeenth-century English Prayer Book

Exterior Ornamentation:
– The pineapples on the roof signify hospitality, friendship and warmth. They are traditional marks of Wren's work; they used to be a symbol of wealth and status. Wren crowned many buildings with pineapples, including St. Paul's Cathedral.

Overall Reconstruction:

– The church exterior is almost exactly the way it existed when Wren designed the church. The one exception is the window on the west side that Sisson added to allow light in the stairway.

Present On-Going Preservation Work:

Gutter System:

– K & M Sheet Metal LLC, in Durham, North Carolina made a new gutter system entirely of heavy copper. Installed by Vogel Sheet Metal, it adds beauty and sophistication to the exterior of the building.

Decking:

– A temporary decking system of thermoplastic polyolefin (TPO) has eliminated water intrusion through the decking. Installed by Kirkberg Roofing, the TPO will eventually be replaced by more permanent decking.

Doors:

– Gorgeous new doors, made entirely of kiln-dried furniture grade clear white oak wood, have been installed in the recent preservation. New locksets replace the old damaged ones. They were made in Montgomery, Alabama by Decora, which makes doors for churches nationwide.

Museum Ceiling:

– Glove Con construction company replaced damaged museum ceiling tile beneath the church with better quality ones.

Roof and Bell Tower:

– Kirgberg Roofing repaired problems with the church roof and the roof of the bell tower to stop roof leaks.

Masonry:

– Marbelite of Wentzville, MO, repaired stonework and grouting on the west side of the church. Now gleaming and beautiful, the wall no longer sheds material.

Glass:

– Blenko Glass Company in Cabell County, West Virginia, made the glass for new windows recently installed by Brady Glass Company in Columbia, MO

New exterior sidewalk and steps and upgraded storm water/sewer connections are in progress.

Other Preservation Work Needed Includes:

– Accessible building updates, permanent decking, masonry work on the three other sides of the church, stone carving repairs, new Blenko windows, new storm windows, and interior repairs are included in the preservation work still needed. All work is proceeding in accordance with the required Department of Interior Standards for Historic Properties.

Church rebuild. Photo courtesy of America's National Churchill Museum.

CHAPTER 25

Preparing for the Big Reveal

Prior to a major reveal, organizations typically build suspense by having a number of other smaller events. Westminster College did the same.

The earliest celebration that occurred was the Winston Churchill Memorial Groundbreaking Ceremony in 1964. President Lyndon B. Johnson announced the fund drive on April 15 of that same year. He held a ceremony at the White House where he praised the accomplishments of Churchill and met with Missouri senators, Stuart Symington and Edward V. Long as well as representative Clarence Cannon.

In Fulton, Harry Truman participated in the groundbreaking ceremony and shoveled the first dirt to kick off the occasion. The Rt. Hon. Lord Harlech (William David Ormsby-Gore), British Ambassador to the United States, represented the British government. A friend of the Kennedy family, he worked with President John F. Kennedy on issues dealing with disarmament and the Cuban missile crisis. After the death of both their spouses, he proposed to Jackie Kennedy, who turned him down and married Aristotle Onassis.[463]

Joyce Hall, Churchill's friend, and CEO of Hallmark, also assisted with the ground turning. Born into poverty in a small Nebraska town,

Hall most likely received his first name due to the arrival of a visiting minister, Reverend Isaac W. Joyce. One of his first ventures came to a halt when the building in which it was located burned in a fire, a tragedy not unfamiliar to historians of St. Mary's church. With hard work, determination, and good marketing skills, he built Hall Bros., Inc., the predecessor to Hallmark Cards, Inc.[464] Churchill owed a great deal to Hall. He did a fantastic job of marketing Churchill's paintings in cards that Hallmark made.[465] As a friend of both Truman and Eisenhower, he helped with the establishment of their libraries in Missouri and Kansas.

Hall's friendship with Churchill began in 1946, when he attended Churchill's speech in Fulton. Hall featured Sarah, Churchill's daughter, in one of his first Hallmark Hall of Fame shows. He also marketed Churchill's paintings once more in an exhibit at the Nelson Gallery of Art in Kansas City. A number of other locations in the United States, Canada, England, and Australia featured his paintings in similar exhibits.[466]

Carl Trauernicht also participated in the ground breaking. During World War II, he piloted a B-17 airplane based in England, probably at a former RAF air base. When Winston Churchill spoke at Westminster, Trauernicht led the honor guard procession in Churchill's honor.

Governor John M. Dalton of Missouri rounded out the group. He chaired the fundraising effort during his term in office. One of his major accomplishments as governor, in addition to his role at Westminster, was furthering the desegregation of schools in the state.

The groundbreaking ceremony highlighted the church as a symbol of the "courage, endurance, and leadership" with which Churchill rallied the British people in their time of crisis.

In October of 1966, another ceremony held at the church site featured the Right Rev. Robert Wright Stopford, Lord Bishop of London who arrived at Westminster to lay the church cornerstone.

A fundraising dinner was held in New York to highlight the memorial. The $100 a plate functions attracted a large group of publishers, celebrities, and Churchillians. Shelton Fisher, president of McGraw Hill chaired the publishing industry's *Salute to Churchill* event.[467] Douglas Fairbanks Jr. had met with him and convinced him that the event at the New York Hilton would be well received. When Fisher made a public announcement of the event he said, "It is fitting that the publishers of America and their associates in the many fields of communications pay homage to this man, who above all others, used words to keep men free."[468]

Co-chairmen of the committee included the following prominent men:

The Hon. William Benton. Former owner of the Encyclopedia Britannica and United States Senator, Benton challenged the tactics of fellow senator, Joseph McCarthy, and his anti-communist crusade that ruined the lives of many people with baseless allegations.[469]

The Hon. David K. E. Bruce, C.B.E. Bruce served as former Assistant Secretary of Commerce, 1947-48, Chief of the Economic Cooperation Administration to France, May 1948-49; United States Ambassador to France, 1949-52; and Under Secretary of State, 1952-53 under President Harry Truman.[470]

Cass Canfield Sr. Senior editor at Harpers Collins from 1967 until his death in 1986. The *New York Times* referred to him as a titan of publishing. His son Michael was the first husband of Lee Radziwill, sister of Jackie Kennedy Onassis. After Michael died, his widow, Frances Charteris, married her fourth husband, the 10th Duke of Marlborough (the eldest son of Consuelo Vanderbilt). She became known as Laura Spencer-Churchill, Duchess of Marlborough.[471]

Bennett Cerf. Publisher and co-founder of Random House, Cerf wrote syndicated columns and appeared on the popular television show, *What's My Line?*

Gardner Cowles. Co-owner of Cowles Media Co., Garner Cowles controlled a number of media publications, including two Minneapolis papers and the *Des Moines Register*, all of which published many articles about Churchill. He owned a half interest in *Harper's Magazine*.[472]

Allen Ferrin. After holding a number of jobs in the publishing business, Ferrin served as president of the American Management Association, International.[473]

Irving Geist. Although he was an apparel manufacturer, Geist gained a powerful reputation for providing rehabilitation services to hasten the recovery of veterans who served in the war. President Truman awarded him a Medal for Merit, one of the highest awards at the time Geist received it in 1947.[474]

The Hon. W. Averell Harriman. A successful businessman, Harriman gained fame for his work as Secretary of Commerce under Truman and, later, his tenure as Governor of New York. He held a number of other prominent government positions, including ambassadorships to Russia and Great Britain. At the time of his death, his widow, Pamela, the former wife of Randolph Churchill, survived him.[475]

Henry A. Laughlin. President of Houghton Mifflin, Laughlin published Churchill's *Memoirs of World War II.* Survivors held his son's memorial service at a church with a British historic name, St. Mary the Virgin in Falmouth, Maine.[476]

Dr. Howard A. Rusk. Founder of the Rusk Institute of Rehabilitation Medicine, Rusk is sometimes referred to as the founder of comprehensive rehabilitation. His rehabilitation programs proved very successful in the military. He later won the Distinguished Service Medal.[477]

Harry Scherman. Scherman's Book of the Month Club published Churchill's Memoirs of the Second World War.

Joseph C. Wilson. President and founder of Xerox Corporation, Wilson gave the John Findley Green lecture in 1965. His photocopying machines transformed the publishing business.[478]

The crowd gathered to hear the program also contained many illustrious people who gave a grand salute to Churchill. They had a great day at Westminster College in Fulton. The museum, not fully constructed at the time of the reveal, is now fully complete, though it changes over time. It is a welcome sight for visitors of all ages to enjoy and learn more about Winston Churchill.

Scene from the parade before the unveiling of the Church of St. Mary the Virgin, Aldermanbury on the campus of Westminster in 1969. Photo courtesy of America's National Churchill Museum.

CHAPTER 26

The Big Reveal

Today and in 1969, Westminster College in Fulton, Missouri, is a private co-educational, Liberal Arts College in the middle of the Midwestern state. The college, over 100-years of age in 1969, seeks to develop leaders in a global community and inspire its students by means of a dynamic and challenging curriculum. Its mission is to graduate future leaders who are committed to the values of integrity, fairness, respect, and responsibility that Churchill exhibited in his leadership of Britain. By so doing, the college is preparing its graduate for the same life that Churchill lived—a life of success, significance, and service.[479]

The months and years leading to the reveal of the completed Churchill memorial motivated some students to acquire a better understanding of the English as Europeans, the concept of liberty, and the spirit of cooperation needed to deal with the crisis of tyranny and loss of freedoms. They appreciated the majestic language of Churchill and came to realize the power of the spoken word. They understood the importance of reaching out beyond personal partisanship and national differences to achieve common goals that benefit society and expand the freedom of mankind. They realized that tyranny and freedom do not peacefully coexist.[480]

It is no wonder that the campus filled with excitement as the completion of the Churchill Memorial came to an end. The Westminster campus and the Fulton community were anxious to participate in the events that filled Churchill Week from Sunday, May 4 through Sunday, May 11, 1969. Several of the opening lectures dealt with personages involved with the church during its days in England. Music of the Shakespeare era was played in honor of the great playwright and his famous publishers, John Heminges and Henry Condell, both of whom had an association with the church. A lecture on John Milton, who married his second wife at the church, enlightened people about his career and importance. Capping the three events was the school-sponsored lecture on Christopher Wren, the genius who designed the church in the seventeenth century, and a pictorial art exhibit of some of Wren's works at the St. Louis Art Museum. A well-attended event, the exhibit gave visitors an in-depth view of his works.

On Tuesday, May 6, a dinner at the fabulous Chase Park Plaza honored both the late Richard Amberg, former newspaper publisher and Westminster Board of Trustee member, and the rebuilt Church of St. Mary. It gave a host of media representatives and Churchillians the chance to celebrate two events along with a delicious dinner.

Among the attendees were representatives of the news media: the Associated Press, the United Press International, KMOX Radio, KPLE-TV, Women's Wear Daily, Business Week Magazine, and Commerce Magazine. Representatives from a number of banks and public relations firms attended. Corporations headquartered in St. Louis included Anheuser Busch, Falstaff Beer, and the May Company. Local influential and notable citizens of Missouri who attended included: T. Ellis Barnes, Arthur Baer, Taylor Desloge, Alfred Fleishman, Clark Gamble, Lee Hunter, Warren Lammert, Morton May, James McDonnell, I.E. Millstone, Walter Orthwein, Vernon Piper, H. Sam Priest, Donald Schnuck, Ethan Shepley, John E. Simon, Frederick Switzer, Charles Thomas, Stuart Symington, and Gupton Vogt.

Other influential and notable people outside of Missouri included: Bromwell Ault, Angier Biddle Duke, Mrs. Chauncey Hamlin, Stanley Mortimer, Vincent Sardi, Nicholas Soames, the Bishop of Dover, Averell Harriman, British Ambassador John Freeman, and the Earl Mountbatten of Burma.[481]

A luncheon was held on Wednesday, May 7, for invited guests. Catered by Vincent Sardi of New York, the food held a special significance. During World War II, Martin Balma, who served as the dinner manager at Sardi's Restaurant in New York, managed a restaurant in the hotel where Mountbatten made his headquarters as Chief of Combined Allied Operations on the Mediterranean island of Malta. Both Balma and Vincent Sardi arrived in Fulton to cater the luncheon.

The church dedication, also held on Wednesday, featured W. Averell Harriman and the toast of the evening, the Earl Mountbatten of Burma. Douglas Fairbanks Jr. had both encouraged and supported Mountbatten's involvement in the dedication. When Fairbanks realized the neither he nor his wife could attend the ceremony due to his commitment to a play in which he starred, Fairbanks thought Mountbatten might change his mind. He had tremendous respect for Mountbatten but realized that his shyness might make it difficult to attend. He needn't have worried. Not only did he attend, he gave an impressive speech that he consistently said he would not give. His admiration for Churchill won the day.

In his speech at the dedication, Harriman expressed his belief that the transporting of the stones from London to Westminster in Fulton, Missouri, "the center of the continent," compared in many respects to the journey of the pilgrims on the Mayflower. So much of history began with the Mayflower; Harriman thought that "much would also come from the transport of the church."[482]

He then went on to say that the dedication was not just about the church but also about the "principles for which Churchill stood." He believed it important that in visiting this site, people understand that very fact. Churchill, he said, used his speech to awaken people to the dangers that he so rightly saw coming after the war, when democracy seemed challenged. He recalled how many people who heard the speech could not accept the warning. Believing that the Soviets were their friends, they rebuffed any suggestions to the contrary. In fact, as he pointed out, Churchill was picketed and booed by people when he gave another speech in New York a few days later. They thought that Churchill was a warmonger.

According to Harriman, Churchill's speech was a great one as he used his famous oratory to convince people to accept the truth. It took time for some to realize the importance of what he said. His use of words did awaken some people initially and others later.

Averell praised Truman for his more active and stronger actions towards containing Russian expansion after hearing Churchill's speech at Westminster. Words can be convincing but Churchill knew how to energize them in his speech. (Note: As the historian, Simon Schama, said in one of his books, "Churchill's oratory, {is} a unique, at times almost Shakespearean marriage between the grandiloquent and the puckishly conversational.")[483]

Harriman believed that the Soviets would have tried to march all the way to the Atlantic if the United States and Britain did not resist. He spoke of Churchill's reminder that "war and tyranny" are great marauders.

> We must ever proclaim in fearless tongues the great principles of freedom and the rights of man.

Churchill repeated those words to highlight the common heritage of both countries and Harriman agreed that the British were "drawn to America" for that reason.

Both Churchill and Harriman agreed that the basic principles of the Declaration of Independence and the Constitution with its Bill of Rights are all drawn from the British tradition. Harriman quoted Churchill as once saying the following words about that connection.

> The Declaration was, in the main, a restatement of the principles which had animated the Whig struggle against the later Stuarts and the English Revolution of 1688.

He then pointed out the connection that the Church of St. Mary had to that same time period before the church succumbed to the Great Fire in the seventeenth century.

At the end of his speech, Harriman recalled Churchill's words about the responsibilities that powerful countries have to help the rest of the world. He thought his wording remarkable. He ended by saying, despite the problems that exist and "even though a complete freedom is not possible, even though the sunshine is not shining on both sides of the Iron Curtain … there is much that can now be done between us."

Mountbatten's speech included more about his long, personal relationship with Churchill. He elaborated on that and the events that led to some of the great speeches that Churchill made during the war. But he began with praise for the Church of St. Mary and the fact that it survived so many struggles over the years. He expressed his pleasure that it is now rebuilt in America's heartland and has received a new life. He recalled Churchill's hope that the church "may symbolize in the eyes of English-speaking peoples the ideal of Anglo-American association on which rest, now as before, so many of our hopes for peace and the future of mankind."[484]

In 1941, Churchill summoned Mountbatten to tell him that he had picked him to replace Admiral Keyes, the Commander-in-Chief of the Mediterranean Fleet. When Mountbatten said he would prefer to return to sea and fight with his friends, Churchill gave him a Churchillian reply.

> Have you no sense of glory? I pick you out of your generation and give you a say in the highest direction of the war and all you want to do is to go back and fight at sea. What could you hope to achieve, except to be sunk in a bigger and more expensive ship this time?
>
> You will carry on with the Commando Raids, but you will prepare for the invasion of the continent itself. You must get the finest brains in the Army, Navy and Air Force to help you with the plans. You must devise the techniques and design the appurtenances and appliances, the landing ships and landing craft needed for the invasion. And you must set up training bases where you can teach the Army, Navy and Air Forces to work as a single unit. All of the south of England is a bastion of defense against German invasion. You must turn it into a springboard for our own attack. All other headquarters in these islands are thinking defensively. Yours is only to think offensively.

Churchill's inspirational speech stirred Mountbatten to action much as his other speeches did during the war and as the *Sinews of Peace* would with time.

Mountbatten then recalled going with General Eisenhower to meet President Roosevelt about a proposed invasion that would later take place at Normandy. Mountbatten felt somewhat like John the Baptist since he had to explain that the British did not have enough landing ships and craft in 1942 and that they preferred having Africa serve as the proposed site for invasion in 1943. The trip did teach him something for he realized the great admiration that Eisenhower had for Churchill. Like Mountbatten, Eisenhower believed that Churchill had "tremendous courage, integrity, and sound common sense."

The friendship that Roosevelt and Churchill shared made the alliance and relationship between the two countries stronger, according to Mountbatten. It also allowed them to have some jovial fun with each other. On one occasion, Roosevelt tried to best Churchill by inviting a woman who crusaded for an India free of British control to have dinner with the two of them. At the dinner, the woman asked Churchill, "Prime Minister, what are you going to do about those wretched Indians?" At first, Churchill seemed surprised by the question; however, he quickly realized the game was on. In great Churchillian fashion, he answered in the following manner.

> Madam, to which Indians do you refer? Do you by chance refer to the second greatest nation on earth, which under benign and beneficent British rule has multiplied and prospered exceedingly or are you referring to those unfortunate Indians of the North American continent, which under the present administration are almost extinct?

When given the responsibility to form the new supreme allied command in Southeast Asia, the special relationship again raised its head. "Remember," said Churchill to Mountbatten, "this is an allied job and you must be a good American as well as a good Englishman." Roosevelt told him, "Your job ought to have been given to an American. Remember you are as much my servant as Eisenhower is a servant to your King." Mountbatten then told the audience, "I tried to be a good American. I hope I was and I am trying again today."

Finally, Mountbatten quoted excerpts from two of Churchill's wartime speeches that he greatly admired as someone who held a high position in the war. One speech was made after Dunkirk, when Churchill spoke at the Commons and referenced Britain and the United States (the old and the new).

> We must be very careful not to assign to this deliverance the attributes of victory. (Referring to the expected invasion) We shall not flag or fail. We shall go on to the end. We shall fight in France. We shall fight in the seas and oceans. We shall fight on the landing grounds. We shall fight in the fields and in the streets. We shall fight in the hills. We shall never surrender. Even if, which I do not for a moment believe, this island or a large part of it were subjugated and starving, then our Empire beyond the seas would carry on the struggle. Until in God's good time, the new world with all its power and might steps forth to the rescue and liberation of the old.

He ended with a portion of the speech that Churchill made on the 18th of June after the fall of France. Churchill, once again, refers to the impact on Christianity.

> The battle of France is over. I expect the battle of Britain is about to begin. Upon this battle depends the survival of Christian civilization. The whole fury and might of the enemy must very soon be turned on us. Hitler knows that he will have to break us in this island or lose the war. If we can stand up to him all Europe may be free—and the life of the world may move forward into broad sunlit uplands. But if we fail, then the whole world will sink into the abyss of a new dark age. Let us therefore so brace ourselves to our duties—and so bear ourselves—that if the British Empire and the Commonwealth last for 1000 years, men will still say, "This was their finest hour."

Among the many people in the audience who heard that speech were Mary Soames, Churchill's daughter, and her son, Christopher. It was the finest hour of the celebration with the exception of the reveal of the rebuilt church, which awed everyone with its craftsmanship and beauty. As all the speakers noted, it symbolized both Churchill and his *Sinews of Peace* speech very well and had the added benefit of symbolizing the special relationship between the two countries that made the church relocation possible.

A number of songs played during the dedication paid homage to all the British representatives present. The one poem missing is one by Arthur Hugh Clough (1819-1861). Clough was an assistant to Florence Nightingale and married to her cousin. Churchill dearly loved the poem and quoted it on many an occasion, including in a radio address in 1941, when he forecast American sea aid to Britain. Entitled "Say Not the Struggle Nought Availeth," its unwavering words remind us that struggles are not hopeless and we should never give up.[485]

Say not the struggle nought availeth,
The labour and the wounds are vain,
The enemy faints not, nor faileth,
And as things have been they remain.

If hopes were dupes; fears may be liars;
It may be, in yon smoke concealed,
Your comrades chase e'en now the fliers,
And, but for you, possess the field.

For while the tired waves, vainly breaking,
Seem here no painful inch to gain,
Far back, through creeks and inlets making,
Comes silent, flooding in, the main.

And not by eastern windows only,
When daylight comes, comes in the light;
In front the sun climbs slow, how slowly,
But westward, look, the land is bright.

Winston Churchill breathed his last on January 24, 1965, four years prior to the church reveal.

For more information on the church, contact America's National Churchill Museum, https://www.nationalchurchillmuseum.org or visit the church and museum located at 501 Westminster Ave., Fulton, MO 65251-1299

Epilogue

On March 24, 1985, Sir John R. Colville, C.B., C.V.O., gave the fourth Crosby Kemper lecture at Westminster College. While at the college, he presented America's National Churchill Museum with a replica of the writing table in the library at Chartwell. Made by the firm of Arthur Brett of Norwich, it came to the museum due to the generosity of Heritage Arts, Ltd. and the efforts of the National Trust of England and Wales and the Royal Oak Society.

The former principal to Winston Churchill and famous diarist spoke about Churchill's character. He prefaced his comments by stating that Churchill, despite all his wonderful qualities, was not a perfect man. Like everyone else, he had his failings and just like the "finest emeralds, he had his flaws." But, he emphasized that Churchill's "defects were not vices."

One point that Colville emphasized was Churchill's belief that the common history and the commonality of speech, law, and literature between the United States and Britain formed the basis for a special relationship that would make it possible to do extraordinary things together, particularly in peacemaking ventures. He heard Churchill say the same on countless occasions.

Did that mean that the two countries would be in lock step or that Britain only wanted to ride the coat tails of the United States? Absolutely not.

While Churchill believed that the two countries could do much as partners, he did not believe that a relationship between the two countries prohibited other relationships. Yes, he believed that the United States was the hope of the future, but he did not give up on Britain. He knew that the United States had more power after World War II, while the power of Britain had diminished but that did not mean he saw an end to Britain's role on the world stage. Yes, Britain needed a loan from the United States as they had spent most of their resources on the war, but that did not mean he had no faith in Britain's ability to revitalize. As he stated at the end of his speech in Fulton, "Let no man underrate the abiding power of Britain or the Commonwealth."

Churchill believed in Britain and its people. His desire to join forces with the United States for the security of the world did not diminish his belief in his own country and its people. He believed in its constitutional monarchy and its unwritten constitution, which he thought gave it the flexibility to better deal with complex, modern problems, and the rights of the individual.

While he had concerns about the rigidness of the American constitution and the problems he thought were inherent in the separation of powers, Churchill did not think all countries should follow the same course in ensuring individual rights and fighting tyranny.

In looking back on what happened at the end of the war, Churchill realized that the Allies lost many opportunities by allowing Russia to expand its control. He tried to warn the world of the communist threat and the "mythological declaration of egalitarianism" by socialism. Alas, the world did not always listen

Churchill knew he made mistakes in life. He would never deny that. Impulsive as a youth, age taught Churchill the importance of responsibility and duty. His core values helped win the war and save democracy. His words, simple but effectively launched, lifted the morale of the British people, when all seem lost. Americans tend to think of Britain as one small island; however, during the World War II, the British Empire represented a quarter of the world's population, according to Colville, and almost a third of its territory. The entire British Commonwealth stood with Churchill during the war and Churchill stood for safety and peace in the world. They stood alone before the United States entered the war. He knew they could lead with or without a special relationship but he thought that together the two countries could accomplish even more.

Churchill had vision, creativeness, imagination, flexibility, and courage. He believed the British people had the enduring qualities and virtues that would always propel them forward. It is hard to imagine a better leader.

As Churchill wrote about Hopkins after his death, we shall not see his like again.

During the period May 3-5, 2019, Westminster hosted a 50th year celebration of the restoration of the Church of St. Mary the Virgin, Aldermanbury on the campus of the college in Fulton, Missouri. The imaginative concept that Churchill described became a reality and stands in memory of Churchill, his prescient speech, and the ability of people to overcome the worst tragedies. Like a phoenix, the church rises above the Fulton skyline and symbolizes the victory of democracy over tyranny.

Many notable people came to Fulton in 2019 to join in the celebration. Among them were descendants of Winston Churchill, including two granddaughters (the Hon. Emma Soames and the Hon. Edwina Sandys, M.B.E.) and two great-grandsons (Duncan Sandys and Jack Churchill). One granddaughter, Edwina Sandys, also gave a talk on the site of her famous *Breakthrough* sculpture.

The Reverend Canon Jonathon Brewster represented St. Paul's Cathedral in London, another remarkable church, which is a beneficiary of some of Christopher Wren's artistry. Also from the British Isles, the Rt. Hon. Lord Watson of Richmond C.B.E. participated in the ceremony. Author of the book, *Churchill's Legacy: Two Speeches to Save the World,* Lord Watson is a permanent High Steward of Cambridge University, a patron of Churchill Archives at Churchill College, former president of the Liberal Party, and Chairman of the Cambridge University. He had a breadth of experience and stories to impart to eager listeners on the college campus.

Andrew Roberts, author of the critically acclaimed biography of Winston Churchill, *Churchill: Walking with Destiny,* gave the Enid and R. Crosby Kemper Lecture at a luncheon on campus. He also signed books at a special luncheon on Friday evening. A highly acclaimed author, Westminster welcomed his presence and participation.

David Rubenstein, co-founder and executive chair of The Carlyle Group, one of the world's largest and most successful investment firms, gave the keynote address at a dinner on campus. Rubenstein hosts a successful cable television show and serves as Chairman of the Board of Trustees for the Kennedy Center, a member of the Board of Regents for the Smithsonian Institution (the world's largest museum and research complex), Trustee of the National Gallery of Art, the University of Chicago, Memorial Sloan-Kettering Cancer Center, Johns Hopkins Medicine, the Institute for Advanced Study, the National Constitution Center, the Brookings Institution, and the World Economic Forum, a Director of the Lincoln Center for the Performing Arts and the American Academy of Arts and Sciences, and the President of the Economic Club in Washington, DC. He previously served as Chairman of the Board of Trustees of Duke University and the Smithsonian Institution, and Co-Chairman of the Board of the Brookings Institution. The talented Mr. Rubenstein is a member of a number of other diverse organizations.

Mr. Rubenstein has been a leader in the area of Patriotic Philanthropy, having made transformative gifts for the restoration or repair of the Washington Monument, Monticello, Montpelier, Mount Vernon, Arlington House, Iwo Jima Memorial, the Kennedy Center, the Smithsonian, the National Archives, the National Zoo, the Library of Congress, and the National Museum of African American History and Culture. Mr. Rubenstein gave the US government long-term loans of his rare copies of the Magna Carta, the Declaration of Independence, the US Constitution, the Bill of Rights, the Emancipation Proclamation, the 13th Amendment, the first map of the US (Abel Buell map), and the first book printed in the US *(Bay Psalm Book).*

Other notable speakers and participants at the event included Esley Hamilton, popular Preservation Historian, who explored the nature of Wren's church designs and varied approaches to their preservation that have been taken in recent years. Bill Hart, Executive Director for Missouri Alliance for Historic Preservation, introduced him. They received a hearty reception from visitors anxious to learn about the history and preservation of the church.

Sculptor Don Wiegand gave a lecture on sculpting and did a hand cast of the hands of Churchill's great grandsons for exhibit at the museum. Frederick Hohman, Concert Organist, gave a musical potpourri on the famed Mandel organ that rests in the church of St. Mary. Dr. William Parish, former Harry S. Truman Professor of history and Professor Emeritus of History at Westminster, introduced him.

The Reverend Kelly Clarkson, a 1987 graduate of Westminster College and Yale Law School, served as officiant at the church service on Sunday. St. Peter's Episcopal Church in St. Louis, where she is Associate Rector, granted her leave to perform the service. The Reverend Canon Jonathon Brewster from St. Paul's Cathedral assisted her. The Choir from St. Peter's graced the service with wonderful music.

At the end of the ceremony the following men and women were inducted as Churchill Fellows: Brock Ayers, James F. Bennett, Prince Erik De Bourbon, Jack Churchill, Clementina "Tina" Santi Flaherty, Deborah G. Lindsay, Ken Murer, Dr. William E. Parrish, the Honorable Emma Soames, David M. Rubenstein, Don Foss, and Benjamin David Stinson (post humous).

A parade was held under brilliant blue and sunny skies in the city of Fulton during the weekend and the community gathered to help celebrate.

The continued preservation of the church was highlighted all weekend as people explored its wonders and soaked in its history.

Honorary Committee (1969)

Randolph Churchill, Co-Chairman
Governor Michael L. Parson, Co-Chairman
Mayor LeRoy D. Benton
Senator Roy Blunt
Philip J. Boeckman, Senior Fellow
Ambassador Stephen F. Brauer
Senator Christopher "Kit" Bond
Jack Churchill
Jennie Churchill
Tricia Nixon Cox
Senator John C. Danforth
Clifton Truman Daniel
Anne Eisenhower
Susan Eisenhower
Vera Fairbanks
Tina Santi-Flaherty
Laurence Geller, C.B.E.
Senator Josh Hawley
R. Crosby Kemper III
Representative Joseph P. Kennedy III
Henry Kissinger, Ph.D.
Fletcher M. Lamkin, Ph.D.
Richard J. Mahoney
The Rt Honorable Sir John Major KG CH
Richmond H. McCluer, Jr.
Jean-Paul Montupet
Governor Jay Nixon
John M. Panettiere
General (Ret) David H. Petraeus, Ph.D.
The Honorable Edwina Sandys, M.B.E.
Duncan Sandys
Monroe E. Trout, M.D.
The Honorable Emma Soames
The Rt. Honorable Sir Nicholas Soames
The Rt. Honorable Lord Watson of Richmond, C.B.E

Board of Governors of Association of Churchill Fellows

Emeriti and Ex Officio

50th Anniversary
America's National Churchill Museum
Event Schedule
May 3rd to 5th, 2019

Friday, May 3rd

11 a.m. -- Registration Opens

America's National Churchill Museum

11 a.m., 1 p.m. and 2 p.m. -- Museum Tours

Meet at the Front Desk of America's National Churchill Museum

1 p.m. -- 50th Anniversary Commemorative Tour

The 1 p.m. tour will be led by author, artist and videographer **Steve Stinson**, who served as one of the original tour guides for the Museum during the 1960s. Mr. Stinson's father, **Dave Stinson**, was the Vice President at Westminster responsible for organizing the remarkable relocation from London to Fulton and rebuilding of the Church of St. Mary the Virgin, Aldermanbury.

3 p.m. -- Opening Lecture: *Preserving the Past: Christopher Wren's Church of St. Mary the Virgin, Aldermanbury*

Church of St. Mary the Virgin, Aldermanbury

Taken together, Sir Christopher Wren's 52 London parish churches constitute one of the greatest architectural achievements of the Baroque era. **Esley Hamilton**, Preservation Historian with St. Louis County Parks, will discuss how war and expanding commerce have taken a major toll on this heritage, however, and today the surviving buildings are doubly precious. This talk will explore the nature of Wren's church designs and varied approaches to their preservation that have been taken in recent years.

4:30 p.m. -- Opening Concert: *A Recital on the Noel Mander Organ*

Church of St. Mary the Virgin, Aldermanbury

Churchill Fellow **Frederick Hohman** transforms the pipe organ from a "Sunday morning" instrument into a virtual symphony orchestra. Critics have noted his intense energy "like a victorious athlete" [*Portland Press Herald, Maine*], thoughtful interpretations "full of fantasy" [*Raleigh News and Observer*], his creative use of organ tone with "registrations appropriately kaleidoscopic" [The American Organist magazine], and his pedal technique "the best you'll ever hear" [*St. Louis Post-Dispatch*]. Fellow Hohman will be playing the Church's Mander organ, built and installed by the well-known British organ builder Noel Mander. While Mander's most famous organ is installed at St. Paul's Cathedral in London, the Aldermanbury organ is considered by many the finest baroque organ in America, while also having a unique hybrid construction and pedal rank allowing contemporary music to be played on the instrument. His concerts have brought appreciative audiences in America and abroad to their feet, sometimes more than once, during a concert.

6:00 p.m. – Reception with Churchill Family Members and a Preview of New Museum Exhibits

(For 50th Anniversary Sponsors Only)

Plaza Outside America's National Churchill Museum

- *Painting as a Pastime: From Winston to the White House*
- *An Imaginative Concept: Christopher Wren's St. Mary the Virgin, Aldermanbury Journey to Fulton*
- *The Special Relationship Project*

Together with members of the Churchill family, guests will have a preview of these three exciting exhibitions. Inspired by **Winston Churchill**, Presidents **Eisenhower**, **Kennedy** and **George W. Bush** became enthusiastic amateur painters. For the first time ever, paintings by these remarkable American presidents will be publicly displayed along with works by Winston Churchill. Another exhibition celebrates the audacious relocation of **Christopher Wren**'s 17th century Church of St. Mary the Virgin, Aldermanbury from London to Fulton in the 1960s. As Churchill himself proclaimed, this "imaginative concept" was the work of many individuals across Missouri, the United States and across the pond in the United Kingdom. A third exhibition features over 4,000 works of art created by **K-12 students** from Mid-Missouri whose paintings explore the idea of "special relationship," a term coined by Winston Churchill in his Fulton speech.

Program of events for 50th Anniversary celebration.

7:00 p.m. -- Dinner and Program with Members of the Churchill Family

Mueller Leadership Hall—Backer Dining Hall

A dinner and spirited program with **Clementine** and **Winston Churchill**'s granddaughters The Hon. **Edwina Sandys**, M.B.E. and The Hon. **Emma Soames**; great-grandsons **Jack Churchill and Duncan Sandys**; former Monsanto CEO and legendary Churchillian **Richard Mahoney;** and, biographer **Andrew Roberts**.

Saturday, May 4th

8:30 a.m. -- Registration Opens

America's National Churchill Museum

9 a.m., 1 p.m. and 3 p.m. -- Museum Tours

Guests will enjoy three new museum exhibits as they tour the museum throughout the weekend. Meet at the Front Desk of America's National Churchill Museum. The exhibits are:

- *Painting as a Pastime: From Winston to the White House:* Inspired by Churchill, Presidents **Eisenhower**, **Kennedy** and **George W. Bush** became enthusiastic amateur painters, and for the first time, their paintings, along with works by **Churchill**, will be publicly exhibited during our 50th anniversary celebration.
- *An Imaginative Concept: Christopher Wren's St. Mary the Virgin, Aldermanbury Journey to Fulton:* This exhibit, which includes historic photos, archival documents, and artifacts regarding the arduous relocation of **Christopher Wren**'s 17th century Church of St. Mary the Virgin, Aldermanbury from London to Fulton in the 1960s.
- *The Special Relationship Project:* Our third exhibit features over 4,000 works of art created by **K-12 students** from Mid-Missouri who explore the idea of "special relationship," a term coined by Churchill in his Fulton speech.

10 a.m., 2:30 p.m. and 4 p.m. -- Walking in Churchill and Truman's Footsteps Tour

Meet Outside the Front Entrance of America's National Churchill Museum

Walk in the footsteps of **Winston Churchill** and President **Harry Truman** when they visited the campus of Westminster College on March 5th, 1946. Tour the **Historic Gymnasium**, where the "Iron Curtain" Speech was given, and **Washington West**, the College President's house where Winston Churchill enjoyed a nap, a meal, and drink. Special guests will include Churchill Fellow **Baxter Watson**, who, as a Westminster College student in 1946, led Winston Churchill and President Truman into the Historic Gymnasium.

9:00 a.m. -- Meet the Authors and Book Signing

Inside America's National Churchill Museum

An opportunity to meet with noted authors **Andrew Roberts**, who's recent biography of Churchill *Walking with Destiny* has made the *New York Times* bestseller list; **Lord Alan Watson**, whose *Two Speeches to Save the World* chronicles the incredible impact of Churchill's Fulton and Zurich speeches; **Jim Wilson**, the award winning author of the historical fiction *Churchill and Roosevelt: The Big Sleepover at the White House;* **Tina Santi Flaherty**, whose *What's Jackie Taught Us* highlights the heroic battles of both Jacqueline Kennedy and Winston Churchill; and, **Edwina Sandys**, whose career and life is captured in *Art.* Her book *Winston Churchill: Painting as a Pastime* remains the Museum's best-selling book.

10:00 a.m. -- Continuing the Special Relationship: Sculptural Life Casting of Special Guests

Inside America's National Churchill Museum

Sculptor and Churchill Fellow **Don Wiegand** will make life casts of two surprise guests--one American, the other British--to symbolize the ongoing special relationship, a term Churchill introduced in his Fulton speech, between the United States and Great Britain.

11:00 a.m. -- Meet the Artist and Experience Breakthrough

In front of *Breakthrough* sculpture (Berlin Wall)

Internationally acclaimed artist and Churchill granddaughter The Hon. **Edwina Sandys**, M.B.E., will discuss her monumental sculpture, ***Breakthrough***, comprised of eight sections of the Berlin Wall, with a dramatic introduction and special guests.

12:00 p.m. -- For Military Level Sponsors and Up, a Private Reception with Andrew Roberts

The Panettiere Room in the Backer Dining Hall

12:30 p.m. -- Enid and R. Crosby Kemper Lecture and Luncheon

Mueller Leadership Hall-Backer Dining Hall

Churchill Fellow **Andrew Roberts** will inform and entertain with "Churchill and Humor," drawn from his recently published and widely acclaimed Churchill biography *Walking with Destiny*, which is a *New York Times* bestseller. Fellow Roberts, who will emphasize Churchill's sense of humor, which he used to good effect in every facet of his life, joins legendary Churchill biographer **Sir Martin Gilbert** as the only other person to give the prestigious Enid and R. Crosby Lecture twice.

2:30 p.m. -- 50th Anniversary Parade

Across from America's National Churchill Museum

Enjoy a fun time with members of the Churchill and Truman families and other VIPs at the 50th Anniversary Parade, which will include U.S. **military bands**, **high school bands**, the St. Andrews Society **Pipes and Drum Corps**, the **Air Attaché British Embassy**, the Commanding **Officer 4th Fighter Group** U.S. Air Force, and other VIPs. There also will be historic **military vehicles**, and much, much more as we retrace the route Winston Churchill and President Harry Truman took when they arrived in Fulton March 5, 1946. There also will be a special salute to the **Eagle Squadrons** of WWII and one of their own, **Lt. John Lutz,** of Fulton.

Parade Route: Starts at the corner of Westminster Avenue and W. 7th Street, South on Westminster Avenue, East on 5th Street, North on Court, West on 7th Street, and ends after passing the Museum.

3:30 p.m. -- Board of Governors Meeting

Clementine Room in America's National Churchill Museum

5:30 p.m. – For Military Level Sponsors and Up, a Private Reception to Meet David Rubenstein

America's National Churchill Museum

6:00 p.m. – Churchill Gala with David Rubenstein (Business Attire)

Historic Gymnasium

Join members of the **Churchill Family** and Co-Founder and Co-Executive Chairman of The Carlyle Group **David Rubenstein** for a gala in Westminster College's Historic Gymnasium, the site of Winston Churchill's historic "Sinews of Peace" (or the "Iron Curtain" speech).

Sunday, May 5th

10:00 a.m. – 11:15 a.m.- Special 50th Anniversary Service

Church of St. Mary the Virgin, Aldermanbury

Join us for a special commemorative service in honor of the Church of St. Mary the Virgin, Aldermanbury's 50th anniversary with Canon Jonathan Brewster, Treasurer of St. Paul's Cathedral in London, the Rev. Kelly Carlson, of Ladue, MO, Lord Alan Watson of Richmond, and others. Nine new Churchill Fellows also will be installed. Coffee, tea and pastries will be served after the ceremonies.

-- **Denotes events that are free and open to the public**

Endnotes

FRONT QUOTATION

1 Winston Churchill, *Churchill by Himself,* edited by Richard Langworth, New York: Public Affairs, 2008, pp. 18

DEDICATION

2 *The 8th Air Force vs. The Luftwaffe,* National World War II Museum, October 18, 2017, https://www.nationalww2museum.org

3 Ibid.

4 Winston Churchill, *The Few,* August 20, 1940, *Winston Churchill by Himself,* edited by Richard Langworth, (Public Affairs: New York, 2008), p. 6

INTRODUCTION

5 *Group to Stop Over Briefly in St. Louis on Way to Fulton for Speech Tomorrow, St. Louis Post Dispatch,* March 4, 1946

6 Max Coffey, *Crowd Plaudit to Churchill,* Omaha World Herald, March 6, 1946, and, Carlos F. Hunt, *Churchill Urges Settlement of Russia Issues, Peril in Delay, St. Louis Post-Dispatch,* March 6, 1936

7 Richard Everrett and Mary Kimbrough, *Churchill Proposes US-British Coalition to Restrain Russia, St. Louis Star,* March 6, 1946.

8 *How Churchill Happened to Accept Fulton Invitation, The St. Louis Star and Times,* January 11, 1946

9 Richard Langworth, *Origins of Churchill's Phrases: 'Special Relationship and Iron Curtain',* September 4, 2019. https://richardlangworth.com/iron-curtain-special-relationship

10 Richard M. Hunt, *Tyranny is Our Foe, Harvard Magazine,* September 6, 1918, https://www.harvardmagazine.com/churchill-18

11 Ibid.

12 National Churchill Muscum, https://www.nationalchurchillmuseum.org/winston-churchill-the-writer.html

13 *Perfect Fit,* St. Louis Post Dispatch, September 2, 1990

14 *Churchill by Himself,* Edited by Richard Langworth, September 9, 1941, p. 7

15 Winston Churchill, *A History of the English-Speaking Peoples, Volume 1: The Birth of Britain,* (London: Cassell, 1956), vii-viii.

16 Winston Churchill, *Winston Churchill: By Himself,* ed. by Richard Langworth, (New York: Public Affairs, 2008), p. 577.

PART ONE: Special Relationship: Winston Churchill's Sinews of Peace (Iron Curtain) Speech

CHAPTER 1

17 *Today in History: The "Show Me" State,* August 10, Library of Congress, https://www.loc.gov

18 Dred Scott, 60 US393 (1856)

19 Jeremy Neely, *Civil War on the Western Border: The Missouri-Kansas Conflict 1 855-1865, Order Number 11,* Missouri State University, https://www.civilwaronthewesternborder.org

20 *Civil War on the Border: The Missouri-Kansas Conflict, 1855-1865, Liberty Arsenal,* Missouri State University, https://www.civilwaronthewesternborder.org

21 Christopher Phillips, *Civil War on the Border: The Missouri-Kansas Conflict 1855-1865, Nathaniel Lyon,* University of Cincinnati, https://www.civilwaronthewesternborder.org

22 Christopher Phillips, *Civil War on the Border: The Missouri-Kansas Conflict 1855-1865, Claiborne Fox Jackson,* University of Cincinnati, https://www.civilwaronthewesternborder.org and, Ibid. *Neosho, Missouri*

23 *Why Are There 13 Stars on the Confederate Flag?,* https://www.confederateflags.org

24 *Agricultural Libraries, Information Notes,* Volume 15, No. 3, p. 5

25 Andrew M. Saeger, *The Kingdom of Callaway: Callaway County, Missouri, During the Civil War,* thesis, Northwest Missouri State College, Maryville, Mo, p. 6, https://www.nwmissouri.edu

26 John E. Pickel, *The Town That Jacks Built,* December 8, 1917, *The Country Gentleman,* p.6, and
History of Jack Stock and Mules in Missouri, Volume 22, Number 3, Missouri Department of Agriculture, Jefferson City, pp. 4-26, https://www.google.books.com

27 University of Missouri Digital Library, https://www.dl.mospace.umsystem.edu

28 *Antebellum Resources of Johnson, Lafayette, Pettis and Saline Counties, Missouri,* October 9, 1997, pp. 3-4, https://www.dnr.mo.gov/shpo and, Saeger, p. 6

29 Michelle Brooks, *190 Years As the Capital City,* (Jefferson City) *News Tribune,* September 20, 2016, https://www.newstribune.com

30 *Survey and Inventory of Boone Historic Area, Phase I,* https://www.dnr.mo.gov

31 William E. Parrish, *A History of Missouri (1860-1875): Radicalism in the Saddle,* Volume III, (University of Missouri Press: Columbia, 2001).

32 *To Thomas Jefferson from Volney, November 16, 1793,* Founders Online, National Archives, https://founders.archives.org , and,
Bushnell Dimond, *Gilbert Stuart's Portrait of Volney Presented by Mrs. Thomas Bayard, Philadelphia Inquirer*, September 24, 1922

33 C. Seymour Bullock, *Centenary of American Commerce, The Connecticut Magazine*: An Illustrated Monthly, Volume 11, p.366, https://www.books.google.com

34 *Old School Presbyterians,* {St. Louis Republican}, *Daily National Intelligencer,* Washington, DC, November 20, 1852

35 B. Waugh, *What Are the Old School and New School?* Presbyterians of the Past, March 28, 2019, https://www.presbyteriansofthepast.com

36 Ovid Bell, *Callaway County: Westminster College,* edited by Walter Williams, (Lewis Publishing Company: Chicago, 1913), p. 300

37 *Laying the Cornerstone, Daily Missouri Republican*, St. Louis, July 5, 1853

38 *Anti-Duel Rule at Westminster College Revoked,* St. *Louis Post Dispatch*, June 6, 1939

39 *The Schism of 1861: Issue of Slavery,* The American Presbyterian Church, Presbyterian Church History, Lesson 7, https://www.americanpresbyterianchurch.org

40 Larry Hall, *Missouri's 'Kingdom of Callaway' Sprucing Up Excitedly for Historic Churchill-Truman Visit, Corpus Christi Caller-Times*, January 27, 1946

CHAPTER 2

41 David McCullough, *Truman,* (Simon & Schuster: New York, 1992), pp. 29-32

42 *Remarks at a Cornerstone Laying of the Westminster Church, Alexandria, Virginia,* Harry S. Truman, 33rd President of the United States (1945-1953),
The American Presidency Project, University of California, Santa Barbara, https://www.presidency.ucsb.edu

43 *Franc L. McCluer, Educator, Dies, St. Louis Post Dispatch*, April 2, 1979

44 *Ex-Premier and Truman Get Ovation from Huge Crowds in Fulton Parade, St. Louis Post Dispatch*, March 5, 1946

45 Thomas Snyder, Editor, *120 Years of American Education: A Statistical Portrait,* Department of Education, Center for Education Studies, January 1993 https://www.nces.ed.gov

46 *Mary Baldwin's Chief Stresses Tradition, Faith, Richmond Times Dispatch*, April 17, 1955

47 *Dr. McCluer Bacalaureate Speaker at Washington University, St. Louis Post Dispatch,* June 5, 1955, and,
Shallow Thinking Perils Democracy Dr., McCluer Suggests, St. Louis Star and Times, June 2, 1947

CHAPTER 3

48 Dr. William E. Parrish, *The Columns,* Westminster College, May 2, 1969

49 *State's New Constitution To Be a Good One, McCluer Says, St. Louis Star and Times,* March 28, 1944

50 Harry Wohl, *The President's Harry Vaughan, St. Louis Star and Times*, August 18, 1949

51 Paul R. Leach, *Who's Who in the News: Maj. Gen. Harry Vaughan, from Salesman to White House Jester,* August 21, 1949

52 Harry Wohl

53 Jerald L. Hill and William D. Stilley, *General Harry H. Vaughan Oral History Interview,* March 20, 1976, Harry S. Truman Library and Museum, https://www.trumanlibrary.gov

54 Harry Wohl

55 J. Y. Smith, *Maj. Gen. Harry Vaughan, Aide to President Truman, Dies, Washington Post*, May 22, 1981, https://www.trumanlibrary.gov

56 Ibid.

57 Chester A. Bradley {in the Kansas City Star}, *Mr. Churchill and the 'Old College Try,' Milwaukee Journal*, January 27, 1946

58 Charles T. Morrissey, *General Harry H. Vaughan Oral History Interview, January 10, 1963,* Harry S. Truman Library and Museum.

59 Charles T. Morrisey, Vaughan's actual description of what Harry Truman wrote on the letter, as described in this interview, is somewhat different than what actually happened. Time caused Vaughan to forget the exact wording. He did not address it to Winnie, as Vaughan thought. His exact words are shown in the text. Vaughan's description was: "Dear Winnie: This is a fine old college out in my state. If you'll come out and make them a speech, I'll take you out and introduce you, Signed, Harry Truman." The Truman Library and Museum did a wonderful job in interviewing Vaughan and the interview may be accessed on their website, https://www.trumanlibrary.gov

CHAPTER 4

60 Ibid.

61 Ibid.

62 Richard Everett, *St. Louis Star and Times,* March 4, 1946

CHAPTER 5

63 St. Louis *Star and Times*, January 15, 1946

64 Haywood Vincent, *Thanks, Texans!—Churchill, Dallas Morning News*, January 20, 1946

65 Ibid.

66 *Churchill Down South, Augusta Chronicle,* January 18, 1946

67 Martin Gilbert, *Winston S. Churchill: Never Despair, 1945-1965,* (Hillsdale: Hillsdale College Press, 1988), p. 182 and, Timothy Riley, *Finest Hour, 178, Fall 2018,* International Churchill Society, https://www.winstonchurchill.org

68 *Where Churchills Relax in Florida, Greensboro Daily News*, January 21, 1946

69 Jimmie Fidler, *In Hollywood, St Louis Star and Times*, April 7, 1946

70 Deborah C. Pollack and Paul S. George, Resident Historian, History Miami Museum, *Vintage Miami Beach Glamour: Celebrities & Socialites in the Heyday of Chic,* (History Press: Charleston, South Carolina, 2019), p. 60

71 Martin Gilbert, *Churchill and America,* (New York: Free Press, 2005), p. 367 and, Letters of 17 and 25 February 1946, Churchill Papers, 2/210, and, Martin Gilbert, *Winston S. Churchill,* pp. 191-193

72 *Truman to Meet Churchill While on Florida Trip, St. Louis Star and Times,* February 1, 1946

73 *For the Record,* C-SPAN, https://www.c-span.org

74 *Bernard Baruch,* Jewish Virtual Library: A Project of AICE, https://www.jewishvirtuallibrary.com and, *Baruch, Bernard M.,* Encyclopedia.com, Oxford University Press, https://www.encyclopedia.com

75 *Bernard Baruch Coins the Term Cold War,* History, https://www.history.com

76 *Baruch, Bernard M.,* Enclyclopedia.com, https://www.encyclopedia.com

77 David McCullough, p. 327

78 Jonathon R. Logsdon, *Power, Ignorance, and Anti-Semitism: Henry Ford and His War on Jews,* Hanover College, Madison, Indiana, https://www.hanover.edu

79 *Maimonides' Eight Levels of Charity,* Chassidic Thought, https://www.chabad.org

80 *Miami Daily News,* January 16, 1946, and, Martin Gilbert, p. 182

81 Martin Gilbert, *Winston S. Churchill,* p. 192

82 *Truman Signs British Loan; Credit for More, He Says, Chicago Sun,* July 16, 1946

83 Drew Pearson, *Byrnes Plans New Combine to Guide US Foreign Policy,* (Quincy (MA) Patriot Ledger, February 1, 1946)

CHAPTER 6

84 *Hopkins Is Eulogized by Winston Churchill, Register-Republic* (Rockford, IL), January 30, 1946

85 *Truman to Meet Churchill While on Florida Trip, St. Louis Star and Times,* February 1, 1946

86 Richard S. Davis, *Folks Pour Into Fulton to Hear Churchill Talk, Milwaukee Journal,* March 4, 1946

87 *Clark M. Clifford Papers, 1946-1950,* Harry S. Truman Library and Museum, https://www.trumanlibrary.gov

88 *Harry S. Truman (1945-1953),* The American Presidency Project, University of California, Santa Barbara, https://www.ucsb.edu

89 W. Dale Nelson, *Standing in for the President, Part 2,* National Archives, Prologue Magazine, Summer 1999, Volume 3, No. 2 and, Transcript, Ross Papers, July 10, 1931, The Harry S. Truman Library and Museum, Independence, MO, https://www.trumanlibrary.gov

90 *Statement by the President on the Death of Charles G. Ross,* The American Presidency Project, University of California, Santa Barbara, https://www.ucsb.edu

91 *Bretton Woods Conference, 1944,* US Department of State, Archive, https://www.2001-2009.state.gov

92 *Nevertheless She Assisted,* Churchill College, Archives Centre, Cambridge, https://www.chu.com.ac.uk

93 Alan Watson, *Churchill's Legacy,* (Bloomsbury Publishing: New York, 2016), p. 58

94 Clark Clifford with Richard Holbrooke, *Counsel to the President: A Memoir,* (Random House: New York, 1991), p. 102

95 Ibid. p. 101

96 Ibid.

97 Ibid. p. 102

CHAPTER 7

98 *President Chats with Friends Here, St. Louis Post Dispatch*, March 5, 1946

99 *Truman Aide Recalls 'Iron Curtain' Speech,* E.F. Porter, Jr., *St. Louis Post Dispatch, The St. Charles Post*, May 8, 1979

100 Richard Langworth, *Churchill, Truman and Poker on the Train to Fulton, March 1946,* July 6, 1986, https://www.richardlangworth.com

101 Andrew M. Saeger, *The Kingdom of Callaway: Callaway County, Missouri, During the Civil War,* A Thesis, Northwest Missouri State University, Maryville, Missouri, April 2013

102 Ibid.

103 *Fulton, Welcome Mat Out, Awaits Truman, Churchill, St. Louis Star and Times,* March 4, 1949

104 *Robert James Paquette, December 19, 1929-November 29, 2018,* Obituary, Legacy, https://www.legacy.com

105 *Radio Favorites,* St. Louis Post Dispatch, Eve*ryday Magazine*, March 4, 1946

106 William E. Parrish, *Westminster College: An Informal History, 1851-1999,* Westminster College, Fulton, 2000, pp. 201-202

CHAPTER 8

107 *Children Perched on Roofs, Sidewalks Packed from Curb to Buildings— Briton Waves Black Cigar to Crowd, St. Louis Post Dispatch*, March 5, 1946 and, *Churchill Proclaims the Pig at the Highest Point of Evolution, St. Louis Post Dispatch*, March 6, 1946

108 Ibid.

109 The text of the speech is contained in the Appendix.

110 Stanley Meisler, *United Nations: A History,* New York: Grove Press, 1995), pp. 1-7

111 Ibid.

112 James B. Reston, *Fear Misuse of Oaks Plan, Boston Herald-New York Times Dispatch,* April 20, 2945

113 Ibid.

114 Ibid. and,
Associated Press and Kennedy Scoop the World, Jersey Journal, May 8, 1945

115 David R. Shribman, *James "Scotty" Reston: Scared and Sinned as He Changed the Style of Journalism,* (John F. Stacks Book Review), *Chicago Tribune*, December 1, 2002, https://www.chicagotribune.com and,
Leonard Miale, *Obituary: James Reston, Independent*, December 8, 1995

116 Philip White, *Our Supreme Task,* (Public Affairs: New York, 2012), p. 182

117 W. Averell Harriman and Elie Abel, *Special Envoy to Churchill and Stalin, 1941-1946,* (Random House: New York, 1975), p. 496

118 Ibid. p. 519

119 Martin Gilbert, Winston S. Churchill, p. 683

CHAPTER 9

120 *Churchill Expected Speech to Be a Major Policy Statement, Jefferson City News Tribune*, March 3, 1996, and,
Phillip White p. 191

121 Anne Applebaum, *Iron Curtain: The Crushing of Eastern Europe, 1944-1956,* (New York: Anchor Books, 2012), 194

122 Martin Gilbert, *The World Crisis, 1911-1918*, (Free Press: New York, 2005), Introduction, p. xv

123 Rob Havers, *Where Was That 'Iron Curtain' Anyway,* America's National Churchill Museum, https://www.nationalchurchillmuseum.org

124 Richard Bessel, *Germany 1945,* (Pocket Books: New York, 2010), pp. 220-239

125 *Szcsecin,* Wikipedia, https://www.en.wikipedia.org and,
Beata Halicka, *The Everyday Life of Children in Polish-German Borderlands During the Early Postwar Period,* from *Borderland Studies Meets Child Studies,* edited by Machteid Venken, Peter Lang, February 5, 2018, https://www.peterlang.com, and
Portion of Port Given to Poles, Milwaukee Journal from New York Times News Service, March 25, 1946

126 Bogden C. Novak, *American Policy Toward the Slovenian Trieste, 1941-1974,* https://www.3442-3281-1-p.13 and,
Slovenes, Encyclopedia of Cleveland History, Case Western Reserve University, https://www.case.edu/ech and,
Trieste, Wikipedia, https://www.en.wikipedia.org and,
Sumner Wells, *Western Powers Must Be Firm on Trieste, Dallas Morning News,* June 29, 1946, and,
Border Plan Hit by Slavs, D*allas Morning News*, September 8, 1946, and,
Anglo-American Policies in Italy Wrong, Dallas Morning News, December 14, 1946, and
Julian March, Wikipedia, https://www.en.wikipedia.org and,
Enakopravnost, Ohio History Central, https://www.ohiohistorycentral.org and,

Trieste Imposes Knotty Problem for Allies, Dallas Morning News, May 16, 1945, and,
Troops in Control, Tito Quits Trieste, Dallas Morning News, May 21, 1945, and,
A. p. Taylor, *Trieste*, Enakopravnost, February 4, 1946, and,
Allies Make Trieste Pact with Tito, Dallas Morning News, June 10, 1945, and,
Drew Pearson, *Washington Merry-Go-Round, Dallas Morning News*, May 26, 1945, and,
Trieste: Stepchild of Many, The *Oregonian*, November 11, 1945, and,
Louis Adamic, *Trieste: A Vital Challenge to the Big 3,* Enakopravnost, June 4, 1945, and,
Frederick Kuh, *Comintern Rebirth Called Russia's Retreat to the Defensive, Chicago Daily Times*, October 12, 1947

127 *US, Britain Join in Recognizing Poles of Warsaw Regime, Dallas Morning News,* July 6, 1945, and,
Polish Envoy Blasts Nod to Warsaw, Dallas Morning News, July 8, 1945

128 Winston Churchill, *Sinews of Peace* speech, America's National Churchill Museum

129 *Communists Emerge as Strongest Party in Czechoslovakia, Washington DC Evening Star*, May 26, 1946

130 Herbert Corn, *Wreckage of Danube Bridge Blocks Trade Restoration, Washington DC Evening Star*, August 2, 1946, and,
Phillip Parrish, *Magic of Vienna Proves Difficult to Miss Despite Stern Realities Brought on by War,* Portland: *The Oregonian*, November 13, 1946, and,
Drew Pearson, *Washington Merry-Go-Round, Dallas Morning News*, June 22, 1945

131 Diana Preston, *Eight Days at Yalta*, (New York: Atlantic Monthly Press, 2019), p.186

132 *Horror Era in Hungary Described, Dallas Morning News*, July 8, 1945, and,
Driven Out of Budapest by Nazis, Thousands Die on Way to Austria, Pittsburgh National Labor Tribune, February 17, 1945 and,
Germans Falter in Budapest Tilt, D*allas Morning News*, January 11, 1945, and,
Budapest Forlorn Heap of Wreckage, Laurel, *Montana Outlook*, February 13, 1945

133 *Did Yugoslavian Dictator Tito Poison Stalin? Historian Claims He Killed Rival After Being the Target of 22 Assassination Attempts,* D*aily Mail Reporter*, July 18, 2012, https://www.dailymail.com

CHAPTER 10

134 *Crimean Conference,* February 27, 1946, https://www.api.parliament.uk

135 *$300,000,000 Reparations is Price Hungary Must Pay, St. Louis Star and Times*, July 21, 1946, and,
Bulgarian Voting Heavy in Single-Slate Election, St. Louis Post Dispatch, November 19, 1945, and,
US Again Warns Bulgaria on Forthcoming Elections, St. Louis Post Dispatch, November 16, 1945, and,
R. H. Markham, *Bulgaria, Wilmington (MC) Morning Star*, March 28, 1945

136 James C. Humes, *The Sir Winston Method: The Five Secrets of Speaking the Language of Leadership,* (William and Morrow Company: New York), 1991, pp. 27-28

137 *Fulton Speech Draws Divergent Comment, St. Louis Post Dispatch*, March 6, 1946

138 Ibid.

139 Comments by senators, *Associated Press, Times-Picayune, New Orleans, LA,* March 6, 1946

CHAPTER 11

140 Comments of representatives, *Congress Divided in Opinions about Churchill's Speech, Dallas Morning News,* March 7, 1946

141 British press comments, *Atlee Link to Alliance Proposal by Churchill Scouted by MPs,* Even*ing Star Washington DC*, March 6, 1946

142 San Francisco Chronicle, March 10, 1946

143 Ibid.

144 Ibid.

145 *Chicago Sun,* March 17, 1946

146 Eleanor Roosevelt, Chicago Daily Times, March 7, 1946

147 Clark Clifford, Oral Interview, April 13, 1976, with Jerry N. Hess, Truman Library and Museum, https://www.trumanlibrary.gov

148 George Washington, *Washington's Farewell Address*, 1796, The Avalon Project, https://www.avalon.law.yale.edu

149 Thomas Jefferson, *First Inaugural Address,* 1801, The Avalon Project, https://www.avalon.law.yale.edu

150 Speech, Harvard University, Cambridge, Massachusetts, September 6, 1943, Richard Langworth editor, *Churchill by Himself,* (Public Affairs: New York, 2008), p. 134

151 Speech, Westminster College, Fulton, Missouri, March 5, 1946

152 ibid, Speech, Ritz-Carlton Hotel, New York, March 25, 1949

153 Thomas Jefferson's *First Inaugural Address,* March 4, 1801

154 Ibid.

155 George Washington's *Farewell Address,* 1796

156 Ibid. Thomas Jefferson

157 *The Language of Liberty,* speech by Margaret Thatcher Speech to the English-Speaking Union in New York, December 7, 1999, Margaret Thatcher Foundation, https://www.margaretthatcher.org

CHAPTER 12

158 Ibid.

159 Ibid.

160 *Bitter Denunciation*, *Daily Illinois State Journal*, March 12, 1946, and, *Russians Not Surprised by Churchill Talk, Daily Illinois State Journal*, March 12, 1946 and, Sidney Fine, *Churchill Incites War say Russia, Chicago Daily Times*, March 11, 1946 and, *Pravda*, *J.V. Stalin on Post-War International Relations,* Stalin's response to *Pravda* correspondent's questions on Churchill's speech at Westminster College, *Soviet News*, 1947, Brian Reid for MIA, 2008, https://www.marxists.org

161 Ibid.

162 Ibid.

163 Ibid.

164 Ibid.

165 *GIs Told: Don't Criticize Russia!, Chicago Daily Times*, March 11, 1946

166 Clark Clifford, Oral History, with Jerry N. Hess, March 16, 1972, Truman Library, https://www.trumanlibrary.gov

167 Winston Churchill, *History of the English-Speaking Peoples, Volume 1*

PART TWO: Special Relationship: British History Explains British-American Ties

CHAPTER 14

168 Winston Churchill, Richard Langworth, Editory, Churchill by Himself, pp. 116-117, Liberty Day Meeting, London, *Winston S. Churchill: His Complete Speeches, 1897-1963,* Volume III, (New York: Cheslea House/Bowker, 1974) and,

169 https://www.Poetryfoundation.org

170 https://www.Shakespeare.org.uk

171 Ibid. and Leslie Dunton-Downer and Alan Riding, *Essential Shakespeare Handbook,* (DK Publishing: New York, 2013), 14.

172 *Shakespeare's First Folio.* https://www.bl.uk/collection-items/shakespeares-first-folio#

173 *Obituary Notice, Fellow, Charles Clement Walker,* Report of the Council of the Seventy-Eighth General Meeting, Monthly Notices of the Royal Astronomical Society, Vol. 58, p. 152, SAO/NASA Astrophysics Data System, https://www.adsbs.harvard.edu

174 E. A. B. Barnard, F. S.A., F. R. Hist. S., *New Links with Shakespeare,* (Cambridge University Press: London, 1930), p. 95

175 Ibid. 96

176 https://www.shakespeare.org.uk/exploreshakespeare/shakespedia/shakespeares-words/

177 All dates are Common Era (CE).

CHAPTER 15
Roman London

178 Library of Congress, *Columbus Day,* https://www.loc.gov.item/today-in-history/October-12

179 Christian E. Hauer Jr. and William S. Young, *A Comprehensive History of the London Church and Parish of St. Mary, the Virgin, Aldermanbury, (*Lewston: New York, 1994), pp. 2-3

180 *London*, March 7, 2019, https://www.History.com

181 Tim Lambert, *A Brief History of London, England,* https://www.localhistories.org

182 Simon Schama, *A History of Britain: At the Edge of the World (3500 BC – 1603 AD),* p. 29

183 Winston Churchill, *Marlborough: His Life and Times, Vol. 1,* (Scribner's Sons: New York, 1968), p. xxviii

184 Rebecca Fraser, *The Story of Britain,* Vol. 1, (New York: W.W. Norton & Company, 2005, pp. 11-13

185 Peter Stone, *The History of the Port of London: A Vast Emporium of All Nations,* Barnsley, (Pen & Sword History: South Yorkshire, 2017), p. 3.

186 Roman London, https://www.projectbritain.com

187 Ibid. pp. 3-5.

188 Ben Johnson, *London's Roman Basilica and Forum, History Magazine*, no page given.

189 *Discover Roman London,* https://www.londonmithraeum.com

190 Strong, p. 15.

191 *Ancient Roman Cuisine,* en.wikipedia.org. and
Roman Britain, "The Romans in Britain Roman Recipe Sauce,"
https://www.romanbritain.org.

192 Strong, p. 12.

193 Strong, pp. 15-16.

194 Saltassociation.co.uk and Wim Hordijk, *From Salt to Salary: Linguistics Takes a Page from Science*, npr.org.

195 Fraser, p. 21.

Anglo-Saxon London

196 Robert Tombs, *The English and their History (*Alfred A. Knopf: New York, 2015*)*, pp. 26-27

197 Tombs, p. 31.

198 Stanley R. Hauer, *Thomas Jefferson and the Anglo-Saxon Language, PMLA,* Vol. 8, No. 5, October 1983, pp. 897-898 and,
Thomas Jefferson, *The Writings of Thomas Jefferson,* "Essay on Anglo-Saxon Language," Vol. 17-18, pp. 365-389.

199 Ibid.

200 George Bernard Shaw, *Thoughts on the Business of Life*, Forbes Magazine, https://www.Forbes.com, no date given.

201 Julian Harrison, *Who Were the Anglo-Saxons?* The British Library, https://www.bl.uk.

202 Stone, p. 18.

203 Editors of *The Encyclopedia Britannica, Encyclopedia Britannica,* "Anglo-Saxon Law," https://www.britannica.com.

204 The Jefferson Monticello, "Seal of the United States," from *The Thomas Jefferson Encyclopedia,* https://www.monticello.org.

205 Thomas Jefferson, "Letter from Thomas Jefferson to John Cartwright," 5 June 1824, US National Archives, "Founders Online," https://www.fournders.Archives.gov.

206 Tombs, p.33.

207 Winston Churchill, *A History of the English-Speaking Peoples,* (Skyhorse Publishing: abridged version, New York, 2011), p. 62.

208 Hauer and Young, p. 12.

209 Strong, pp. 27-28 and Schama, p. 61.

210 Stone, p.16

211 British Library, *Anglo-Saxons*: *Religion in Anglo-Saxon Kingdoms*, https://www.bl.uk.

Norman and Angevin Rule

212 Winston Churchill, *A History of the English-Speaking Peoples, The Birth of Britain,* Volume 1 (Cassell & Co. Ltd.: London, 1980), pp. 124, 130.

213 Tombs, p. 51.

214 Tombs, p. 50 and
C. Brooke, *From Alfred to Henry III, 871-1272,* The Norton Library History of England, Harvard Law School, Sec. 3A, (Edinburgh: New York, 1961), pp. 82-93. https://www.law.harvard.edu/faculty/cdonahue/courses/ELH/mats

215 Fraser, p. 100

216 Strong, p. 44 and Fraser, p. 104.

217 Tombs, p. 55.

218 Tombs, p. 73.

219 The Editors of *The Encyclopedia Britannica, The Encyclopedia Britannica,* "Assize of Clarendon." https://www.britannica.com

220 Marc Morris, *King John,* (Pegasus Books: New York, 2015), 290-298

221 Yale Law School, Lillian Goldman Law Library, Avalon Project, "Magna Carta 1215." https://www.avalonlaw.yale.edu.

222 Tombs, p.24

The Plantagenet Rule

223 Tombs, p. 65

224 Strong, p. 56

225 *How Artillery Evolved with the 100 Years War,* Naval History Online, https://www.warhistory.com/medical/artillery/100yearswar

226 Victoria Masson, *The Black Death,* historic-uk.com, and
London Plagues, 1348-1665, Museum of London,
https://www.mUeumoflondon.org.uk and,
Strong, pp. 96-97.

227 Masson

Tudor Rule

228 Winston Churchill, p. 215 and Tombs, p. 68 and Churchill's granddaughter, Edwina Sandys, December 15, 2019

229 Peter Marshall, *1517: Martin Luther and the Invention of the Revolution,* (Oxford University Press: New York, 2017). p. 38

230 Fraser, p. 269 and Strong, pp. 152-153

231 Thomas Cahill, *Heretics and Heroes: How Renaissance Artists and Reformation Priests Created Our World,* (New York: Anchor Books, 2014), p. 277

232 Living Heritage, Religion and Belief, *Act of Uniformity, 1559,* https://www.parliament.uk

233 Steven Ellis, *Turning Ireland English,* February 17, 2011, https://www.bbc.co.uk

234 *Dictionary of Canadian Biography* and Canadian Museum of History, *Sir Humphrey Gilbert, https://www.*biographi.cn

Stuart Rule

235 En*cyclopedia Britannica*, *Hampton Court Conference,* (January 16, 2020), https://www.britannica.com/event/Hampton-court-conference

236 Winston Churchill, Volume 2, *A History of the English-Speaking Peoples: The New World,* (London: Cassell, 1980, p. 136)

237 Edwina Sandys, December 15, 2019.

238 Willard Wallace, *Sir Edwin Sandys and the First Parliament of James I,* (Philadelphia, 1940), pp. 74-76

239 William Renwick Riddell, *Death of King James I: A Medico-Legal Study, Journal of Criminal Law and Criminology*, Volume 19, Issue: Article 4, May, Spring 1928, https://www.scholarlycommons.law.nortwestern.edu

240 *Witches and King James*, http://www.internetshakespeare.uvic.ca

241 *The Civil War, Charles I and the Petition of Right*, https://www.parliament.uk

Interregnum Rule

242 Joshua Dorsey Warfield, *Founders of Anne Arundel and Howard Counties, Maryland,* (Kohn & Pollock Publishing Co.: Baltimore, 1905), pp. 6-7

243 Ibid. pp. 186-187

244 Carmen Miner Smith, edited by William S. Powell, *Navigation Acts (1651-1660), Encyclopedia of North Carolina*, 2006, https://www.ncpedia.org

245 Pierson Cathrick Carter, *The History of the Church and Parish of St. Mary the Virgin, Aldermanbury,* (W. H. & L. Collingridge: London, 1913), p. 86

246 Tai Liu, *Puritan London: A Study of Religion and Society in the City Parishes,* (University of Delaware Press: Newark, 1986), pp. 151, 173

The Restoration Period (Stuart Reign—Part 2)

247 Antonia Fraser, *King Charles II,* (Weidenfield and Nicholson Ltd.: London, 1979), p. 128

248 Rev. S. C. Damon, *The Sailors' Magazine and Seamen's Friend,* "Charles II, John Bunyan and the Quaker Sailor," Volume 45, (American Seamen's Friend Society: New York, 1873), pp. 332, https://www.books.google.com

249 J. Reaney Kelly, *Quakers in the Founding of Anne Arundel County, Maryland,* (Maryland Historical Society: Baltimore, 1963), pp. 79-81.

250 Matthew Jenkinson, *Charles I's Killers in America,* (Oxford University Press: Oxford, 2018), p. 53

251 Jenkinson, p. 74

252 Jenkinson, pp. 145-148

253 Robert Charles Winthrop, *The Life and Letters of John Winthrop: Governor of the Massachusetts Bay Company,* Volume 1, (Little, Brown and Co.: Boston, 1869), p. 26, https://www.google.books.com

254 *Connecticut History,* "The Charter of 1662", (July 18, 2019), https://www.connecticuthistory.org

255 J.F.D. Shrewsbury, *A History of Bubonic Plague in the British Isles,* (Cambridge University Press: Cambridge, 1970) p. 459

256 Walter George Bell, *The Great Fire of London in 1666,* (Bodley Head: London, 1951), p. 17

257 Westminster College, *WestMoNews*, October 25, 2016

258 Magna Carta TrU.S.t, *The History of the Magna Carta,* https://www.magnacarta800th.com

259 *New Amsterdam,* History, History Today, https://www.history.com

260 Field Marshal Viscount Wolseley, K. P., *The Life of John Churchill, Duke of Marlborough, to the Accession of Queen Anne,* Cornell University Library, (Richard Bently and Son: London, 1894), p. 248, https://www.internet.archive

261 Hudson Bay History Foundation, *King Charles II and the Early Governors of HBC,* https://www.hbcheritage.ca

262 Tombs, p. 263

263 H. Jenkinson, *The Antiquarians Journal,* Volume 23, Issue 1-2, January 1943, "What Happened to the Great Seal of James II?" https://www.cambridge.org

264 Tombs, pp. 262-263

265 Kate Whitfield, *Battle of Boyne Explained, Express,* July 12, 2019, https://www.express.co.uk

The Great Fires of London (1666) and Chicago (1871)

266 Bell, p. 1, 6, 22,and 337

267 Daniel Hautzinger, *Out of the Ashes: The Birth of the Chicago Public Library,* January 1, 2017, https://www.interactive.wttw.com and
History Channel, *Chicago Fire of 1871,* March 4, 2010, https://www.history.com and
Mary Schloss, *National Geographic, The Chicago Fire of 1871 and the "Great Rebuilding,"* January 25, 2011, https://www.nationalgeographic.org

The Glorious Revolution and the Stuart Rule (Part 3)

268 Alison Freehling, *Sir Christopher Wren Building: Architectural Mystery Part of Wren's History,* (Daily Press: Hampton, Virginia, August 6, 1995)

269 Michael L. Wilson, *Happy and Glorious: The Revolution of 1688,* (The History Press: Gloucestershire, 2014, p. 144

270 Tombs, p. 307

271 Ibid.

Queen Anne (Stuart Rule, Part 4)

272 Winston Churchill, *A History of the English-Speaking Peoples,* Skyhorse Publishing, p. 396

273 Guest Submission, *Blenheim Palace: A Gift from the Queen,* Royal Central, (*The Guardian*: London, September 24, 2015)

274 History Editors, *American Indian Wars: Queen Anne's Wars,* November 17, 2019, https://www.history.com

275 *The Treaty of Utrecht, The Canadian Encyclopedia*, https://canadianencyclopedia.ca

276 United States Government, Office of the Historian, *French and Indian War/ Seven Years' War 1754-1763,* https://wwww.state.gov and,
The Society of Colonial Wars in the State of Connecticut, *The French and Indian Wars,* https://www.colonialwarsct.org

277 John Kerrigan, *The Secret Agent,* (*The Guardian:* London, March 7, 2008)

278 Fraser, p. 405

Hanoverian Rule

279 *The Act of Settlement,* The Royal Family, https://www.royal.uk

280 *Sophia Dorothea of Brunswick-Celle, 1666-1726,* Encyclopedia, https://www.encyclopedia.com and,
Skeleton Discovery Reignites 300 Year-Old Royal Murder Mystery, National Geographic, November 11, 2016, https://nationalgeographic.com

281 James Henretta, *Salutory Neglect, Encyclopedia Virginia,* Virginia Humanities, no date, and,
Rebecca Beatrice Brooks, *What Was the British Policy of Salutary Neglect?* March 30, 2016, https://historyofmassachusetts.org

282 Julie Ann Sweets, *War of Jenkins Ear, New Georgia Encyclopedia*, October 12, 2019. https://www.newencyclopediageorgia.org, and
Winston Churchill, *A History of the English-Speaking Peoples,* Skyhorse Publishing, 428

283 Ellen Castelow, *War of Jenkins' Ear, History Magazine*, History of England, https://www.historic-uk.com

284 Winston Churchill, *A History of the English-Speaking Peoples,* Skyhorse Publishing, p. 431

285 Richard Middleton, *Colonial America,* (Blackwell: Cambridge, MA, 1992), pp. 177-179 and,
Provincial Troops in the French and Indian War, Wikipedia, https://en.m.wikipedia.org

286 *Atlantic Virginia,* (Philadelphia: University of Pennsylvania Press, 2004), pp. 49-50

287 Winston Churchill, *A History of the English-Speaking Peoples,* Skyhorse Publishing, p. 444

288 *No Taxation without Representation,* Magna Carta: Muse and Mentor, Library of Congress, https://www.loc.gov

289 *The Tea Act: The Catalyst of the Boston Tea Party,* Boston Tea Party, https://www.bostonteapartyship.com

290 Winston Churchill, *A History of the English-Speaking Peoples,* Skyhorse Publishing, p. 452

291 First Continental Congress, https://u-s-history.com

292 *Declaration of Rights and Grievances, October 14, 1774,* The American Revolution, 1763-1783, Library of Congress, https://www.loc.gov

293 Thom, *Common Sense,* (Signet Books: New York, 2003)

294 Harlow Giles Under, *Thomas Paine and the Clarion Call for American Independence,* (DeCapo Press: US, 2019), p. 42.

295 *Washington's Letter,* George Washington Institute for Religious Freedom, 2020, https://www.gwirf.org

296 *John Jay Treaty, 1794-1795,* United States Government, US History, https://www.history.state.gov

297 *Pinckney's Treaty, Encyclopedia Britannica,* https://www.britannica.ca

298 *To Anacreon in Heaven,* National Park Service, Fort McHenry, https://www.nps.gov

299 Ibid. and Noel D. Johnson and Mark Koyama, *Persecution & Toleration,* (Cambridge University Press: New York, 2018), p. 179

300 Dr. Marjorie Bloy, *Peel and Emancipation,* A Web of English History, The Peel Web, https://www.historyhome.co.uk

301 *The Monroe Doctrine (1823),* United States Government, US Embassy, https://www.US.embassy.de

302 Ibid.

303 Natasha Henry, *Slavery Abolition Act, United Kingdom, 1833,* Britannica, https://www.britannica.com

304 Kris Manjapa, *When will Britain Face Up to its Crimes Against Humanity,* (*The Guardian*: March 29, 2018) https://www.theguardian.com

305 *Today in History* and Library of Congress, *Abolition in the District of Columbia,* April 16, 2019, https://www.loc.gov

306 *King William IV (1830-37),* British Royals, https://www.britroyals.com

307 *Americans Caught in 'Victoria Fever': The British Queen's 1838 Coronation,* https://www.smithsonianmag.coms

308 Tracy Borman, *Nothing Could Have Gone Off Better: The Wedding of Queen Victoria and Prince Albert,* https://www.historyextra.com

309 *The Pill: Anthony Comstock's Chastity Laws,* https://www.npr.org

Queen Victoria, Last of the Hanoverians

310 Ben Johnson, *The Great Exhibition of 1851, History Magazine,* https://historic-uk.com and Lisa Picard, *The Great Exhibition,* October 14, 2019, British Library, https://bl.uk

311 Jesse Greenspan, *Why the Purchase of Alaska Was Far from 'Folly',* History, https://www.history.com

312 *Cotton Is King: Cotton Diplomacy in the Confederate States,* American Battlefield Trust, https://www.battlefields.org

313 H. C. G. Matthews and K. D. Reynolds, *Victoria, Oxford Dictionary of Biography,* https://www.oxforddnb.com

314 Kristin Hunt, *Victor and Abdul: The Friendship that Scandalized England,* (Smithsonian Magazine: September 20, 2017)

King George V Reign

315 *Four Underlying Causes of War,* BBC, https://www.bbc.co.uk

316 R. G. Grant, *Did Britain Go to War over Belgium?* (British) National Archives, The Great War—1914-1918, National Archives, https://www.nationalarchives.gov.uk and *World War I: The Definitive Visual History, Smithsonian*, (Penguin Random House: New York, 2018), pp. 42, 46

317 Ibid. pp. 166-167 and,
The National Archives, Educator Resources, The Zimmerman Telegram, https://www.archives.gov

318 *Talk of Europe, The Living Age*, Volume 300, Thirteenth Quarterly, Volume of the Eighth Series, January-March, 1919, p.249

319 Winston Churchill, *The World Crisis: 1911-1918, (*Free Press: New York, 2005), p. 169

320 Mitchell Yockelson, *They Answered the Call,* National Archives, *Prologue Magazine,* Fall, 1998, Volume 30. Number 3

321 *The American Expeditionary Forces,* Library of Congress, https://www.loc.gov and *Military Figure – John J. Pershing, General (1860-1948),* Biography, July 16, 2019, https://www.biography.com

322 Mitchell Yockelson, p. 100

323 Martin Gilbert, video, *What Did the United States Mean to Winston Churchill?* Hillsdale College, July 17, 2015

324 General John J. Pershing, http://www.nps.gov

325 *The Meuse-Argonne Offensive,* US National Archives, Military Records, https://www.archives.gov and
H. p. Willmott, *World War I,* (New York: DK Publishing, 2009), pp. 265-266

326 John F. McGrath, Regimental Historian, *War Diary of the 354th Infantry, 89th Division,* pp. 176-177, https://www.babel.hathitrust.org

327 George H. English, *History of the 89th Division, in World War I,* National World War I Museum and Memorial, Office of the Secretary of State, Missouri, Digital Heritage, (War Society of the 89th Division: no city given, 1920), pp. 71, 133, 150, 163, 165, 178, 179, 190, 191, and 240, https://www.sos.mo.gov

328 George H. English, Ibid.

329 Mary Soames, *Clementine Churchill: A Biography,* (Houghton Mifflin: New York, 2002), pp. 160-161

330 Roy Jenkins, *Churchill: A Biography,* (Farrar, Straus and Giroux: New York, 2001), p. 297

331 Peter Apps, *Churchill in the Trenches,* Amazon, 2015

332 George Sylvester Viereck, *The Fatherland,* New York, February 23, 1916

333 Andrew Roberts, *Churchill: Walking with Destiny,* (Viking: New York, 2018), p. 262

334 *World War I: Killed, Wounded, and Missing,* As Reported by the US War Department, February 1926, *Encyclopedia Britannica*, https://www.britannica.com

335 Richard Langworth, "Churchill and the President: Woodrow Wilson," Hillsdale College, August 5, 2015, https://www.winstonchurchill.hillsdalecollege.edu and, Andrew Roberts, p. 269 and,
Winston Churchill, *The World Crisis,* pp. 694-695

336 *Man Who Hit British Statesman Tells How It Feels to Run Down Churchill: They're Now Friends, Milwaukee Journal*, February 11, 1932

337 Constantine Brown, *Churchill's Peace Formula, Washington DC Evening Star,* February 12, 1932

338 *Why Did the US Abandon the Gold Standard?* Mental Floss, October 3, 2012, https://www.mentalfloss.org and
H R Knickerbocker, *Gold Standard Return Awaits Recovery, The Seattle Daily,* October 13, 1932 via *The New York Evening Post*

339 Edward H. Judge and John W. Langdon, *The Struggle Against Imperialism: Anti-colonialism and the Cold War,* (Rowman and Littlefield: Maryland, 2018), p. 21 and
Japanese Troops Swarm to Shore for Chapei Drive, New Orleans Picayune, February 15, 1932, and
Constantine Brown, *Shanghai Threat is Held Alarming, San Francisco Chronicle,* January 28, 1932

340 *Lebensraum,* United States Holocaust Memorial Museum, https://encyclopedia.U.S.hmm.org

King Edward VIII Reign

341 *Letter reveals Churchill's Anger with Edward Over Abdication,* T*elegraph*, October 21, 2001

George VI Reign

342 World War II and the events leading up to it have been covered extensively in many books, newspapers, and magazines. As previously mentioned, this coverage is intended to cover examples of the evolution of the special relationship between the United States and Britain, not the entire war.

343 *Chamberlain Addresses the Nation on Peace Negotiations,* BBC, https://www.bbc.co.uk and *Chamberlain Declares "Peace for our Time One Return from Munich,* T*he Guardian,* October 1, 1938

344 Washington's *Farewell Address* (1796) and Jefferson's *First Inaugural Address* (1801)

345 Fireside Chat No. 15

346 *Destroyers-for-Bases Agreement,* BBC, https://www.bbc.co.uk, and
Destroyers for Bases, History Central, https://www.historycentral.com

347 R. G. D. Allen, *Mutual Aid Between the United States and the British Empire: 1941-1945,* Journal of the Royal Statistical Society, Volume 109, Number 3, pp. 243-277

348 *Remarks on Signing Honorary Citizenship for Sir Winston Churchill,* John F. Kennedy Library, April 4, 1963, https://www.jfklibrary.org

349 America's National Churchill Museum, https://www.nationalchurchillmuseum.org

350 *Prime Minister Winston Churchill's Broadcast to the World about the Meeting with President Roosevelt,* British Library of Information, https://www.ibiblio.org

351 *The Atlantic Conference,* Office of the Historian (US), Milestones 1937-1945, https://history.state.gov

352 *Norman Rockwell's Four Freedoms,* Norman Rockwell Museum, https://www.nrm.org

353 *Pearl Harbor,* History, https://www.history.com

354 *Pearl Harbor Attack: How Did Churchill React?* Ch*ristian Science Monitor,* https://www.csmonitor.org

355 *The Eighth Air Force vs. the Luftwaffe,* National World War II Museum, https://www.nationalwwIImuseum.org

356 Interview with Al Villagran, March 2, 2020

357 Ibid.

358 Ibid.

359 Ibid.

360 Ibid. and *6 July 1944: Rose of York,* This Day in Aviation, https://www.thisdayinaviation.com

361 Interview with Al Villagran, March 2, 2020

362 Simon Worrall, *The Inside Story of How Three Unlikely Allies Won World War II, National Geographic,* Culture, Book Talk, January 11, 2019, https://www.nationalgeographic.com

363 *The Potsdam Conference, 1945,* Office of the Historian, https://www.history.state.gov, and *The Cold War and Its Origins,* BBC, https://www.bbc.co.uk and, Andrew M. Goldstein, *Truman at Potsdam: The First Battle of the Cold War,* Eastern Illinois University, https://elu.edu

364 History, June 7, 2019, https://www.history.com

365 Philip Nobile, *Were They War Criminals? The Independent,* https://www.independent.co.uk

366 Interview with Ed Tilles, his brother, 1999

367 Interview with Ed Tilles

368 Ibid. pp. 47, 48, 60, 61, 144

PART THREE: Special Relationship: Christopher Wren's Church

CHAPTER 16

369 Mike Hutton, *Life in 1940s London,* Amberley Publishing: U.K., 2014, pp. 159-160

370 Peter J. Larkham and Joe L. Nasr, *Decision-Making Under Duress: The Treatment of Churchies in the City of London During and After World War II,* Volume 39, No. 2, 285-309, Cambridge University Press, May 2012, https://www.jstor/stable/26398139

371 Ibid.

372 Ibid.

373 Ibid.

CHAPTER 17

374 English-Speaking Union Website, https://www.esuus.org

375 Parrish, *History of Westminster College*

376 *On Horsbrugh's Leaving, Omaha World-Herald*, January 27, 1965

377 *World Nearly Jumps Gun on Burying Sir Winston, Omaha World-Herald*, April 16, 1964

378 James Denney, *The Professor's Memorial to Winston Churchill, Omaha World-Herald*, May 24, 1970

379 Patrick Horsbrugh, *A Wren Church for the United States: Problems of Choice, Transportation, Siting and Reconstruction,* An Address Given before the Members of the Iowa Chapter of the American Institute of Architects, Des, Moines, Iowa, January 24, 1964.

CHAPTER 18

380 Patrick Horsbrugh, Ibid.

381 Patrick Horsbrugh, Ibid. and,
Mansion Coming to US, San Diego Evening Tribune, January 28, 1926 and,
Leave Buildings for England, Cincinnati Post, September 15, 1926 and,
The Flight of Agecroft Hall, Boston Herald, March 7, 1926 and,
Hall US Is to Get Was Built Four Centuries Ago, Denver Post, January 31, 1926 and,
Betty Pettinger, *Ancient Bed Comes to Rest in Historic Virginia Home, Richmond Times Dispatch*, November 24, 1974 and,
Doug Childers, *Agecroft Hall: A Tudor Manor House, Transported,* January 25, 2020, https://www.richmond.com/realestate/features/great-homes/agecroft-hall

382 Ibid.

CHAPTER 19

383 Horsbrugh

384 V. Maevsky, *The Stones are Groaning, Pravda*, December 26, 1961, America's National Churchill Museum

385 Horsbrugh, Ibid.

386 Horsbrugh, Ibid.

387 Horsbrugh, Ibid.

388 Horsbrugh, Ibid.

389 Horsbrugh, ibid,

390 Horsbrugh, Ibid.

391 Horsbrugh, Ibid.

392 Letter from Winston Churchill to Westminster College, America's National Churchill Museum, November 22, 1962

CHAPTER 20

393 *Christopher Wren*, *Encyclopedia Britannica*, https://www.britannica.com and,
History – Sir Christopher Wren, BBC, https://www.bbc.co.uk, and
Sir Christopher Wren, Math History, https://wwww.mathshistory.co.st-andrews.ac.uk

394 Ibid.

395 Ibid.

396 Ibid.

397 Ibid.

398 Ibid.

399 Ibid.

400 Colin Amery, *Wren's Churches,* (Lennard Publishing: England, 1988), pp.6-7

401 *Sir Christopher Wren,* Math History

402 Christopher Wren Jr., Ernest J. Enthoven, Editor. *The Life and Works of Sir Christopher Wren from the Parentalia or Memoirs.* (Samuel Buckley & Co. and Bruce Rogers: New York, 1903), pp. 117-118.

403 Ibid.

404 Ibid. 119-120

405 Colin Amory, pp. 6-7

CHAPTER 21

406 Jenkinson, Wilberforce, *London Churches Before the Great Fire,* (Society for Promoting Christian Knowledge: London, 1917), p. 172

407 Jenkinson, Wilberforce, *London Churches Before the Great Fire,* (Society for Promoting Christian Knowledge: London, 1917), p. 172

408 Westminster College, *The Columns,* February 28, 1969, p. 9

409 Liu, p. 74

410 Ibid. pp. 73-76

411 J. F. D. Shrewsbury, *A History of the Bubonic Plague in the British Isles,* (Cambridge University Press: Cambridge, 1970), p. 468 and appendix

412 Walter George Bell, *The Great Fire of London,* (The Bodley Head: London, 1951) (Washington University, St. Louis, Library collection), p. 1

413 Ibid. p. 2

414 Ibid. p. 2

415 Ibid. pp. 22-24

416 *The Living Age, Manchester Guardian,* January –March, 1919, Volume XIII

417 *Impressions of the Airship Raids Over London on October 13, 1915,* Holborn, Princeton Street (B) School, Bedford Row, W.C., British Library Collection, MS 39257-39258, Manuscript, Essay, Ephemera, https://www.bl.uk

418 Ibid.

419 John Colville, *The Fringes of Power: Downing Street Diaries,* Volume One, 1939-October 1941 (Great Britain: Spectre, 1986), p. 385.

420 Mrs. Robert Henrey, *The Virgin of Aldermanbury: Rebirth of the City of London,* (J. M. Dent & Sons Ltd.: London, 1958), pp. 110-111

421 Westminster College, *The Columns*, February 28, 1969, p. 9

CHAPTER 22

422 Douglas Fairbanks, Jr., *A Hell of a War,* Robson Books, Butler & Tanner, Ltd.: Great Britain, 1993, Dedication

423 Fairbanks, pp. 240, 260

424 Steve Stinson Remarks, son of Dave Stinson

425 Stinson, Ibid.

426 Stinson, Ibid.

427 Letter to Dave Stinson, courtesy of Steve Stinson

428 America's National Churchill Museum

CHAPTER 23

429 David Eisenhower with Julie Nixon Eisenhower, *Going Home to Glory: A Memoir of Life with Dwight D. Eisenhower, 1961-1969,* (Simon & Schuster Paperback: New York, 2010), p. 158

430 Ibid.

431 Ibid.

432 Ibid.

433 Abigail Malangone, *Sir Winston Churchill's Path to United States Citizenship,* April 9, 2002, John F. Kennedy Presidential Library and Museum, National Archives, https://jfk.blogs.archives.gov

434 Ibid.

435 Valerie Lynn Adams, *A Fine Group of Fellows: Civilian Advisors, Eisenhower, and National Security Planning,* Spring 2001, Doctoral Dissertation, University of New Hampshire, Durham, Scholars' Repository, https://www.scholars.unh.edu

CHAPTER 24

436 American Institute of Architects, St. Louis, https://www.aia.org

437 Royal Academy of Arts, Marshall Sisson (1897-1978), https://www.royalaceademy.org.uk

438 *Sisson Speaks about the Chapel, The Columns,* Westminster College, May 2, 1969

439 *Sisson Speaks, Ibid.*

440 *Westminster Words,* February 11, 1963

441 Ibid.

442 *Architects' Plans for Fulton Project, St. Louis Post Dispatch*, March 5, 1965

443 *Sisson Speaks*, Ibid.

444 *British Stones Going to Fulton for Rebuilding of Old Church, St. Louis Post Dispatch,* February 23, 1966

445 *Westminster College Magazine,* Summer 1969

446 *Sisson Speaks,* Ibid.

447 *Sisson Speaks,* Ibid.

448 *Sisson Speaks,* Ibid.

449 *Architects' Plans for Fulton Project, St. Louis Post Dispatch*, March 5, 1965

450 *Westminster College Magazine,* Summer 1969

451 *A Ship of Wren's Mighty Fleet, St. Louis Post Dispatch*, March 7, 1966

452 *London Church Being Moved to Small College in Missouri, Trenton Evening Times*, May 3, 1964 and,
School Eyes Church Ruin as Memorial, San Diego Union, April 30, 1964

453 *London Church Being Moved to Small College in Missouri, Trenton Evening Times*, May 3, 1964

454 William R. Plunkett, *Fitting Church Puzzle Pieces Together at Fulton, St. Louis Post Dispatch*, September 11, 1966

455 *Sisson Speaks about the Chapel, The Columns,* Westminster College, May 2, 1969

456 *Westminster College Magazine,* Summer 1969

457 Ibid.

458 Ibid.

459 Ibid.

460 *The Words of Man,* Westminster College, (The Westphalia Press: Fulton, no date provided and,
Olivia Skinner, *Tokens of Honor for Churchill, St. Louis Post Dispatch*, November 20, 1974 and,
Curt Matthews, *Rebuilding of Old English Church Draws on Skills in Several St. Louis Companies, St. Louis Post Dispatch*, June 1, 1967 and,
Steve Stinson, video, 2019 and,
America's National Churchill Museum, archival collection of donations, as of 2019 and,
Steve Stinson, son of Dave Stinson

461 Sheila M. Hannah, Church of St. Mary the Virgin (Winston Churchill Memorial), Aldermanbury, Nomination Form, National Register of Historic Places, US Department of the Interior, National Park Service, October 13, 1970, https://www.dnr.mo.gov

462 *The Words of Man,* and,
Sisson Speaks, Ibid. and,
British Stones, Ibid. and,
Steve Stinson, Ibid.

CHAPTER 25

463 Hilary Weaver, *The Marriage Proposal Jackie Turned Down,* Vanity Fair, February 9, 2017, https://www.vanityfair.com

464 Hallmark website, https://www.corporate.hallmark.com

465 Ibid.

466 Philip and SU.S.an Larson, *When You Care Enough: Joyce Hall and Hallmark's Churchill Connection, Finest Hour*, 137, Winter, 2007-8, https://www.winstonchurchill.org

467 *The Daily Advocate,* (Stamford, CT), October 5, 1967

468 *The Daily Advocate,* (Stamford, CT), October 18, 1967

469 *William Benton,* Ency*clopedia Britannica*, https://www.britannica.com

470 Jerry N. Hess, *Oral History Interview with David K. E. Bruce,* Harry S. Truman Library and Museum, https://trumanlibrary.gov

471 *Cass Canfield, Jr.,* Wikipedia, https://www.wikipedia.org and, *Laura Spencer-Churchill, Duchess of Marlborough,* Wikipedia, https://www.wikipedia.org

472 *Cowles Family, Encyclopedia Britannica*, https://www.britannica.com

473 *Allan Wheeler Ferrin*, *Palm Beach Post*, obituary, Mary 25, 2014

474 *Harry S. Truman 1947 Document Signed as President—Awarding the Medal for Merit—with the Actual Medal,* Shafran Collectibles, https://www.shrafrancollectibles.com

475 Richard D. McKinzie and Theodore A. Wilson, *W. Averell Harriman*, Oral History Interview, Harry S. Truman Library and Museum, Washington, DC, 1971, https://www.trumanlibrary.com

476 Henry A. Laughlin, Jr. Obituary, *Boston Globe*, Boston, MA, Legacy, https://www.legacy.com

477 *Howard A. Rusk (1901–1989) From Military Medicine to Comprehensive Rehabilitation,* American Journal of Public Health, February 2008, https://www.ncbi.nim.nhih.gov

478 *Joseph C. Wilson*: The Founder of Xerox Who Brought an Innovation in the Printing Industry, Your Tech Story, https://www.yourtechstory.com

CHAPTER 26

479 Westminster College website, https://www.wcmo.edu

480 Rt. Hon. Quinton Hogg, *Salute to Winston Churchill Speech,* River Club, New York, NY, 1964 and, *Westminster College Magazine*, Summer 1969

481 List of Attendees, America's National Churchill Museum

482 *Thoughts on the Dedication of the Churchill Memorial; Some Remembrances, Observations and Auguries, Westminster College Magazine*, Summer 1969. All portions of this chapter dealing with Harriman's speech were sourced from this document.

483 Simon Schama, *Scribble, Scribble, Scribble,* (Bodley Head: London, April 12, 2011), Chapter 3, pp. 150-155

484 *Mountbatten at Westminster, Westminster College Magazine*, Summer 1969. All portions of this chapter dealing with Mountbatten's speech were sourced from this document.

485 Arthur Hugh Clough, *Say Not the Struggle Nought Availeth,* The New York Times, July 10, 1941

Selected Bibliography

BOOKS

Ackroyd, Peter. *Civil War*. London: Pan Macmillan, 2014.

Ackroyd, Peter. 2018. *Dominion: The History of England from the Battle of Waterloo to Victoria's Diamond Jubilee*. New York: Thomas Dunne Books, St.Martin's Press, 2018.

Ackroyd, Peter. *Foundation: The History of England from Its Earliest Beginnings to the Tudors*. New York: Thomas Dunne Books/St. Martin's Griffin, 2013.

Ackroyd, Peter. *Tudors: The History of England from Henry VIII to Elizabeth I*. New York: Thomas Dunne Books; St. Martins Griffin, 2014.

Amery, Colin. *Wren's London*. Luton: Lenard., 1988.

Applebaum, Anne. *Iron Curtain: The Crushing of Eastern Europe 1944-1956*. New York: Anchor Books, 2012.

Apps, Peter. *Churchill in the Trenches*. San Bernardino, CA: {Create Space Independent Publishing Platform}: 2017.

Baker, Kevin. *America: The Story of US: An Illustrated History*. New York: A&E Television Networks, 2010.

Barratt, Nick. *Restless Kings: The Story of Henry II and His Sons*. U.S.A: Faber & Faber, Incorporated, 2019.

Bell, Christopher M. *Churchill and the Dardanelles: Myth, Memory, and Reputation*. Oxford: Oxford University Press, 2017

Bell, Walter George. *The Great Fire of London in 1666*. London: Bodley Head, 1923.

Bessel, Richard. *Germany 1945: From War to Peace*. New York: Harper Perennial, 2009.

Billings, Warren M. *The Old Dominion in the Seventeenth Century: A Documentary History of Virginia, 1606-1700*. Chapel Hill: University of North Carolina Press, 1975.

Bremer, Francis J. *The Puritan Experiment: New England Society from Bradford to Edwards*. Hanover, NH: University Press of New England, 1995.

Bryson, Bill. *Mother Tongue: English and How It Got That Way*. New York: Harper Collins, 2001.

Bryson, Bill. *William Shakespeare: The World as Stage*. New York: Atlas Books, 2007.

Butman, John, and Simon Targett. *New World, Inc.: How England's Merchants Founded America and Launched the British Empire*. New York: Little Brown and Company, 2018.

Carr, Lois Green. *Colonial Chesapeake Society.* Chapel Hill, N.C.: University of North Carolina Press, 1988.

Charmley, John. *Churchill's Grand Alliance: The Anglo-American Special Relationship, 1940-1957.* New York: Harcourt Brace & Company, 1995.

Christopher, John. *Wren's City of London Churches.* Gloucestershire: Amberley Publishing, 2012

Churchill, Winston S. *A History of the English-Speaking Peoples: The Birth of Britain, Vol. 1.* New York: Macmillan Publishing Company, 1980.

Churchill, Winston. *A History of the English-Speaking Peoples: The New World, Vol. 2.* New York: Macmillan Publishing Company, 1980.

Churchill, Winston. *A History of the English Speaking Peoples: The Age of Revolution, Vol. 3.* New York: Macmillan Publishing Company, 1980.

Churchill, Winston. *A History of the English Speaking Peoples: The Great Democracies, Vol. 4.* New York: Macmillan Publishing Company, 1980.

Churchill, Winston. *The World Crisis: 1911-1918.* New York: Free Press, 2005.

Churchill, Winston. *Closing the Ring.* New York: The Riverside Press, 1951.

Churchill, Winston Spencer. *Marlborough: His Life and Times.* United States: Charles Scribner's Sons, 1968

Churchill, Winston. *Memoirs of the Second World War: An Abridgement of the Six Volumes. of the Second World War with an Epilogue by the Author on the Post-war Years Written for this Volume.* Boston: Houghton Mifflin, 1959.

Churchill, Winston, Richard M. Langworth, ed. *Churchill by Himself: The Definitive Collection of Quotations.* New York: Public Affairs, 2008.

Churchill, Winston, Richard M. Langworth, ed. *The Patriot's Churchill: An Inspiring Collection of Churchill's Finest Words.* London: Ebury Press, 2011.

Cimino, Al. *Roosevelt and Churchill: A Friendship That Saved the World.* New York: Chartwell Books, 2018.

Clark, Clifford with Richard Holbroke. *Counsel to the President, a Memoir.* New York: Random House, 1991.

Craven, Wesley Frank. *The Southern Colonies in the Seventeenth Century: 1607-1689.* Baton Rouge: Louisiana State University Press, 1970.

Currie, Stephen. *The Renaissance.* San Diego: Reference Point Press, 2013.

De Lisle, Leanda. *White King: Traitor, Murderer, Martyr.* New York: Hachette Book Group, 2018.

Dunton Downer, Leslie and Alan Riding, Ed. *Essential Shakespeare Handbook: The Definitive, Fully Illustrated Guide to the World's Greatest Playwright and His Works.* United States: DK, 2013.

Enthoven, Ernest. *The Life and Works of Sir Winston Churchill.* New York: Samuel Benchley & Co., 1750, reprinted 1903. Gloucestershire: Essex House Press, 1903.

Fairbanks Jr.,Douglas. *Salad Days.* New York: Doubleday, 1988.

Fairbanks Jr., Douglas. *A Hell of a War.* Great Britain: Robson Books, 1995.

Fraser, Antonia. *Faith and Treason: The Story of the Gunpowder Plot.* U.S.A: Anchor Books, 1997.

Fraser, Antonia. *The King and the Catholics: England, Ireland, and the Fight for Religious Freedom, 1780-1829.* {S.l.}: ANCHOR, 2019.

Fraser, Antonia. *King Charles II.* London: Weidenfeld and Nicolson, 1979.

Fraser, Rebecca. *The Mayflower: The Families, The Voyage, and the Founding of America.* New York: St. Martin's Griffin, 2017.

Fraser, Rebecca. *The Story of Britain: From the Romans to the Present : A Narrative History.* New York: W.W. Norton & Company, 2003.

Gallay, Alan. 2019. *Walter Ralegh: Architect of Empire.* New York: Hachette Book Group, 2019.

Gardiner, Juliet, and Neil Wenborn. *The Columbia Companion to British History.* New York: Columbia University Press, 1997.

Gerteis, Louis S. *Civil War St. Louis.* United States: University Press of Kansas, 2001.

Gilbert, Martin. *Churchill and America.* New York, NY: Free Press, 2005.

Gilbert, Martin, *Never Despair 1945-1965, Volume VIII.* Hillsdale: Hillsdale College Press, 1988.

Gilbert, Martin. *The First World War.* New York: Holt, 2004.

Goodman, Ruth, and Heather Wilds. *How to be a Tudor: A Dawn-to-Dusk Guide to Tudor Life.* New York: Liveright Publishing Corporation, 2016.

Hall, David D. 2019. *The Puritans: A Transatlantic History.* Princeton: Princeton University Press, 2019.

Ham, Paul. *Hiroshima Nagaski: The Real Story of the Atomic Bombings and Their Aftermath.* New York: Thomas Dunne Books, St. Martin's Press, 2014.

Grant, R. G. *World War I: The Definitive Visual History from Sarajevo to Versailles.* New York: DK Publishing, 2018.

Harbutt, Fraser J. *The Iron Curtain: Churchill, America, and The Origins of the Cold War.* Oxford: Oxford Univ. Press, 1988.

Harper, Karen. *The Queen's Governess.* New York: G.P. Putnam's Sons, 2010.

Harriman, William Averell, and Elie Abel. *Special Envoy to Churchill and Stalin: 1941-1946.* New York: Random House, 1975.

John Harte. *How Churchill Saved Civilization: The Epic Story of 13 Years That Almost Destroyed the Civilized World.* New York: Skyhorse Publishing, 2016.

Hatfield, April Lee. *Atlantic Virginia: Intercolonial Relations in the Seventeenth Century.* Philadelphia, PA: University of Pennsylvania Press, 2004.

Hauer, Christian E., and William A. Young. *A Comprehensive History of the London Church and Parish of St. Mary, the Virgin, Aldermanbury: The Phoenix of Aldermanbury.* Lewiston {N.Y.}: E. Mellen Press, 1994.

Heimert, Alan, and Nicholas Delbanco. *Puritans in America: A Narrative Anthology.* Cambridge: Harvard University Press, 1985.

Hicks, Pamela. *Daughter of Empire: My Life as a Mountbatten.* New York: Simon & Schuster Paperbacks, 2012.

Higham, Nicholas J., and Martin J. Ryan. *The Anglo-Saxon World.* New Haven: Yale University Press, 2013.

Hornak, Angelo. *After the Fire: London Churches in the Age of Wren, Hooke, Hawksmoor, and Gibbs.* London: Pimpernel Press, 2016.

Humes, James C. *The Sir Winston Method: The Five Secrets of Speaking the Language of Leadership.* New York: William Morrow and Co., 1991.

Hutton, Mike. *Life in 1940s London.* Stroud, Gloucestershire: Amberley, 2013.

Jenkins, Roy. *Churchill.* Farrar, New York: Straus and Giroux, 2001.

Jenkinson, Matthew. *Charles I's Killers in America: The Lives and Afterlives of Edward Whalley and William Goffe.* Oxford: Oxford University Press, 2019.

Jenkinson, Wilberforce. *London Churches Before the Great Fire.* London: Society for Promoting Christian Knowledge, 1917.

Johnson, Boris. *The Churchill Factor.* New York: Riverhead Books, 2014.

Johnson, Noel D., and Mark Koyama. *Persecution and Toleration: The Long Road to Religious Freedom.* Cambridge: Cambridge University Press, 2019.

Kershaw, Ian. *Fateful Choices: Ten Decisions That Changed the World, 1940-1941.* New York: Penguin, 2007.

Langworth, Richard M. Editor. *The Patriot's Churchill: An Inspiring Collection of Churchill's Finest Work.* United Kingdom: Ebury Press, 2011.

Lehrman, Lewis E. *Lincoln and Churchill: Statesmen at War.* Guilford, CT: Stackpole Books, 2018

Liu, Tai. *Puritan London: A Study of Religion and Society in the City Parishes.* Newark: University of Delaware Press, 1986.

Lovell, Mary S. *The Churchills: A Family at the Heart of History - from the Duke of Marlborough to Winston Churchill.* London: Abacus, 2012.

Macaulay, Thomas Babington Macaulay. *The History of England.* New York: Penguin Books, 1986.

Maier, Thomas. *When Lions Roar: The Churchills and the Kennedys.* New York: Crown Archetype, 2015.

Marshall, Peter. *1517: Martin Luther and the Invention of the Reformation.* Great Britain: Oxford University Press, 2011.

Meacham, Jon, and Grover Gardner. *Franklin and Winston: An Intimate Portrait of an Epic Friendship.* New York: Random House Trade Paperbooks, 2003.

McCandless, Perry. *A History of Missouri, Volume II 1820 to 1860.* Columbia: University of Missouri Press, 2000.

McCullough, David. *Truman.* New York: Simon and Schuster, 1992.

Meider, Wolfgang and George B. Bryan, Compilers. *The Proverbial Winston Churchill: An Index to Proverbs in the Works of Winston Churchill.* Westport, CT: Greenwood Press, 1995.

Meisler, Stanley. *United Nations: A History.* New York: Grove Press, 2011.

Middleton, Richard. *Colonial America: A History, 1607-1760.* Cambridge Mass: Blackwell, 1994.

Millard, Candice. *Hero of the Empire: the Boer War, a Daring Escape, and the Making of Winston Churchill.* New York: Anchor Books, 2017.

Morgan, Edmund S. *The Puritan Dilemma: The Story of John Winthrop.* United States: Harper Collins Publishers, 1958.

Morris, Marc. *King john: Treachery, Tyranny and the Road to Magna Carta.* New York: PegasU.S. Books Ltd., 2015.

Muller, James W. *Churchill's "Iron Curtain" Speech Fifty Years Later.* Columbia: University of Missouri Press, 1999.

Neal, Larry. *The Economics of Europe and the European Union.* United Kingdom: Cambridge University Press, 2008.

Pagliuco, Christopher. *The Great Escape of Edward Whalley and William Goffe: Smuggled through Connecticut.* Charleston, SC: History Press, 2012.

Paine, Thomas, Jack Fruchtman, and Sidney Hook. *Common Sense, the Rights of Man, and Other Essential Writings.* New York: Signet Classic, 2003.

Parrish, William E. *Westminster College: An Informal History, 1851-1999.* Fulton, Missouri: Westminster College, 1971.

Plokhy, S. M. *Yalta: The Price of Peace.* New York: Penguin, 2011.

Pollack, Deborah. *Vintage Miami: Beach Glamour.* Charleston, S.C., 2019.

Preston, Diane. *Eight Days at Yalta: How Churchill, Roosevelt, and Stalin Shaped the Post-War World.* New York: Atlantic Monthly Press, 2019.

Quinn, Arthur. *A New World: An Epic of Colonial America from the Founding of Jamestown to the Fall of Quebec.* New York: Berkley Books, 1995.

Roberts, Andrew. *Walking with Destiny.* United States: Viking, 2018.

Roberts, Steven. *King George III: England's Struggle to Keep America.* New York, Crabtree Publishing, 2013.

Roosevelt, Franklin D., and Elliott Roosevelt. *F.D.R.: His Personal Letters, 1928-1945.* New York: Duell, Sloan, and Pearce, 1950.

Rose, Jill. *Nursing Churchill: Wartime Life from the Private Letters of Winston Churchill's Nurse.* United Kingdom: Amberley Publishing, 2018.

Schama, Simon. *A History of Britain: The End of the World? 3000 B.C. - A.D. 1603.* New York: Hyperion, 2000.

Schama, Simon. *A History of Britain: The British Wars, 1603-1776, Volume 2.* New York: Hyperion, 2001.

Schama, Simon. *A History of Britain: The Fate of the Empire, 1776-2000, Volume 3.* New York: Hyperion, 2002.

Shrewsbury, J. F. D. *A History of the Bubonic Plague in the British Isles.* Cambridge: University Press,1970.

Spencer, Charles. *To Catch a King: Charles II's Great Escape.* London: William Collins, 2018

Steil, Benn. *The Marshall Plan: Dawn of the Cold War.* New York: Simon & Schuster, 2018.

Stelzer, Cita. *Working with Winston.* New York: Pegasus Books, 2019.

Stone, Peter, and Nick Buxey. *The History of the Port of London: A Vast Emporium of All Nations.* Arnsley, South Yorkshire : Pen & Sword History, 2017.

Strong, Roy. *The Story of Britain: A History of the Great Ages from the Romans to the Present.* New York: Pegasus, 2019.

Tilles, Stanley, and Jeffrey Denhart. *By the Neck Until Dead: The Gallows of Nuremberg.* Bedford, Indiana: JoNa Books, 1999.

Tombs, Robert. *The English and Their History.* New York: Alfred A. Knopf, 2015.

Unger, Harlow Giles. *Thomas Paine and the Clarion Call for American Independence.* New York: DaCapo Press, 2019.

Watson, Alan. *Churchill's Legacy: Two Speeches to Save the World.* New York: Bloomsbury, 2016.

West, Ed. *1215 and All That: Magna Carta and King John.* New York: Skyhorse Publishing, 2017.

White, Philip. *Churchill's Cold War: The Iron Curtain Speech That Shaped the Postwar World.* New York: Public Affairs, 2012.

Wilford, John, and John Jones. *Memorials and Characters, Together with theLlives of Divers Eminent and Worthy Persons ... among the Nobility, Gentry and Clergy, from the Year One Thousand Six Hundred to the Present Time. Collected and Compiled from above One Hundred and Fifty Different Authors ... To Which is Added, an Appendix of Monumental Inscriptions, in Latin and English.* London: Printed for John Wilford, 1741.

Willmott, H. P. *World War I.* New York: DK Publishing, 2009.

Wilson, Michael. *Happy and Glorious., the Revolution of 1688.* Stroud, Gloucestershire: The History Press, 2014.

Wood, Adrian Tinnis Wood. *Behind the Throne: A Domestic History of the British Royal Household.* New York: Basic Books, 2018.

Yero, Judith Lloyd. *The Mayflower Compact.* Washington, D.C.: National Geographic Society, 2006

DISSERTATION

Wallace, Willard Mosher, and Edwin Sandys. 1940. *Sir Edwin Sandys and the First Parliament of James I. A Dissertation, etc.*, 1940.

Appendix

Sinews of Peace (Iron Curtain) Speech

I am glad to come to Westminster College this afternoon, and am complimented that you should give me a degree. The name "Westminster" is somehow familiar to me.

I seem to have heard of it before. Indeed, it was at Westminster that I received a very large part of my education in politics, dialectic, rhetoric, and one or two other things. In fact we have both been educated at the same, or similar, or, at any rate, kindred establishments.

It is also an honour, perhaps almost unique, for a private visitor to be introduced to an academic audience by the President of the United States. Amid his heavy burdens, duties, and responsibilities-unsought but not recoiled from-the President has travelled a thousand miles to dignify and magnify our meeting here to-day and to give me an opportunity of addressing this kindred nation, as well as my own countrymen across the ocean, and perhaps some other countries too. The President has told you that it is his wish, as I am sure it is yours, that I should have full liberty to give my true and faithful counsel in these anxious and baffling times. I shall certainly avail myself of this freedom, and feel the more right to do so because any private ambitions I may have cherished in my younger days have been satisfied beyond my wildest dreams. Let me, however, make it clear that I have no official mission or status of any kind, and that I speak only for myself. There is nothing here but what you see.

I can therefore allow my mind, with the experience of a lifetime, to play over the problems which beset us on the morrow of our absolute victory in arms, and to try to make sure with what strength I have that what has been gained with so much sacrifice and suffering shall be preserved for the future glory and safety of mankind.

The United States stands at this time at the pinnacle of world power. It is a solemn moment for the American Democracy. For with primacy in power is also joined an awe inspiring accountability to the future. If you look around you, you must feel not only the sense of duty done but also you must feel anxiety lest you fall below the level of achievement. Opportunity is here now, clear and shining for both our countries. To reject it or ignore it or fritter it away will bring upon us all the long reproaches of the after-time. It is necessary that constancy of mind, persistency of purpose, and the grand simplicity of decision shall guide and rule the conduct of the English-speaking peoples in peace as they did in war. We must, and I believe we shall, prove ourselves equal to this severe requirement.

When American military men approach some serious situation they are wont to write at the head of their directive the words "over-all strategic concept." There is wisdom in this, as it leads to clarity of thought. What then is the over-all strategic concept which we should inscribe today? It is nothing less than the safety and welfare, the freedom and progress, of all the homes and families of all the men and women in all the lands. And here I speak particularly of the myriad cottage or apartment homes where the wage-earner strives amid the accidents and difficulties of life to guard his wife and children from privation and bring the family up in the fear of the Lord, or upon ethical conceptions which often play their potent part.

To give security to these countless homes, they must be shielded from the two giant marauders, war and tyranny. We all know the frightful disturbances in which the ordinary family is plunged when the curse of war swoops down upon the bread-winner and those for whom he works and contrives. The awful ruin of Europe, with all its vanished glories, and of large parts of Asia glares us in the eyes. When the designs of wicked men or the aggressive urge of mighty States dissolve over large areas the frame of civilised society, humble folk are confronted with difficulties with which they cannot cope. For them all is distorted, all is broken, even ground to pulp.

When I stand here this quiet afternoon I shudder to visualise what is actually happening to millions now and what is going to happen in this period when famine stalks the earth. None can compute what has been called "the unestimated sum of human pain." Our supreme task and duty is to guard the homes of the common people from the horrors and miseries of another war. We are all agreed on that.

Our American military colleagues, after having proclaimed their "over-all strategic concept" and computed available resources, always proceed to the next step-namely, the method. Here again there is widespread agreement. A world organisation has already been erected for the prime purpose of preventing war, UNO, the successor of the League of Nations, with the decisive addition of the United States and all that that means, is already at work. We must make sure that its work is fruitful, that it is a reality and not a sham, that it is a force for action, and not merely a frothing of words, that it is a true temple of peace in which the shields of many nations can some day be hung up, and not merely a cockpit in a Tower of Babel. Before we cast away the solid assurances of national armaments for self-preservation we must be certain that our temple is built, not upon shifting sands or quagmires, but upon the rock. Anyone can see with his eyes open that our path will be difficult and also long, but if we persevere together as we did in the two world wars-though not, alas, in the interval between them-I cannot doubt that we shall achieve our common purpose in the end.

I have, however, a definite and practical proposal to make for action. Courts and magistrates may be set up but they cannot function without sheriffs and constables. The United Nations Organisation must immediately begin to be equipped with an international armed force. In such a matter we can only go step by step, but we must begin now. I propose that each of the Powers and States should be invited to delegate a certain number of air squadrons to the service of the world organisation. These squadrons would be trained and prepared in their own countries, but would move around in rotation from one country to another. They would wear the uniform of their own countries but with different badges. They would not be required to act against their own nation, but in other respects they would be directed by the world organisation. This might be started on a modest scale and would grow as confidence grew. I wished to see this done after the First World War, and I devoutly trust it may be done forthwith.

It would nevertheless be wrong and imprudent to entrust the secret knowledge or experience of the atomic bomb, which the United States, Great Britain, and Canada now share, to the world organisation, while it is still in its infancy. It would be criminal madness to cast it adrift in this still agitated and un-united world. No one in any country has slept less well in their beds because this knowledge and the method and the raw materials to apply it, are at present largely retained in American hands. I do not believe we should all have slept so soundly had the positions been reversed and if some Communist or neo-Fascist State monopolised for the time being these dread agencies. The fear of them alone might easily have been used to enforce totalitarian systems upon the free democratic world, with consequences appalling to human imagination. God has willed that this shall not be and we have at least a breathing space to set our house in order before this peril has to be encountered: and even then, if no effort is spared, we should still possess so formidable a superiority as to impose effective deterrents upon its employment, or threat of employment, by others. Ultimately, when the essential brotherhood of man is truly embodied and expressed in a world organisation with all the necessary practical safeguards to make it effective, these powers would naturally be confided to that world organisation.

Now I come to the second danger of these two marauders which threatens the cottage, the home, and the ordinary people-namely, tyranny. We cannot be blind to the fact that the liberties enjoyed by individual citizens throughout the British Empire are not valid in a considerable number of countries, some of which are very powerful. In these States control is enforced upon the common people by various kinds of all-embracing police governments. The power of the State is exercised without restraint, either by dictators or by compact oligarchies operating through a privileged party and a political police. It is not our duty at this time when difficulties are so numerous to interfere forcibly in the internal affairs of countries which we have not conquered in war. But we must never cease to proclaim in fearless tones the great principles of freedom and the rights of man which are the joint inheritance of the English-speaking world and which through Magna Carta, the Bill of Rights, the Habeas Corpus, trial by jury, and the English common law find their most famous expression in the American Declaration of Independence.

All this means that the people of any country have the right, and should have the power by constitutional action, by free unfettered elections, with secret ballot, to choose or change the character or form of government under which they dwell; that freedom of speech and thought should reign; that courts of justice, independent of the executive, unbiased by any party, should administer laws which have received the broad assent of large majorities or are consecrated by time and custom. Here are the title deeds of freedom which should lie in every cottage home. Here is the message of the British and American peoples to mankind. Let us preach what we practise – let us practise what we preach.

I have now stated the two great dangers which menace the homes of the people: War and Tyranny. I have not yet spoken of poverty and privation which are in many cases the prevailing anxiety. But if the dangers of war and tyranny are removed, there is no doubt that science and co-operation can bring in the next few years to the world, certainly in the next few decades newly taught in the sharpening school of war, an expansion of material well-being beyond anything that has yet occurred in human experience. Now, at this sad and breathless moment, we are plunged in the hunger and distress which are the aftermath of our stupendous struggle; but this will pass and may pass quickly, and there is no reason except human folly or sub-human crime which should deny to all the nations the inauguration and enjoyment of an age of plenty. I have often used words which I learned fifty years ago from a great Irish-American orator, a friend of mine, Mr. Bourke Cockran. "There is enough for all. The earth is a generous mother; she will provide in plentiful abundance food for all her children if they will but cultivate her soil in justice and in peace." So far I feel that we are in full agreement.

Now, while still pursuing the method of realising our overall strategic concept, I come to the crux of what I have travelled here to Say. Neither the sure prevention of war, nor the continuous rise of world organisation will be gained without what I have called the fraternal association of the English-speaking peoples. This means a special relationship between the British Commonwealth and Empire and the United States. This is no time for generalities, and I will venture to be precise. Fraternal association requires not only the growing friendship and mutual understanding between our two vast but kindred Systems of society, but the continuance of the intimate relationship between our military advisers, leading to common study of potential dangers, the similarity of weapons and manuals of instructions, and to the interchange of officers and cadets at technical colleges. It should carry with it the continuance of the present facilities for mutual security by the joint use of all Naval and Air Force bases in the possession of either country all over the world. This would perhaps double the mobility of the American Navy and Air Force. It would greatly expand that of the British Empire Forces and it might well lead, if and as the world calms down, to important financial savings. Already we use together a large number of islands; more may well be entrusted to our joint care in the near future.

The United States has already a Permanent Defence Agreement with the Do-minion of Canada, which is so devotedly attached to the British Commonwealth and Empire. This Agreement is more effective than many of those which have often been made under formal alliances. This principle should be extended to all British Commonwealths with full reciprocity. Thus, whatever happens, and thus only, shall we be secure ourselves and able to work together for the high and simple causes that are dear to us and bode no ill to any. Eventually there may come-I feel eventually there will come-the principle of common citizenship, but that we may be content to leave to destiny, whose outstretched arm many of us can already clearly see.

There is however an important question we must ask ourselves. Would a special relationship between the United States and the British Commonwealth be inconsistent with our over-riding loyalties to the World Organisation? I reply that, on the contrary, it is probably the only means by which that organisation will achieve its full stature and strength. There are already the special United States relations with Canada which I have just mentioned, and there are the special relations between the United States and the South American Republics. We British have our twenty years Treaty of Collaboration and Mutual Assistance with Soviet Russia. I agree with Mr. Bevin, the Foreign Secretary of Great Britain, that it might well be a fifty years Treaty so far as we are concerned. We aim at nothing but mutual assistance and collaboration. The British have an alliance with Portugal unbroken since 1384, and which produced fruitful results at critical moments in the late war. None of these clash with the general interest of a world agreement, or a world organisation; on the contrary they help it. "In my father's house are many mansions." Special associations between members of the United Nations which have no aggressive point against any other country, which harbour no design incompatible with the Charter of the United Nations, far from being harmful, are beneficial and, as I believe, indispensable.

I spoke earlier of the Temple of Peace. Workmen from all countries must build that temple. If two of the workmen know each other particularly well and are old friends, if their families are inter-mingled, and if they have "faith in each other's purpose, hope in each other's future and charity towards each other's shortcomings"-to quote some good words I read here the other day-why cannot they work together at the common task as friends and partners? Why cannot they share their tools and thus increase each other's working powers? Indeed they must do so or else the temple may not be built, or, being built, it may collapse, and we shall all be proved again unteachable and have to go and try to learn again for a third time in a school of war, incomparably more rigorous than that from which we have just been released. The dark ages may return, the Stone Age may return on the gleaming wings of science, and what might now shower immeasurable material blessings upon mankind, may even bring about its total destruction. Beware, I say; time may be short. Do not let us take the course of allowing events to drift along until it is too late. If there is to be a fraternal association of the kind I have described, with all the extra strength and security which both our countries can derive from it, let us make sure that that great fact is known to the world, and that it plays its part in steadying and stabilising the foundations of peace. There is the path of wisdom. Prevention is better than cure.

A shadow has fallen upon the scenes so lately lighted by the Allied victory. Nobody knows what Soviet Russia and its Communist international organisation intends to do in the immediate future, or what are the limits, if any, to their expansive and proselytising tendencies. I have a strong admiration and regard for the valiant Russian people and for my wartime comrade, Marshal Stalin. There is deep sympathy and goodwill in Britain—and I doubt not here also—towards the peoples of all the Russias and a resolve to persevere through many differences and rebuffs in establishing lasting friendships. We understand the Russian need to be secure on her western frontiers by the removal of all possibility of German aggression. We welcome Russia to her rightful place among the leading nations of the world. We welcome her flag upon the seas. Above all, we welcome constant, frequent and growing contacts between the Russian people and our own people on both sides of the Atlantic. It is my duty however, for I am sure you would wish me to state the facts as I see them to you, to place before you certain facts about the present position in Europe.

From Stettin in the Baltic to Trieste in the Adriatic, an iron curtain has descended across the Continent. Behind that line lie all the capitals of the ancient states of Central and Eastern Europe. Warsaw, Berlin, Prague, Vienna, Budapest, Belgrade, Bucharest and Sofia, all these famous cities and the populations around them lie in what I must call the Soviet sphere, and all are subject in one form or another, not only to Soviet influence but to a very high and, in many cases, increasing measure of control from Moscow. Athens alone-Greece with its immortal glories-is free to decide its future at an election under British, American and French observation. The Russian-dominated Polish Government has been encouraged to make enormous and wrongful inroads upon Germany, and mass expulsions of millions of Germans on a scale grievous and undreamed-of are now taking place. The Communist parties, which were very small in all these Eastern States of Europe, have been raised to pre-eminence and power far beyond their numbers and are seeking everywhere to obtain totalitarian control. Police governments are prevailing in nearly every case, and so far, except in Czechoslovakia, there is no true democracy.

Turkey and Persia are both profoundly alarmed and disturbed at the claims which are being made upon them and at the pressure being exerted by the Moscow Government. An attempt is being made by the Russians in Berlin to build up a quasi-Communist party in their zone of Occupied Germany by showing special favours to groups of left-wing German leaders. At the end of the fighting last June, the American and British Armies withdrew westwards, in accordance with an earlier agreement, to a depth at some points of 150 miles upon a front of nearly four hundred miles, in order to allow our Russian allies to occupy this vast expanse of territory which the Western Democracies had conquered.

If now the Soviet Government tries, by separate action, to build up a pro-Communist Germany in their areas, this will cause new serious difficulties in the British and American zones, and will give the defeated Germans the power of putting themselves up to auction between the Soviets and the Western Democracies. Whatever conclusions may be drawn from these facts-and facts they are-this is certainly not the Liberated Europe we fought to build up. Nor is it one which contains the essentials of permanent peace.

The safety of the world requires a new unity in Europe, from which no nation should be permanently outcast. It is from the quarrels of the strong parent races in Europe that the world wars we have witnessed, or which occurred in former times, have sprung. Twice in our own lifetime we have seen the United States, against their wishes and their traditions, against arguments, the force of which it is impossible not to comprehend, drawn by irresistible forces, into these wars in time to secure the victory of the good cause, but only after frightful slaughter and devastation had occurred. Twice the United States has had to send several millions of its young men across the Atlantic to find the war; but now war can find any nation, wherever it may dwell between dusk and dawn. Surely we should work with conscious purpose for a grand pacification of Europe, within the structure of the United Nations and in accordance with its Charter. That I feel is an open cause of policy of very great importance.

In front of the iron curtain which lies across Europe are other causes for anxiety. In Italy the Communist Party is seriously hampered by having to Support the Communist-trained Marshal Tito's claims to former Italian territory at the head of the Adriatic. Nevertheless the future of Italy hangs in the balance. Again one cannot imagine a regenerated Europe without a strong France. All my public life I have worked for a Strong France and I never lost faith in her destiny, even in the darkest hours. I will not lose faith now. However, in a great number of countries, far from the Russian frontiers and throughout the world, Communist fifth columns are established and work in complete unity and absolute obedience to the directions they receive from the Communist centre. Except in the British Commonwealth and in the United States where Communism is in its infancy, the Communist parties or fifth columns constitute a growing challenge and peril to Christian civilisation. These are sombre facts for anyone to have to recite on the morrow of a victory gained by so much splendid comradeship in arms and in the cause of freedom and democracy; but we should be most unwise not to face them squarely while time remains.

The outlook is also anxious in the Far East and especially in Manchuria. The Agreement which was made at Yalta, to which I was a party, was extremely favourable to Soviet Russia, but it was made at a time when no one could say that the German war might not extend all through the summer and autumn of 1945 and when the Japanese war was expected to last for a further 18 months from the end of the German war. In this country you are all so well-informed about the Far East, and such devoted friends of China, that I do not need to expatiate on the situation there.

I have felt bound to portray the shadow which, alike in the west and in the east, falls upon the world. I was a high minister at the time of the

Versailles Treaty and a close friend of Mr. Lloyd-George, who was the head of the British delegation at Versailles. I did not myself agree with many things that were done, but I have a very Strong impression in my mind of that situation, and I find it painful to contrast it with that which prevails now. In those days there were high hopes and unbounded confidence that the wars were over, and that the League of Nations would become all-powerful. I do not see or feel that same confidence or even the same hopes in the haggard world at the present time.

On the other hand I repulse the idea that a new war is inevitable; still more that it is imminent. It is because I am sure that our fortunes are still in our own hands and that we hold the power to save the future, that I feel the duty to speak out now that I have the occasion and the opportunity to do so. I do not believe that Soviet Russia desires war. What they desire is the fruits of war and the indefinite expansion of their power and doctrines. But what we have to consider here to-day while time remains, is the permanent prevention of war and the establishment of conditions of freedom and democracy as rapidly as possible in all countries. Our difficulties and dangers will not be removed by closing our eyes to them. They will not be removed by mere waiting to see what happens; nor will they be removed by a policy of appeasement. What is needed is a settlement, and the longer this is delayed, the more difficult it will be and the greater our dangers will become.

From what I have seen of our Russian friends and Allies during the war, I am convinced that there is nothing they admire so much as strength, and there is nothing for which they have less respect than for weakness, especially military weakness. For that reason the old doctrine of a balance of power is unsound. We cannot afford, if we can help it, to work on narrow margins, offering temptations to a trial of strength. If the Western Democracies stand together in strict adherence to the principles of the United Nations Charter, their influence for furthering those principles will be immense and no one is likely to molest them. If however they become divided or falter in their duty and if these all-important years are allowed to slip away then indeed catastrophe may overwhelm us all. Last time I saw it all coming and cried aloud to my own fellow-countrymen and to the world, but no one paid any attention. Up till the year 1933 or even 1935, Germany might have been saved from the awful fate which has overtaken her and we might all have been spared the miseries Hitler let loose upon mankind. There never was a war in all history easier to prevent by timely action than the one which has just desolated such great areas of the globe. It could have been prevented in my belief without the firing of a single shot, and Germany might be powerful, prosperous and honoured to-day; but no one would listen and one by one we were all sucked into the awful whirlpool. We surely must not let that happen again. This can only be achieved by reaching now, in 1946, a good understanding on all points with Russia under the general authority of the United Nations Organisation and by the maintenance of that good understanding through many peaceful years, by the world instrument, supported by the whole strength of the English-speaking world and all its connections. There is the solution which I respectfully offer to you in this Address to which I have given the title "The Sinews of Peace."

Let no man underrate the abiding power of the British Empire and Commonwealth. Because you see the 46 millions in our island harassed about their food supply, of which they only grow one half, even in war-time, or because we have difficulty in restarting our industries and export trade after six years of passionate war effort, do not suppose that we shall not come through these dark years of privation as we have come through the glorious years of agony, or that half a century from now, you will not see 70 or 80 millions of Britons spread about the world and united in defence of our traditions, our way of life, and of the world causes which you and we espouse. If the population of the English-speaking Commonwealths be added to that of the United States with all that such co-operation implies in the air, on the sea, all over the globe and in science and in industry, and in moral force, there will be no quivering, precarious balance of power to offer its temptation to ambition or adventure. On the contrary, there will be an overwhelming assurance of security. If we adhere faithfully to the Charter of the United Nations and walk forward in sedate and sober strength seeking no one's land or treasure, seeking to lay no arbitrary control upon the thoughts of men; if all British moral and material forces and convictions are joined with your own in fraternal association, the high-roads of the future will be clear, not only for us but for all, not only for our time, but for a century to come.

Index